Is There a Transition
to Democracy in
El Salvador?

W Woodrow Wilson Center
Current Studies on Latin America

Published with the Latin American Program
of the Woodrow Wilson International Center for Scholars
Joseph S. Tulchin, Director

Is There a Transition to Democracy in El Salvador?

edited by
Joseph S. Tulchin
with Gary Bland

Lynne Rienner Publishers • Boulder & London

Published in the United States of America in 1992 by
Lynne Rienner Publishers, Inc.
1800 30th Street, Boulder, Colorado 80301

and in the United Kingdom by
Lynne Rienner Publishers, Inc.
3 Henrietta Street, Covent Garden, London WC2E 8LU

Library of Congress Cataloging-in-Publication Data
Is there a transition to democracy in El Salvador? / edited by
    Joseph S. Tulchin, with Gary Bland
    (Woodrow Wilson Center current studies on Latin America)
    Includes bibliographical references and index.
    ISBN 1-55587-310-3
    1. El Salvador—Politics and government—1979- 2. Democracy—
El Salvador. I. Tulchin, Joseph S., 1939- . II. Bland, Gary.
III. Series.
F1488.3.I8   1992
320.97284—dc20   92-12264
                                                            CIP

British Cataloguing in Publication Data
A Cataloguing in Publication record for this book
is available from the British Library.

Printed and bound in the United States of America

The paper used in this publication meets the requirements
of the American National Standard for Permanence of
Paper for Printed Library Materials Z39.48-1984.

Contents

Preface

Today, from a geopolitical point of view, it would appear absurd to argue that El Salvador is of vital strategic interest to either the United States or Russia. Yet, not long ago, El Salvador was a focal point of US policy, with all of its ramifications, because the Reagan administration viewed the situation there as a challenge to US national will and a threat to US national security. Salvadorans consequently paid a heavy price for their entanglement in the Cold War—the loss of tens of thousands of lives, and economic devastation.

With the fall of the Berlin Wall and the collapse of communism, we have seen a complete reversal: the Soviet Union no longer exists, the United States is working for a permanent peace, and the idea of democratic government has taken hold worldwide. What does this mean for El Salvador? Can we assume as a result of the dramatic shift in these external factors that the country will inevitably achieve democratic government? Most observers would agree that such an assumption is unfounded. To the contrary, the transition to democracy in El Salvador is a fragile process resulting from a combination of many elements.

With that in mind, the Latin American Program of the Woodrow Wilson Center organized a conference to study the United Nations-sponsored peace negotiations and the transition to democracy in El Salvador. Although a peace settlement was anticipated by the end of 1991, its timing was in doubt, which complicated the preparation for the event because the availability of key participants was compromised by their commitments to the talks in Mexico and New York. As it turned out, the US Department of State refused to allow members of the Farabundo Martí National Liberation Front (FMLN) negotiating team to attend the April conference, so we ultimately decided to hold two conferences, not one.

This volume is the product of these two meetings. It is an attempt to consider El Salvador as a case of the transition to democracy in Latin America. In doing so, it records landmarks in the history of El Salvador and of Central America. It records events that have taken place only recently and also puts them in historical and theoretical perspective. El Salvador has received a great deal of attention in recent years, but it has not been a focus in the study of democratic transitions. We believe there are many lessons to be learned from the country's experience. We therefore hope this volume adds to the literature on transitions and spurs other students to investigate these issues more closely, not only in El Salvador but in the rest of Central America.

The Latin American Program's staff deserves many thanks for the work they put into this volume. Gary Bland organized the two conferences, coauthored the introduction, wrote the concluding chapter, and guided the manuscript through the publication process. Lucy Hetrick provided valuable assistance in preparing the events. Leah Florence, who continues to amaze us with her insightful comments on grammar, sentence structure, and word choice, tried to help us avoid serious infelicities of expression.

Joseph S. Tulchin

Introduction

Joseph S. Tulchin & Gary Bland

How does one measure the transition to democracy in El Salvador? The most positive trend is represented by the dramatic cease-fire accord reached on New Year's Eve in the waning hours of Javier Pérez de Cuéllar's tenure as secretary-general of the United Nations and by the emotional public reconciliation among President Alfredo Cristiani, the leadership of the Farabundo Martí National Liberation Front (FMLN), and the United States at the signing ceremony some two weeks later in Mexico City. There are other favorable signs, including the election of leftist leader Rubén Zamora as Vice-President of the National Assembly, the United Nation's role in monitoring human rights violations and ensuring the peace, and the widespread public expression of relief that the civil war had come to an end. On the other hand, a host of formidable obstacles to democracy remain: El Salvador is devoid of democratic tradition and strong institutions; the country is faced with continuing human rights abuses; and it is devastated economically and torn politically as a result of twelve years of civil war.

This apparent contradiction captures the complexity and the precariousness of the changes under way in El Salvador. The country is progressing, but it is also carrying the baggage of decades of dictatorial rule, of a bloody legacy of repression, and of a conflict over the establishment of representative government and social justice that has cost an estimated 75,000 lives, deep social polarization, and the destruction of billions of dollars of economic resources. The government and the FMLN have reached extraordinary agreements on political, economic, and military reform. Peace accords alone, however, do not resolve

Joseph S. Tulchin is director of the Latin American Program at the Woodrow Wilson International Center for Scholars. Gary Bland is program associate of the Latin American Program there.

age-old problems, such as a judiciary with virtually no independent power that will remain weak even after substantial reform. Lasting change will take time and sustained commitment. What is certain is that El Salvador is at a critical juncture, and the next few years will determine the extent to which democracy takes hold.

The transition to democracy in El Salvador has been severely hindered not only by the country's oligarchical past, but also by its having been caught up in the Cold War and US domestic politics during the 1980s. Some scholars view October 15, 1979, when reformist officers of the Salvadoran military led a coup deposing the old regime, as the start of the country's transition. A series of reformist juntas composed of civilian and military representatives ruled in the months following the overthrow. But the mass popular mobilization that ensued was met with brutal and widespread army repression, which hastened the descent into civil war by spring 1980. The groups that would unite to create the FMLN, allied with exiled leftist politicians, took up the banner of social justice in armed opposition to the government. The ruling junta, essentially powerless to control the resurgent hard-line military, managed to institute banking and land reforms with US backing in 1980 in an unsuccessful attempt to relieve the social pressure for radical change.

Soon after Reagan took office, his administration selected El Salvador as its first Central American test case in launching its crusade against Soviet-inspired Communist aggression in the Western hemisphere. The central components of the Reagan strategy included the following: providing massive military and economic assistance to build a powerful, professionalized army, to prevent the overthrow of the Salvadoran regime, and to marginalize the FMLN; managing the transition to democratic government; making Congress's support for the regime a high-profile test of its support for President Reagan and his anti-Communist foreign policy; and largely overlooking the tens of thousands of killings perpetrated by the armed forces against laborers, peasants, and FMLN sympathizers while insisting that social unrest was the result of external subversion conducted by puppets of the Soviet Union. The debate over US policy toward El Salvador resounded in the halls of Congress as policymakers objected to the Reagan administration's inattention to gross human rights abuses and its steadfast refusal to acknowledge the internal causes of the conflict.

By 1982, the Reagan strategy also included elections in an effort to provide the Salvadoran government with democratic legitimacy in the eyes of Congress and the US public. Over the course of the decade, five more elections were held for legislative, municipal, and presidential offices, which ultimately created an electoral framework for helping resolve the war but impeded efforts to bring both sides to the negotiating table. In fact, the Reagan administration had no interest in resolving the conflict, which was soon stalemated, in any way other than by military and political defeat of the rebel movement. Human rights violations began to decline significantly in 1984. With the election to the presidency of José Napoleón Duarte, a Christian Democrat perceived in the United States as a moderate between two extremes, and with evidence of political liberalization, congressional opposition to the Reagan policy effectively vanished. Not until five years later, following the election of new US and Salvadoran presidents, a radical shift in the FMLN's view of the war, and the end of the Cold War, did prevailing circumstances allow the possibility of a peaceful settlement to emerge.

The warring sides began discussions in fall 1989. While the process was quickly cut short by increased right-wing violence and a massive FMLN offensive, the parties returned to the negotiating table with surprising speed under the auspices of the United Nations. By April 1990, as El Salvador looked ahead to a seventh round of elections to be held the following March, the government and the FMLN agreed in Geneva to the framework for an extended process of peace negotiations.

As the talks began in Geneva, the public positions of the two warring parties were well known. President Cristiani and his supporters argued that El Salvador had become increasingly democratic since the early 1980s. In subsequent years, they noted, six successive free and fair elections had been conducted in accordance with the country's constitution. Cristiani himself, taking office after President Duarte's term expired in 1989, was the first democratically elected president to succeed another in El Salvador's history. In addition, President Cristiani's position was that human rights abuses were the result of a small minority within the military. The armed forces were more disciplined than they were at the beginning of the decade, he pointed out, and when violations came to light they were subject to investigation with the support of the army. The military, Cristiani intimated, was an increasingly professional institution respectful of the rights of citizens to express their points of view and subject to civilian control. Moreover, he argued, the electoral process ensured the right of all societal groups to vote and to have their point of view represented in government. In short, El Salvador was one of Latin America's youngest democracies.[1]

Those who advocated this position called on the FMLN rebels to unilaterally lay down their arms and participate in the elections, in the belief that change could be accomplished through the ballot box. The idea was that civilian government with such a popular mandate, coupled with international pressure, would ensure that the military respected election results and preserved the right of all views in Salvadoran society to be heard.

In contrast, the FMLN recounted the country's long history of institutionalized repression of Salvadoran political life and social protest and rejected the idea that El Salvador was "democratic." From the perspective of the armed rebels, for decades prior to the October 1979 coup the powerful Salvadoran military in alliance with the economic oligarchy had ruled the country with an iron fist. The armed forces continually thwarted attempts to hold free elections and killed labor unionists, peasants, and anyone else who tried to change the status quo or tampered with the elite's control over the country's wealth. The only way to change society and achieve social justice, they argued, was through armed revolution and, for many, the establishment of some form of state-dominated, socialist regime. Civilian democrats who faced the repression saw no alternative to support for the armed rebel movement.

From the FMLN's point of view, in the early 1980s the military continued to repress the population, murdering tens of thousands more people, including religious leaders and opposition politicians, while the United States mounted a counterinsurgency program to marginalize the rebels and instituted a farcical electoral process. Democracy, as the various elements of the movement defined it, existed in name only. As the decade evolved, the United States exerted pressure on the military to halt the killing and pushed the elected Duarte government to implement limited reform. But US policies were part of the ongoing counterinsurgency project; they produced no fundamental change in the country's power structure.

By January 1989, the FMLN was compelled to adopt a new strategy of change because of the realities of a changing international system, especially the ending of the Cold War, the popular desire for peace, their failure to achieve victory on the battlefield, and the increased political space in the country, among other factors. The rebels now believed that the war ultimately had to be settled at the negotiating table—that is, where they could receive concessions and guarantees such that if they were to lay down their arms they would be entering a "truly democratic," pluralistic society. Democracy in El Salvador, they emphasized, meant the ability to engage freely in legal political activity, to take and exercise power if it were won fairly at the ballot box, and to curb, if not dissolve, the armed forces in an effort to halt human rights abuse and protect their own safety. The main obstacle to these goals, the FMLN argued, was the continuing power of the military and its ally, US imperialism.[2]

Advocates of this position called for a continuation of the war as well as negotiations for a carrot-and-stick policy that could achieve true democracy and deep-seated reform in El Salvador. The FMLN appeared determined and capable of holding onto its arms and prosecuting the war until it was confident, above all, that the impunity of the military would be broken.

Since the negotiations began in 1989, there has been a dramatic meeting of the minds. As indicated by the peace agreements to date, especially the more than 100-page accord reached on December 31, 1991, and finalized on January 16, 1992, the FMLN, the Cristiani government, and the Salvadoran armed forces have moved away from some of their long-held positions, although groups on the right especially have refused to support compromise. Over the course of the peace process, which involved numerous major meetings, a number of smaller, secret encounters, and six formal agreements, their opposing views have moderated significantly. In Geneva on April 4, 1990, the warring parties established a framework for a peaceful settlement in the first major step in the peace process. Less than two months later, on May 21, they agreed in Caracas to a general agenda—including human rights, the armed forces, and constitutional, judicial, and economic reform—and a timetable for the negotiations.

By July 26, 1990, in San José, Costa Rica, the FMLN and the Cristiani government completed a landmark accord for the protection of human rights that provided for a United Nations mission to verify not only respect for human rights but also all other agreements reached. The two parties met the following spring in Mexico City and held intensive talks for three weeks, at the conclusion of which they agreed, on April 27, 1991, to constitutional reforms and a commission to help ensure prosecution for the most egregious human rights offenses. At the direct request of the United Nations secretary-general, who was prompted by both the United States and the Soviet Union, the two negotiating teams met five months later in New York. There, on September 25, 1991, the two sides held overnight sessions to break a major impasse, settled several critical points of contention, such as the FMLN's demand to be incorporated into the Salvadoran army, and created a framework for a final accord.

Finally, the two parties began the last stage of the talks. Progress was slow in meetings in Mexico during fall 1991. The two parties then decided to return to the United Nations in December in response to a second invitation from Pérez de Cuéllar. Again the negotiations were difficult. Under tremendous international pressure, however, and realizing that the peace process would lose critical momentum if Pérez de Cuéllar left office without securing an accord, the negotiators, supported by a high-level US delegation and the presence of President Cristiani, reached a last-minute breakthrough. The FMLN and the Cristiani government found solutions to the remaining key issues essential to peace: reduction of the armed forces, social and economic reform, cease-fire provisions, creation of a new national police, and disarmament of the FMLN. The accords were finalized over the following two weeks after another series of arduous discussions.

The ceremonial signing of the peace agreement held in Mexico City on January 16 was both a historic event and an emotion-filled and joyous celebration. The scene was remarkable: Former adversaries embraced and wept, President Cristiani and US secretary of state James Baker met the FMLN leaders for the first time and warmly congratulated each other, and the presidents of nations deeply involved in talks, such as Carlos Salinas de Gotari of Mexico and Felipe González of Spain, offered their continued support. Baker later traveled to El Salvador and the following day before the National Assembly issued a stern warning to right-wing elements who might use violence to oppose the accord. Most important, although the peace process neither has been nor promises to be a smooth road, it clearly represents the beginning of societal reconciliation. Without the desire and political will to broach differences on the part of both the FMLN and President Cristiani, as well as the United States and the international community, the success of the past two years could not have occurred.

This book is primarily the result of two meetings on El Salvador held by the Latin American Program of the Woodrow Wilson International Center for Scholars in Washington, D.C. First, the Latin American Program held a day-long conference on April 25, 1991. The conference was divided into three parts: (1) the March 1991 elections, (2) US policy, and (3) key issues for the future: human rights, the military, and the economy. The second meeting was an afternoon presentation on October 1, 1991, by United Nations mediator Alvaro de Soto, who addressed the negotiations and prospects for peace. Finally, this work is based in part on independent research and interviews, including meetings in New York during the final round of peace talks in December and in Mexico City during the January 16 signing of the accord.

The program originally planned to hold a single conference on April 25 that would have included a final session on the peace process with the participation of one negotiator each from the FMLN, the Cristiani government, and the United Nations mediating team. Unfortunately, as a result of the ongoing negotiations and because one of the participants, Eduardo Sancho of the FMLN General Command, was refused a visa, that session was postponed. At this point, the Bush administration continued to be intransigent in its dealings with the FMLN. Given our continuing desire to discuss the search for peace and continuing inability to convene the original panel, we invited Alvaro de Soto to speak in the wake of the New York Agreement. He proved to be an intriguing alternative.

The general objective of the two events was to analyze the political reality in El Salvador and the prospects for an end to the war. The overriding theme of both was the degree to which democracy had developed in El Salvador and could become a basis for lasting political and socioeconomic reconciliation. A subordinate theme was the role of external forces—the United States, the Organization of American States, the United Nations, and other international actors—in shaping Salvadoran democracy.

Our interest in El Salvador had several dimensions. First, the Latin American Program had long maintained a concern for transitions to democracy.[3] The meetings on El Salvador were the fourth case study over two years emphasizing aspects of democratization, a series that also included Chile, Cuba, and Venezuela.[4]

Second, during the 1980s the passion of many political scientists, especially Latin Americanists, was transition theory: creating typologies to explain why and how countries develop democratic regimes. With authoritarian governments collapsing across the continent—from Peru, Argentina, and Brazil to Chile and Paraguay—and with surprisingly durable democracies emerging to replace them, that motivation is easily understandable. And the scholarly contribution in this area was immense. O'Donnell and Schmitter's *Transitions from Authoritarian Rule*, noted previously, and Diamond, Linz, and Lipset's *Democracy in Developing Countries*,[5] each in four volumes, are large testaments to that trend.

These studies concentrated on the large Latin American countries, countries that had emerged from bureaucratic authoritarian regimes, or countries that had some experience with democratic politics. Perhaps because the country is relatively tiny or more likely because, despite the rhetoric of the Reagan administration, any evidence of democratization at that time was at best debatable, El Salvador was never a focus of the major works of transition theory. Today, however, El Salvador is a country that is emerging—a bit late for the academics who now have moved on to issues in structural adjustment and post-transition theory— as a fascinating candidate for the study of a country on the path of democratization. It is interesting to note that in the 1980s El Salvador (along with Nicaragua) dominated the agenda of US policy in Latin America and received massive amounts of foreign assistance and attention. It was South America that was largely ignored. As the Central American conflicts come to an end, as deficits limit US ability to provide aid where it is sorely need in the war-torn region, and as the Enterprise for the Americas, free markets, and free trade take hold in the south, one can argue that the reverse may prove true in the 1990s.

The obsessive focus of the United States on El Salvador during the 1980s is the third reason for addressing the question of the transition to democracy there today. Although the obsession has passed, the influence of the United States in the country remains essentially the same today—pervasive—even though its policy has shifted in favor of dialogue and the Cold War has ended. As the civil conflict winds down, there is no reason to believe that US policy, even at a time when less attention is being accorded Central America, will be any less critical to the future of El Salvador or any less intriguing for students of Latin America. If attendance at our events is any indication, interest in El Salvador's future has not diminished in the least. Both events were extraordinarily well attended by representatives of various government agencies, nongovernmental organizations, the private sector, and the general public.

During our April and October events, the discussion centered on whether one could accurately label El Salvador a democratic country. To the extent that El Salvador has democratized over the past decade—if it has indeed moved forward at all—can the progress that has been made be reversed as the pressure of a rebel armed force is removed? Can the military and economic elite return to dominate the government's decisionmaking processes on critical issues?

Perhaps El Salvador is not a democracy but is in transition to becoming one. What will be the quality of that democracy? Will, or can, the rebels successfully lay down their arms, join the process, and help build a democratic regime? Will the final group of reforms agreed to in the peace talks, from the creation of a new electoral council to the remaking of the national police, be sufficient to bring about democracy? How strong will the armed forces be after the accords are fully implemented? Fear still pervades Salvadoran society, though it can be expected to decline, and there exists a visible lack of institutional strength, particularly in the judicial system, that is unlikely to be remedied fully by the peace agreements. Viewed in this light, is democracy in El Salvador a realistic goal for the short or medium term?

By providing a forum for scholars and policymakers to discuss events in El Salvador soon after the March 10 election and in the wake of the New York Agreement, we sought to highlight the central issues of the civil conflict. We also sought to provide an opportunity for dialogue between scholars and policymakers from opposing perspectives both in the United States and El Salvador. Shedding light on these key questions can help strengthen the efforts under way to end the long war and build democratic government in El Salvador. Some of the questions we attempted to raise may have been partially answered by the quick pace of events of recent months. Indeed, as former US ambassador to El Salvador Edwin Corr recently remarked, writing about El Salvador today is like trying to paint a moving train. Nevertheless, we expect this volume to provide a large snapshot of the situation during an especially important period as well as to be timely enough to provide insight into current events, even as they continue to unfold.

The Rest of the Book

Part 1 addresses the legislative assembly elections of March 1991 and the political context in which they were conducted. In Chapter 1, Tom Gibb, a veteran analyst who has researched the death squads, among many other areas, emphasizes that ending the war means transferring the conflict from the battlefield to the political system. The March elections, when for the first time there was widespread participation and for the first time the FMLN did not disrupt the vote, demonstrated that this transition already has started. But deficiencies in the areas of societal consensus, the protection of minority rights, and rule of law ensure that the process will be "difficult and messy." 1994, the year the Salvadoran president, national assembly, and municipal officeholders will all be up for reelection, is a critical date in the calendar of the peace process. In less than three years, El Salvador's "entire power structure will be up for grabs" and the clear prospect exists that "a real set of options will be put before the Salvadoran people," according to Gibb.

Gibb argues that the conduct of the elections raises a number of concerns. First, the registration process is open to abuse, especially in the countryside. Second, an extraordinary number of names were lost from the voting register without explanation, so tens of thousands of people who were registered were not able to vote. Yet, the election results probably reflected broadly how the public actually voted and were highly favorable for the peace process, largely because of the participation of two parties on the left, whose strong performance was the surprise of the election. The Christian Democrats were the biggest vote losers; the Nationalist Republican Alliance (ARENA) on the right remained the dominant political force in the country.

In Chapter 2, George Vickers puts the electoral process in El Salvador in historical perspective. His review of the six elections between 1982 and 1989 does not provide much room for optimism. The increasing pluralism demonstrated by the participation of parties on the left is offset by trends that suggest a repolarization of voters and a disintegration of the center. "Votes for rightist parties increased by 12 percent from 1989 to 1991, while votes for centrist parties declined by 8 percent," he writes, "parties on the Left of the Salvadoran political spectrum got 15 percent of the valid votes, up from 3.8 percent" two years earlier.

In this electoral climate, Vickers sees the peace negotiations going through a difficult period in the short term. None of the parties has shifted position since early April 1991 and much more fighting can be expected prior to reaching a settlement because the FMLN will be forced to demonstrate that it has the military capacity to maintain its political demands. All sides will have to shed completely the illusions of the past. For the FMLN, that means discarding the idea that popular insurrection will bring them to power. For the extreme Right, it means discarding the belief that demands for social justice are the result of Communist agitation. Finally, the United States must realize that formal mechanisms of electoral democracy cannot necessarily be equated with democratic values.

In Chapter 3, John McAward, an analyst of El Salvador and US policy for well over a decade, disagrees with Vicker's assessment of the efficacy of elections. In the early 1980s, one could oppose the US policy of supporting elections, but today that policy should be viewed as far-sighted. The vision of this policy can be seen today in increased political pluralism and in the improved behavior of the military, although the 1989 killing of the Jesuit priests illustrates that it is an imperfect process. The recent elections were not perfect, he argues; the process can be improved. Difficult challenges remain, and the most important US role is to give "a strong signal to the Salvadoran military that a resolution of this conflict has to come now" and that backpedaling is unacceptable.

Part 2 addresses US policy toward El Salvador. In Chapter 5, Bernard Aronson, an assistant secretary who has closely examined the history and political life of El Salvador, emphasizes that the "United States fully and unequivocally supports the negotiating process." But the United States is also "unequivocally committed to the defense of the security of the government of El Salvador" and hopes that commitment will not be tested. The United States would be pleased to use its military assistance to support a cease-fire and the reintroduction of combatants from both sides into civilian life.

Aronson notes that with regard to the armed forces, the reform of which the FMLN rebels argue is critical to ending the war, the two parties had agreed on 80 to 90 percent of the toughest issues. The FMLN is wrong to believe that reform will be impossible once a cease-fire is reached because a reduced level of violence will create an atmosphere more conducive to change. Furthermore, the March elections "were a major achievement and one of the most profound changes" during the preceding year. The process of reconciliation will not be easy; one can be optimistic yet should not be surprised if something happens that threatens to setback the process. Ultimately, however, it will succeed because democratization, the creation of political space for everyone to compete for power peacefully, is occurring in El Salvador today.

In Chapter 6, Heather Foote, a veteran analyst of the Salvadoran crisis and congressional policy in the region, raises questions about the consistency of the U.S. role. The Bush administration's support "for both negotiations and elections has been fairly clear." But five examples—the decision to release military aid, sharp criticism of UN mediator Alvaro de Soto, Chief of Staff Colin Powell's remarks on a trip to the region, the replacement of aging helicopters for the Salvadoran army, and raising expectations about the negotiations—produce doubts as to the administration's commitment to peace. Foote sees the gains for political pluralism in the elections diverting attention from the voting irregularities. A sense of fair play in the electoral process will be a critical factor in the transformation of the FMLN into a political force—and Capitol Hill policymakers may be missing this point.

Three key issues in the transition to democracy—human rights, military reform, and the economy—are the topics of Part 3. In Chapter 8, Cynthia Arnson, an expert on human rights and US policy toward Central America, traces the progress, or lack thereof, in the protection of human rights. The crucial issue is how to put an end to human rights atrocities and implement the institutional changes to ensure that they are not repeated. A human rights accord reached between the government and the FMLN, and a 50 percent cut in US military aid to El Salvador by Congress, she argues, helped improve the situation in the second half of 1990. Preelectoral violence in 1991, however, was greater than it was in 1989.

In an update to her presentation, Arnson writes that "El Salvador has traversed a political universe" since April 1991 with the signing of a final peace accord. She provides a review of the important elements of the settlement as they relate to human rights, such as the dissolution of the notorious security forces. Violence in El Salvador in the coming years may emerge from groups opposed to the accord or, because of a lack of prosecutions, from unrepentant criminals either within or outside the military. The first test, Arnson notes, will be the treatment afforded former FMLN combatants as they return to civilian life.

Chapter 9, by José García, who has extensively studied the Salvadoran military, most recently with the US Army School of the Americas, addresses the institutional basis of the Salvadoran armed forces, particularly the *tanda*, or class rotation, system of promotion. He argues that many US policymakers and human rights advocates criticize the *tanda* system for its evils. It should, however, be viewed in historical context as a largely successful effort to create internal stability in the military. Evil still exists within the institution, but it is the result of extremely weak civilian democratic institutions, not the system itself.

"Ironically," García believes, "in some ways the armed forces [of all the principal actors] have had the least coherent idea of what they were fighting for" because they continually accepted the ideas of their allies and benefactors, particularly the United States, whose policy often changed over time. The ability of the military to engage in "collective introspection about their wartime experience" will be important to its future behavior. Continued international monitoring of human rights and democratic practices will be useful because, in the past, this work has helped restrain antidemocratic activity. Generally, he highlights three factors: (1) that US leverage over the army has decreased, (2) that cooperation between the army and the government has improved, and (3) that the autonomy of the armed forces has increased.

In Chapter 10, Salvadoran businessman Roberto Murray Meza expresses an "an air of optimism" about the state of El Salvador's economy. He argues that the progress in the peace negotiations is being mirrored in the economic arena. Thanks to President Cristiani's market-oriented policies, the overall economic situation has improved over the past year, bringing about increased business confidence and the first real steps toward economic recovery.

According to Murray Meza, the 1991 economic plan includes the "deepening of the structural adjustments begun in 1989" and "safety net programs" for Salvadorans "not immediately benefiting from the current economic growth." Equally important to the future, however, is negotiating an end to the extremely destructive war. And reintegrating tens of thousands of combatants into civilian life will be a major challenge.

In Chapter 11, Enrique Baloyra, author of *El Salvador in Transition*[6] and numerous articles on the country, highlights the dramatic changes in both parties to the conflict since the war began. Who would have thought ten years ago, he writes, that a candidate from the rightist ARENA party would run for president vowing to seek dialogue with the guerrillas or that the FMLN leaders would announce that they are Social Democrats? A cease-fire would be achieved because "one can see at each level of Salvadoran society a process of replacement and substitution that points to a quantitative improvement." In addition, he insists, today "there is a prevalence of democratic discourse." Progress will be difficult, however, and one should not be surprised by gross acts of provocation against those who support the process.

In Chapter 13, Alvaro de Soto provides a detailed outline of the peace negotiations and examines the prospects for a settlement. From the initial involvement in 1989 to the latest major accord in New York, he emphasizes, the United Nations has offered many ideas and done a great deal of persuading in an effort to bring the parties together on controversial points. When the secretary-general invited the FMLN and the Cristiani government to New York, he assumed that "the political cost of the two parties returning empty-handed would be so high that they would be very flexible" and reach agreements that were not possible previously. The gamble paid off.

De Soto asserts that there is "a lot of work still to be done." But after the New York Agreement, only the issue of the reduction of the armed forces had not been addressed in some fashion. If there are no major bumps, the talks should flow smoothly, but if another deadlock emerges, the possibility always exists of the secretary-general gambling on another invitation at the highest levels.

In Chapter 15, Gary Bland, who has closely followed and written about El Salvador, applies broadly to the country democratic transition theory developed in the 1980s. The case of El Salvador, he argues, demonstrates that steps toward democratization—an electoral process, a freer press, and increased political pluralism—are significant in starting the democratic transition. But societal accommodation and increasing acceptance of the political uncertainty that characterizes democracy, both of which were central to the success of the peace talks, were the essential criteria for democratization itself to begin.

Bland is cautiously optimistic about the prospects for democracy. El Salvador began democratizing, he writes, when the warring parties reached negotiated agreements and began implementing them for the benefit of all Salvadoran citizens. This process will continue as the conflict ends and as the country prepares for and conducts elections regarded as open and fair in 1994, after which one will be able to speak of Salvadoran democracy. In the 1980s, according to Bland, the Reagan administration attempted to export democracy to El Salvador while seeking a military victory over the FMLN, deliberately increasing, rather than seeking to halt, societal conflict. The result was, naturally, failure. Today, he argues, with all the major actors supporting the accords and in light of the trends evident throughout society, a fledgling democracy, the first in El Salvador's history, is likely to be achieved in roughly two years.

Included as a chapter at the end of each section is an edited transcript of the conference discussion sessions. We find these sessions informative, especially the remarks of the two public officials. They may be of special interest to the reader.

Notes

1. See, for example, Alfredo Cristiani, "In El Salvador, a New Arena Party," *New York Times,* March 15, 1989, p. A27; and Alfredo Cristiani, "El Salvador: A Defense," *Washington Post,* April 27, 1990, p. A29.

2. See, for example, Joaquín Villalobos, "A Democratic Revolution for El Salvador," *Foreign Policy* 74 (Spring 1989): 103–122.

3. See, for example, Guillermo O'Donnell, Philippe C. Schmitter, and Laurence Whitehead, *Transitions from Authoritarian Rule* (Baltimore: Johns Hopkins University Press, 1986).

4. See Joseph S. Tulchin and Augusto Varas, eds., *From Dictatorship to Democracy: Rebuilding Political Consensus in Chile;* and Joseph S. Tulchin and Rafael Hernández, eds., *Cuba and the United States: Will the Cold War in the Caribbean End?* (Boulder: Lynne Rienner Publishers, 1990). A Woodrow Wilson Center publication on the Venezuela event is forthcoming.

5. Larry Diamond, Juan J. Linz, and Seymour Martin Lipset, eds., *Democracy in Developing Countries, Volume Four: Latin America* (Boulder: Lynne Rienner Publishers, 1989).

6. Enrique A. Baloyra, *El Salvador in Transition* (Chapel Hill: University of North Carolina Press, 1982).

PART 1

El Salvador After the March 1991 Elections

1

Elections and the Road to Peace

Tom Gibb

Ending the war in El Salvador essentially means transferring the conflict from the battlefield to the political arena. In practice, although the fighting continues, politics—including electoral politics—is already taking on an increasingly important role. It is now recognized by all that at some point there will be a political settlement in El Salvador; when and in what form is still open to question.

In many ways, the National Assembly and municipal elections in March 1991 demonstrated that the transition from war to politics has already started. There were a number of firsts: There was wide participation, from the leftist Nationalist Democratic Union (UDN) to the governing right-wing Nationalist Republican Alliance (ARENA) party; the rebels did not disrupt the poll, although in most areas they did not actively participate either; and leftist politicians are due to take up seats in the National Assembly.

On the minus side, the elections demonstrated that the transition to politics is going to be difficult and messy. Building a democracy in El Salvador, or anywhere else for that matter, is not just about instituting majority rule by elections. It is more about building a consensus among the major sectors of society on how the society should work; that is difficult in a country polarized by civil war. Democracy is less about majority rule than minority rights, so that whoever loses the elections does not lose everything else as well. Rule of law to protect individuals, especially from institutions that hold power, is key for any democratic system to work. The population as a whole must have faith in the law and the judicial system. In El Salvador these are areas of serious deficiency,

Tom Gibb is a freelance journalist for the *Washington Post.*

and the elections have to be seen in this light.

1994 will be especially important because presidential, National Assembly, and municipal elections will all be held at the same time. In 1994 the country's entire power structure will be up for grabs—and this will be the crux of the peace process.

The Context of the Elections

Opinion polls by the Jesuit-run University of Central America suggest that the majority of Salvadorans are not firmly lined up behind either side in the conflict (political activists, though very vocal and determined on both sides, are a minority in El Salvador). More than 40 percent believed there would be fraud in the March election. Most believe that all politicians, even those in the party they support, lie and are interested only in winning votes. There is a profound disillusionment with and skepticism about anything or anyone involved in politics. This explains why there was a relatively low turnout—and a great number of spoiled votes—in these elections in a country where many people still regard voting as a duty.

The great majority (73.9 percent) believe that people in El Salvador are afraid to express their opinions publicly. This picture was reinforced by my conversations with Salvadorans. There is a feeling, more marked in the countryside, that it is better not to have a political opinion; "I don't get involved in that kind of thing" is a typical comment. People tend to believe that they have no control over what happens in their lives and that they have little possibility of improving their lot—that nothing ever changes.

These types of attitudes in the electorate have been generated by decades of military dictatorship, during which elections were a farce. And the war itself has produced conditions in El Salvador that clearly affect the results of elections. The most obvious is the level of fear in the countryside. This is a civil war that is more a rebellion than a conventional conflict. Many families and communities are divided. In small communities people look over their shoulders to see who is spying for the government or for the guerrillas. Only a few years ago, getting fingered could mean getting killed. Although this situation affects all parties, it clearly affects the Left a great deal more. In the March elections the leftist coalition, the Democratic Convergence (CD), was able to find candidates for only 70 of the country's 262 municipalities.

In the small town of Santa Clara, in the central province of San Vicente, for example, the Left clearly has much potential support. The town organized a couple of years ago to stand up to the army and abolish the civil defense patrol. The rebels maintain a permanent presence in the countryside around the town. Many people I talked with said that they would support the Convergence. Yet there was no candidate for mayor because "no one was prepared to take the risk and lift his head." About a week before the vote the Christian Democrats held a meeting in the town. Afterward the rebels held their own meeting (borrowing the Christian Democrats' sound equipment). The rebels said that they did not believe elections were the way to solve the problem of the war—that must come through a negotiated settlement—but that the people were free to vote for whom they wanted. Even the ARENA candidate for mayor, who narrowly won the vote on a very low turnout, complimented the guerrillas for holding an "honest meeting." It would be hard, however, to argue that the result reflects the real political balance in the town.

The Conduct of the Elections

There are a number of areas of concern that need to be addressed before 1994. The first is the registration system, which is a badly organized and highly chaotic two-stage process that can take months and that is clearly open to widespread abuse, especially in the countryside.

At the start of the war there was a clear geographic division in the countryside. Families who were part of the military structure, or longtime retainers loyal to the landlords, were often targeted by the rebels. They moved to the nearest town to live under the protection of the local army base or National Guard post. Major Roberto D'Aubuisson is their hero; they hate the guerrillas. These people tend to be the support base for ARENA. Half a mile out of town, the opposite is true: People support the rebels and have often been targeted by the army. In the past, these people did not vote. Often these two sets of people know each other or are even related. People in the towns know exactly which hamlets and which families support the rebels. At the moment, the administration of registration, and much of the rest of the work of the elections, are done by the local mayor's office in each municipality—in other words, by the people who moved to town. Thus the system is clearly open to abuse.

But most worrisome is that the actual electoral register contains many errors. A group of journalists and observers calculated, by taking a sample of voting tables as the polls closed, that up to 60,000 people who had been issued voter ID cards found that their names were not on the register when they came to the polling station. It is possible that losing so many names from the computer register was a result of incompetence and not conspiracy or fraud. Even so, how do we know that many more thousands of names were not lost from the register, as only about half of the registered voters turned out?

The answer is that we do not know, and for an election that is not good enough. The onus must be on the authorities to show a clean and fair vote—not on others to show that there was fraud. The election authorities failed to do that in El Salvador. The problems continued into the vote count. It took almost two weeks to get a result. This, too, raised the level of uncertainty about and degree of mistrust in the process. And respected international observers, who have given a clean bill of health to previous elections in El Salvador, were more critical this time. There was general agreement that compared to the 1990 elections in Nicaragua the vote in El Salvador was a shambles.

The United States has a degree of responsibility for these problems. This year again a large number of official US observers turned up a few days before the vote and were loud in their praise of a "festival of democracy" the day afterward. As the polls were closing, I pointed out to a group of these observers that many people with ID cards had not been able to vote and suggested that they make a check; they did not. If the United States wants democracy to take root in the minds of the Salvadoran people, it should do more than rubber-stamp elections.

The Results: A Push for the Peace Process

Yet no one is seriously disputing that the official results broadly reflect how votes were cast. The outcome has been extremely favorable in pushing forward the peace talks. Now there is a clear prospect of a genuine electoral race in 1994, in which a real set of options will be put before the Salvadoran people for the first time.

The results once again show the strength of the organization that ARENA has built up. However, the party did have certain advantages. It flagrantly violated agreements on spending levels for advertising and placed government advertisements throughout the campaign, dominating radio and television. But the result owed as much to a party organization that is present in every small town as well as the cities; although ARENA lost its overall majority in the National Assembly and got fewer votes than in the 1989 presidential elections, it is still the dominant political force in the country.

It is worth noting, however, the change that is taking place in the party. As the name suggests, it is an alliance of unlikely bedfellows. The government of President Alfredo Cristiani has crystallized around a free-market ideology. Cristiani has brought in a number of highly capable business people and technocrats who are united by the relatively new ideas of removing all influence of the state and equalizing opportunities in the market. Their main interest is not in controlling power or government for itself but in creating the best conditions for their own businesses to flourish. It is a Salvadoran version of Margaret Thatcher's philosophy. If ARENA can continue to develop as a conservative party based on free-market ideology, then it will have a strong position on the Salvadoran political scene.

However, the party machinery, which fought this election campaign and is still under the control of Major Roberto D'Aubuisson, contains many people with differing sets of values. They owe their position to a party that won power. Their loyalty is to the party and, in the case of many of the ex-military officers, the army. These individuals are united by a rabid anticommunism but are at the same time populists. They would not be too happy about selling off the state assets that give them influence. In fact, some of them would like to extend the functions of the state, especially in security areas. Many are personally extremely ambitious. Much will depend on Major D'Aubuisson himself; he has, ironically, acted as a moderator within ARENA and kept many of the ambitious hard-liners in check. In the past few months he has been seriously ill. If his illness (cancer) continues, ARENA has an uncertain future as a unified force.

In many ways the elections helped the Cristiani line of the party, because he and the mayor of San Salvador, Armando Calderon Sol, are far more popular than anyone else in ARENA. (The fact that ARENA's share of the vote fell has been blamed partly on Major D'Aubuisson, who chose all the candidates.) However, Cristiani is facing a serious challenge from the right wing of ARENA. This challenge has centered around opposition to the concessions being made by the government in peace talks. Calderon Sol especially has come under vitriolic attack—he was accused of being a traitor. If the Cristiani wing is going to win in the party, Calderon Sol is the obvious successor for the presidency (by law, Cristiani cannot run again). But there is likely to be a messy succession battle.

Within the government camp there is a great deal of suspicion between the business community and groups within, or allied to, the military. Many business people agree with the Left that the military should be brought under civilian control and the justice system re-formed. They are highly critical of the military's performance in the war and believe that it has become a big business for many senior officers. They are also frightened of the military because earlier in the war military officers were responsible for kidnapping a number of wealthy business-men and demanding multimillion-dollar ransoms. This action caused capital flight from the country. The kidnap ring was broken after an FBI-aided investigation. But only one person is now in jail; the cases against all the others were dropped. The kidnappings have recently started up again, sending a wave of alarm through the business community.

The Christian Democrats were in many ways the real losers of the elections. Even though they came in a respectable second, their share of the pie dropped dramatically from the days when José Napoleón Duarte led them to victory in 1984. Part of the problem is that the party has not clearly defined whether it will be a moderate conservative party, be allied to the Cristiani wing of ARENA, or be a moderate socialist party. Their heaviest loss was in the capital, where they were nearly beaten by the Democratic Convergence. San Salvador used to be their stronghold; their main strength now is in the countryside, where they are still regarded as (and in fact often are) the only legal opposition.

The surprise in the election was provided by the left-wing Democratic Convergence, which did much better than the polls suggested it would. The Convergence was formed three years ago by leftist social democrat–style politicians, allied to the rebels, who have returned to the country from exile. Nationally they obtained 12 percent of the vote, but this result is not an accurate test of their potential. In the capital, the only place they really campaigned, they came in a narrow third with more than 19 percent despite a shoestring campaign and their lack of candidates. Most significant, they received little help from the largest rebel organizations, which, up until the very last minute, virtually boycotted the elections (though they did not actively disrupt them). The performance of the Convergence suggests that there is a hidden vote for the Left that opinion polls cannot pick up. This possibility is not really surprising given that the Left has been acting as a clandestine underground movement for the past fifteen years.

If there is a peace settlement and the rebels put their extensive resources behind a broad left-wing or opposition alliance campaigning on issues of demilitarization and reforms to the judicial system, there could be some surprises in 1994. The key lesson for the Convergence and the left in general is that they are unlikely to continue to grow as an open movement while the war carries on; they need a cease-fire at least within the next year.

The FMLN Guerrillas

Like ARENA, the FMLN is an alliance of sometimes contradictory points of view. The past three or four years have seen an enormous change in the mainstream thought of the FMLN, but there is still a strong internal debate going on. The change is partly a result of the stalemate of the war and the realization that they will have to win politically rather than militarily. More important, international conditions have changed radically. As early as 1987, socialist-bloc allies were telling the rebels that there would be no money to support new regimes in Latin America. This should not be misunderstood: The Eastern bloc has not had much influence over the rebels in terms of how they were fighting the war—the guerrillas are relatively self-sufficient—but they have a great deal of influence in terms of what happens afterward. A Sandinista-type taking of power is no longer a real option because the rebels would be isolated internationally, they would face a US boycott and a ruined economy, and there would be no Eastern bloc to bail them out.

The crisis faced by the Sandinistas in Nicaragua in the past few years and the fall of communism in Eastern Europe have reinforced the message to the point that there is sufficient consensus between the government and the FMLN for a peace process. Both sides say they want to set up a pluralist, democratic society where power is won by elections. Ideas of a one-party state have been dropped by all but the radical minorities in the rebel alliance. It is this change that has made the peace talks possible.

The rebels are clearly looking at a timetable for peace leading up to the 1994 elections. During that time they want to obtain the best conditions possible for reentering the system. They need enough assurance, in terms of security, to convince their supporters, many of whom have lost family members to the army and tend to be more radical than the leadership, that it is safe to come above ground. Above all, they must arrange a settlement in which they can say they were not defeated; otherwise, they will not only lose face, but also be in a weaker position as the conflict moves to the political field.

So why did the FMLN not come out and support the latest elections? The problem is more practical than ideological. Throughout the war years the guerrillas developed an extensive clandestine network throughout the country, a network structured along military lines for fighting a war. This network is the guerrillas' real strength and is often ignored by US officials and the right wing. The dominant sector within the rebel alliance argued that to support the Convergence would, in practice, mean loosening military discipline, bringing structures above ground. They feel the real effort should be to continue military pressure to get concessions at the negotiating table. The way the elections were organized and run has strengthened those within the rebel alliance who argue that to disarm before the elections in 1994 would be committing political, and possibly literal, suicide.

Others argued that the best way to put pressure on the government would be for the Left to make a good showing in the elections, which would demonstrate that they are a real political force. In the end, the rebel attitude toward the elections was confused and divided. The rebels did not boycott the poll, but neither did they participate. The crucial point is that the surprisingly strong showing by the Convergence has given a big push to those arguing that they should go political. Although the results have encouraged the Left to enter the political process, the conduct of the elections has increased the distrust of the government. To have a chance in 1994, the Left will need at least two years after a cease-fire to campaign and to try to build up a broad-based movement to beat ARENA. Forging some kind of unity on the left is going to be a tough challenge, but it is their most attractive option.

Conclusion

For the past eleven years the two sides in the civil war have been trying to win on the battlefield. That is where the fight for power has been. In a situation of extreme polarization many people have been forced to choose sides and have made alliances in time of war that will not necessarily hold in times of peace.

Both sides now say they are willing to support electoral politics. The test of that cannot be until 1994, when we will really know if the rebels are serious or if the right wing will give up power if they lose. Likewise, we will not know for some years whether the agreements that everyone hopes will be reached at the negotiating table—about reforming the army and the judicial system—can really change these institutions and bring the military under civilian control. Reforming the military has been a constantly stated aim of US policy since the start of the war, and it has in many ways been one of the United States' largest policy failures in El Salvador. US influence over the army is based on the knowledge within the Salvadoran military that without US aid they may lose the war. Take away the war and US influence is bound to decline. One wonders how easy it will be to change the institution once the war ends.

A cease-fire will be just the start of a period of change in El Salvador. Whether the rest of the process, including the final steps when the FMLN demobilizes as a military force, goes smoothly will depend largely on the political will of those now holding power. I predict that the process will not be smooth at all; in fact, I think it will be long and messy. I strongly doubt that there is likely to be a definitive resolution of the conflict until after a new set of elections in 1994 in which both sides have participated and after which both sides have accepted the results.

2

The Political Reality
After Eleven Years of War

George R. Vickers

For more than a decade the ebb and flow of the revolutionary civil war in El Salvador has fostered, then shattered, illusions that a decisive turning point has been reached. For the leftist insurgents of the Farabundo Martí National Liberation Front (FMLN), the principal illusion has been of an imminent popular insurrection in the face of which the Salvadoran armed forces will collapse, thus enabling the insurgency to seize power.[1] For the Salvadoran extreme Right, the conviction that popular protest is an artifice of international communism without a genuine social base has been no less an illusion than the certainty that massive repression can crush the desire for social justice.[2] At times the very existence of a political center has seemed illusory. And for the United States the ability to implant on Salvadoran soil formal mechanisms of electoral democracy has sometimes been confused with the creation of a "radically new political culture" of democratic values.[3]

In May 1990 the Salvadoran government and the FMLN began negotiations, mediated by the United Nations, that aimed at reaching a political settlement of the conflict. One year later, expectations that a cease-fire was near were tempered by the reality of continuing intense combat on the battlefield.[4] Are the efforts to achieve a negotiated peace also based on illusion? Not necessarily. The political reality in El Salvador after eleven years of war does contain elements that could provide a foundation for a political accord to end the fighting. Successfully converting those elements into an agreement will require a combination of luck, timing, daring, and skill that recent Salvadoran history suggests is probably less, rather than more, likely.

George R. Vickers is professor of sociology at the City University of New York.

Real opportunities for peace occur when the correlation of political and social forces gives all parties to the conflict greater reasons to seek a political settlement than to prolong the armed struggle. The only consistent feature of Salvadoran political reality over the past eleven years has been the transitory quality of opportunities to achieve a negotiated political solution to the civil war. If the current window of opportunity is not going to be missed, the major actors in the Salvadoran conflict must ruthlessly shed the illusions that have blinded them in the past. They are going to have to stop confusing desire with capacity, form with substance, partial truths with contradictory reality.

In this chapter I review the competing strategic visions and tactical maneuvers that have imparted a dynamic quality to the correlation of political and military forces in El Salvador over the past decade. From an examination of these dynamics we can better understand the illusions that have inhibited a peaceful settlement up to now and the prospects for overcoming those illusions and achieving a negotiated solution in the near future.

Electoral Trends and Democratic Process: 1982–1989

On March 28, 1982, more than 1.5 million Salvadoran voters elected a Constituent Assembly, which was charged with drafting a new constitution and electing an interim government to rule until new elections based on the constitution could be organized.[5] Hope that democratic elections could lead to peace did not last long, however. Over the course of five elections from 1984 to 1989 some 35 percent of the 1982 electorate dropped out of the process.[6]

The March 10, 1991, Legislative Assembly elections brought increased voter turnout for the first time since 1982; it was up 15 percent from the preceding election. This number of voters was still less than three-quarters of the 1982 turnout, however.[7] For the Reagan and Bush administrations, evidence that a democratic consensus was growing in El Salvador was found in the institutionalization of elections, the acceptance of electoral results by losing parties, and the broadening of the ideological spectrum to include leftist political parties competing in elections.[8]

There is, certainly, an important element of truth in this perspective. The 1987 return to El Salvador of social democratic politicians who had been allied with the FMLN, and their subsequent decision to compete in elections in 1989 and 1991, is testimony to the fact that political space has widened significantly since they had to flee the country in 1980. The willingness of right-wing political forces to seek power through electoral competition rather than military coup also provides evidence of a change from El Salvador's troubled political past.

Coexisting with this evidence of El Salvador's increasing political pluralism, however, are trends that suggest a much less encouraging assessment of the prospects for electoral democracy. As disturbing as the decline in turnout are electoral trends suggesting a repolarization of voters, with the right-wing consolidating behind the Nationalist Republican Alliance (ARENA) and centrist voters dropping out of the electoral arena. Although ARENA got 16 percent more votes in March 1991 than in 1982, all rightist parties together got 80 percent of their 1982 total.[9] The centrist Christian Democratic party (PDC), by contrast, got only 54 percent as many votes in 1991 as it received in 1982. All centrist parties together received in 1991 only 46 percent of the votes they received in 1982.[10] Votes for rightist parties increased by 2.5 percent from 1989 to 1991, whereas votes for centrist parties declined by 14 percent over the same period.[11]

In their first appearance in Legislative Assembly elections, parties on the left of the Salvadoran political spectrum got 15 percent of the valid votes in 1991, up from 3.8 percent in the 1989 presidential election.[12] Participation by leftist parties may account for the increased voter turnout compared with 1989. Voter turnout increased by just under 150,000 votes, whereas leftist parties received 130,000 more votes than in 1989.

Added to these disturbing electoral patterns is the fact that the scope and intensity of military struggle has grown dramatically since 1987, after declining from 1984 through 1986. Although elections have provided a new arena for contesting political power in Salvadoran society, there is little evidence to support claims that they have supplanted other, more violent, forms of political struggle.

Revolution and "Democratization": 1979 Through 1989

Revolutions are seldom smooth, linear progressions that steadily build to some final denouement. On the contrary, modern revolutions are much more likely to exhibit the characteristics that Marx discerned in the failed French revolution of 1848: They

> criticise themselves constantly, interrupt themselves continually in their own course, come back to the apparently accomplished in order to begin it afresh, deride with unmerciful thoroughness the inadequacies, weaknesses and paltriness of their first attempts, seem to throw down their adversary only in order that he may draw new strength from the earth and rise again, more gigantic, before them, recoil ever and anon from the indefinite prodigiousness of their own aims, until a situation

has been created which makes all turning back impossible.[13]

The past eleven years provide ample evidence of the ebb and flow of revolutionary fortunes in El Salvador. At times the FMLN has seemed on the verge of triumph, at other times on the verge of collapse. The changing correlation of forces is not a result of some invisible hand of fate but emerges directly out of strategic and tactical decisions by the FMLN, the Salvadoran government, and the armed forces of El Salvador. External support and pressure, particularly from the United States, has been an important factor in these strategic and tactical considerations.

Reform and Repression: 1979–1981

In El Salvador momentum has shifted several times between those forces calling for the revolutionary overthrow of the Salvadoran government and those trying to stave off the revolutionary challenge. Beginning with the military coup by younger, reform-minded officers in October 1979 through much of 1980, forces opposed to the traditional oligarchy organized and mobilized to demand fundamental redistribution of economic and political power. Their efforts were countered by members of the oligarchy and more conservative military officers who initiated a campaign of terror and assassination against activists of the reform movement. By the end of 1980 the conservatives had gained the upper hand in urban areas, and remnants of the reform movement fled the country or joined guerrillas in the mountains.[14]

In January 1981 the newly united guerrilla front, the FMLN, launched a military "final offensive" designed to trigger a popular insurrection to overthrow the conservative regime, but the Salvadoran military (with the help of emergency matériel and financial assistance from the United States) was able to beat back the offensive. The FMLN then retreated to the countryside to wage a protracted guerrilla war.

The Beginnings of Democratization: 1982–1986[15]

In late 1981 the United States began to support a political-military strategy aimed at strengthening the Salvadoran military's ability to combat the FMLN while at the same time establishing a legitimate government through democratic elections. Although the strategy sought to build up the Christian Democratic party into a reformist alternative to both the FMLN and the traditional oligarchy, in the March 1982 elections for a Constituent Assembly right-wing parties headed by ARENA won thirty-six of the sixty seats. The conservative majority proceeded to draft a new constitution that gave broad powers to a Legislative Assembly but limited the powers of the executive branch.[16] The Constitution also placed obstacles in the way of economic reform and made it very difficult to amend the Constitution itself.[17]

Despite this initial political setback, the political-military democratization strategy supported by the United States began to show results over the next several years. The Salvadoran armed forces increased in size from 15,000 to almost 60,000. Special counterinsurgency battalions were trained by the United States and began to take the war to the guerrillas in their own strongholds. The air force received helicopters and gunships that dramatically increased the mobility and firepower of the armed forces. A combination of electronic and human intelligence-gathering techniques improved the government's knowledge of the FMLN and ability to counter its tactics.

There were substantial improvements in the command structure of the armed forces and a corresponding decrease in human rights abuses by the military and security forces. Some officers who were identified as being connected with major abuses were removed from key positions. The officer corps, which traditionally acted as enforcers to maintain the economic power of the oligarchy in exchange for power and wealth, began to discover that support for US policies was now key to career advancement and continued military aid for the armed forces as a whole. Although it would be a mistake to overemphasize the degree of such changes, it is important to note that at this point the armed forces could no longer be accurately described as merely a dependent appendage of the traditional oligarchy.

In response to the improvements in the armed forces, the guerrillas broke down into small units and dispersed throughout the country. Large-scale actions by the guerrillas (which had reached the level of set-piece battles by the end of 1983) became the exception by late 1984 and were more symbolic than militarily significant. During 1985 and 1986, the armed forces launched prolonged campaigns into guerrilla-controlled zones designed to root out the guerrilla infrastructure and disrupt their network of peasant support. These campaigns culminated in the "Phoenix" operation from January through April 1986, when the armed forces attacked and seized the Guazapa volcano. They cleared out peasant supporters of the guerrillas, captured and destroyed guerrilla bases and supplies, drove the guerrillas away, and then selectively resettled peasants into the area under close government control.

The United States, using political and financial support, built up the Christian Democratic party (which was headed by José Napoleón Duarte) as an alternative to both the guerrillas and right-wing parties allied with the oligarchy. Duarte won the presidential election in 1984, and the Christian Democrats regained control of the Legislative Assembly in 1985. Duarte proposed a dialogue with the guerrillas to seek an end to the civil war, and two meetings among the government, the armed forces, and the guerrillas were held. Although this dialogue ultimately broke down, it did produce significant popular support for Duarte and was strongly backed by the Catholic church. Duarte also provided legitimacy to the Salvadoran government and was able to end the international isolation of El Salvador that developed during the period from 1980 to 1982, when military security forces and death squads murdered some 30,000 people. The US Congress restored economic aid, and European governments also renewed political relations and economic assistance.

Despite surface appearances, underlying forces in the social and economic arenas were developing in ways that undermined and endangered the political gains of the prior two years. These forces were partly independent of US policies, partly a consequence of those policies, and partly a consequence of FMLN strategy and tactics. Throughout 1986 these developments gradually eroded the political strength of the Duarte government and, combined with changes in the military arena, allowed the FMLN to gradually regain the political and military initiative in El Salvador.

For example, despite the gains on political and military fronts, the Salvadoran economy continued to deteriorate. Real gross domestic product (GDP) growth was negative or essentially static between 1983 and 1986, and export earnings declined. On a per capita basis, real GDP in 1985 was about 67 percent of the 1978 level.[18] Inflation, which ranged between 11 and 15 percent from 1981 through 1984, rose to 22 percent in 1985 and 32 percent in 1986.[19] Official US estimates indicate that unemployment remained somewhere between 30 and 50 percent.[20] There was virtually no increase in private investment by domestic or foreign sources. These overall economic trends reflected the continued depressed world market for the basic agricultural commodities on which El Salvador's economy depends (coffee, cotton, and sugar) and the special difficulty faced by a nation torn by civil war.

The full significance of the latter fact is evident when the damage to El Salvador's economy from the war is taken into account. The FMLN waged an announced campaign of economic sabotage directed against infrastructure targets like bridges and the electrical system and also disrupted production through periodic strikes to shut down transportation. Direct war-related damage to the infrastructure between 1979 and the end of 1984 is estimated at $146 million; damage resulting from destroyed and lost production for the same period is estimated at $537 million. When indirect costs of the war are included, US estimates of war-related damage to the economy in that period amount to more than $1.2 billion, and through 1986 the total reached $2 billion.[21] During the same period, from 1979 through 1984, total US aid to El Salvador was about $1.386 billion, with an additional $1.2 in 1985 and 1986. Put somewhat differently, total US aid from 1979 through 1986 was roughly equivalent to the economic damage that the war caused to the economy.

As a final nail in the economic coffin, the October 1986 earthquake caused an estimated $1 billion in additional economic damage and its effect was particularly severe in damaging the infrastructure in the capital of San Salvador.[22] More than 300,000 Salvadorans were made homeless by the earthquake, and more than 50,000 homes were destroyed.[23]

In January 1986 President Duarte introduced an economic austerity program to deal with the growing economic crisis. The key elements of this program included a devaluation of the *colón*, an increase in interest rates, a selective consumption tax and value-added tax on coffee, price controls, and an increase in public-sector wages. The wage increases were less than the inflation rate, however, and the austerity program was widely perceived as an additional burden on the poor and the working class (although coffee producers also opposed the tax on coffee).

The most important political result of the austerity program was a fragmentation of union support for Duarte and the Christian Democrats and a resurgence of public demonstrations by unions in San Salvador. During 1986 the Popular Democratic Union (UPD), a pro-Duarte coalition composed of several unions of rural agricultural cooperative workers, broke apart with the majority and joined a new coalition with unions opposed to Duarte.[24] The new anti-Duarte coalition, the National Union of Salvadoran Workers (UNTS), began public demonstrations against the austerity program that grew in size, frequency, militancy, and breadth of representation through most of 1986.

During Duarte's campaign for the presidency in 1984, he promised a series of economic reforms that would redistribute land to peasants and redistribute wealth downward. It was these promises, and his pledge to seek a dialogue with the guerrillas to end the war, that enabled him to gain significant political support from key agricultural unions. After his election and throughout most of 1985, Duarte explained his failure to deliver on promised reforms as resulting from right-wing control of the Legislative Assembly, which blocked his proposals. With the achievement of a Christian Democratic majority in the 1985 Legislative Assembly elections, however, he was no longer able to blame the Right for his failure to produce economic reforms. During late 1985 the government came under increasing pressure from these unions to make good on its promises.

Duarte's inability to produce reforms resulted not only from right-

31

wing opposition but also from US pressure. From the time of Duarte's election in 1984, US Embassy officials believed that the greatest threat to his government came from opposition by the business community to his policies and person, not from the FMLN. The predominantly right-wing business community viewed Duarte as pro-Communist, and US officials were concerned that members of the business community would seek to undermine his government by economic sabotage or by promoting a military coup. These officials urged Duarte to not take actions that would offend the private sector.[25] In practical terms this meant that Duarte could not raise taxes on the wealthy or redistribute income downward and that in seeking measures to cope with the economic crisis his options were severely limited.[26]

The erosion of Duarte's political base and the resurgence of the Right undermined a key element of US policy in El Salvador—the creation of a democratic and reformist alternative to the traditional oligarchy on the one hand and Marxist guerrillas on the other. Accompanying this political erosion was a less visible change in the military situation. The military initiative that was held by the Salvadoran armed forces from 1984 through early 1986 dissipated. The forces of the FMLN shifted to an offensive phase.

US military aid increased from $81.3 million in 1983 to over $206 million in 1984 and exceeded $100 million in each of the subsequent years. In the face of the dramatic quantitative and qualitative improvement in the Salvadoran armed forces described earlier, it is not surprising that the FMLN was forced onto the defensive. What is more surprising in retrospect is that the tactical response of the FMLN to these improvements succeeded in preventing a more decisive strategic victory on the military front by government forces.

The FMLN's tactical response had three principal elements: (1) breaking down into small units to avoid destruction of main-force guerrilla units and to stretch out enemy forces; (2) concentration on economic sabotage, hit-and-run ambushes, and the use of mines to wear down the government forces and to keep them off balance; and (3) placing new emphasis on political propaganda and organizing, particularly in the western provinces and urban centers, to build an infrastructure for spreading the war throughout the country and into the urban areas (particularly San Salvador).[27] In a sense, the first two elements were designed to buy time for the third to bear fruit.

To a significant degree these tactics were successful. Despite the offensives of the armed forces, traditional guerrilla-controlled zones remained largely outside of government control into 1986. While the guerrillas launched fewer and smaller offensive actions against government forces, guerrilla casualties were relatively small and guerrilla units remained intact. By contrast, government casualties rose steadily, with a growing proportion the result of mines rather than direct combat.[28] The predominant view of observers at the outset of 1986 was that the military situation was in a dynamic equilibrium in which neither the guerrillas nor the government forces had a decisive edge. Instead, both sides seemed to be settling into a war of attrition.

Repolarization: 1987–1989

By summer 1986, subtle changes in the military balance began to occur. The dramatic buildup and qualitative improvement of the Salvadoran armed forces began to level off. In terms of size and equipment, if not of training, the armed forces began to reach a saturation point.[29] At about the same time, it became clear that the FMLN had achieved some success in building an infrastructure in the western provinces. For the first time, guerrilla units carried out military operations in Sonsonate and Ahuachapan, which had been essentially free of guerrilla activity.[30]

By early 1987, the shift in military initiative became more pronounced. On January 21, 1987, the FMLN called a nationwide strike against transport that was—for the first time—100 percent effective in the west as well as in the east. In March a large-scale guerrilla attack overran a key government outpost at El Paraiso in Chalatenango Province, killing a US adviser, and in May the guerrillas had partial success with an attack on the regional military command headquarters at San Francisco Gotera in Morazan province. During this same period, guerrilla units became active in the capital, carrying out highly visible attacks against two large supermarkets and engaging in almost nightly attacks against police.[31]

As guerrilla units began to take the offensive, supporters and sympathizers of the guerrillas also were active. Civilians who had been driven out of guerrilla-controlled zones by army offensives in 1985 and 1986 began to resettle near their old homes either informally (by slipping back through army lines) or formally (by relocating en masse with the church and international supporters as guarantors against army retribution). In the capital, students and unions began a campaign of daily demonstrations against the government.

During the second half of 1986 and throughout 1987 the strategic and tactical approaches of the Salvadoran government and armed forces on the one hand, and the FMLN on the other, were diametrically opposed. In March 1986 the armed forces, under US tutelage, developed a new national plan for a counterinsurgency campaign. Entitled "Unidos para Reconstruir" ("United to Reconstruct"), the plan outlined a program designed to bring government services to areas recaptured from the guerrillas and to win the "hearts and minds" of the people. Under the plan, all international resources coming into the country would be channeled into the program beginning in July 1986, and by January 1987 all domestic and international resources were to be focused through the plan.[32]

The difference between this plan and earlier pacification efforts was that the military intended to control the entire project, including distribution of government services. Gen. Adolfo Blandón, the chief of staff, personally announced the plan and went around to the private sector and to government ministries to tell them what was expected of them in terms of their role in the effort. In effect, the military declared that it was taking control of key areas that had been part of civilian government responsibility.[33]

The October 1986 earthquake in San Salvador severely disrupted the timetable for the plan and the financial planning central to its execution. In November 1986 the FMLN General Command met to evaluate the war and concluded that the army project required an acceleration of FMLN plans to intensify urban fighting and to increase the size of FMLN combat units.[34] They laid out a three-stage plan intended to culminate in a counteroffensive and popular insurrection: (1) a preparatory phase that would amass forces while defeating the *Unidos para Reconstruir* campaign; (2) a stage immediately prior to the counteroffensive that would intensify the destabilization of the Salvadoran government and strengthen the insurgent apparatus in urban areas, particularly in San Salvador; and (3) a major national counteroffensive designed to trigger an insurrection.

The FMLN leaders viewed the army counterinsurgency plan as an effort to establish firm control of urban areas and then gradually to extend government control over the countryside. The weakness in this plan was the fact that the cities were not a secure rearguard area because of the presence of large numbers of workers and poor people. To prevent the army from devoting most of its forces to pressuring FMLN zones of control, the FMLN General Command ordered a "reactivation" of urban struggle with five goals: weakening the armed forces, increasing FMLN military forces, economic and political destabilization, organization of the masses, and expansion of the war.[35]

During 1987 and 1988 the army infiltrated unions, human rights organizations, and other popular organizations that surfaced to oppose the Salvadoran government. Although FMLN urban commandos launched increasingly bold attacks in San Salvador, US officials and Salvadoran army commanders dismissed them as terrorist attacks that demonstrated the growing desperation of the FMLN.[36]

It appears that the Salvadoran army intelligence structure was misled by FMLN misdirection. Known FMLN cadre were released from prison during this period, and many reappeared as leaders of unions or popular organizations challenging the government. Army leaders assumed that FMLN urban commando units were run out of these organizations and felt confident that successful infiltration of these groups would provide the armed forces with sufficient information about the capabilities of the FMLN in San Salvador to control the course of events. In fact, however, FMLN urban commandos were primarily recruited from an entirely different sector of the urban population and a clandestine structure was established before the Salvadoran armed forces and US intelligence officials realized that they had been deceived.

ARENA's victory in the 1988 elections for Legislative Assembly and for municipal councils was viewed by FMLN leaders as a vindication of their strategy of undermining the Christian Democrats, and they believed it would sharpen the political polarization within the country.[37] The overwhelming ARENA victory in the 1989 presidential election convinced them that conditions were rapidly maturing to a point where the population was ready to rise up in insurrection. In January 1989 the FMLN announced for the first time its willingness to lay down arms and participate in elections after a negotiated settlement rather than demanding a coalition government prior to elections. In exchange for this concession, the FMLN called for a six-month postponement of the presidential elections scheduled for March 1989. The offer was quickly rejected, and the timing and ambiguity of the offer suggest that it was primarily a tactical move aimed at complicating the electoral process.[38]

Near the end of 1988, Joaquín Villalobos argued that the objective conditions for an insurrection already existed and that the subjective conditions were nearing a point of explosion.[39] He maintained that the FMLN could not afford to pass up the opportunity to seize the moment: "To fail to act would not only constitute a strategic political error, but it would also leave space for the recovery of the politico-economic model of domination that led to the war and to U.S. intervention."[40]

The moment came in November 1989 when the FMLN launched its long-threatened offensive. Despite prior warning, the Salvadoran army was caught off guard by the scale and scope of the attack and was on the defensive for the first three days. Inspired by initial successes, the FMLN ordered its units to hold on to territory taken in the initial assault and called for a general uprising. This proved to be a serious error, however. The urban population in barrios not occupied by FMLN units did not rise up and air power directed against FMLN logistical and command operations inflicted serious casualties. Within two weeks the FMLN units had to withdraw main-force units from urban areas.[41]

Fighting and Talking: 1990–May 1991

The November 1989 FMLN offensive and the killings of the Jesuits brought about a fundamental reexamination of strategy and tactics by the FMLN, the Salvadoran government and armed forces, the Bush administration, and the US Congress. As a result of these evaluations, all parties concluded that negotiations aimed at achieving a cease-fire and political settlement were the best available policy option in the short term.

For the FMLN, the November offensive demonstrated clearly that hopes for a popular insurrection in the cities were not realistic in the immediate future. The offensive also took a heavy material and human toll, necessitating a slowdown in military operations in order to resupply and regroup. Although Villalobos and some other FMLN leaders had begun to argue that the changes taking place in the socialist world required the FMLN to pursue seriously a negotiated settlement to the war, the basic strategic plan of the FMLN from 1985 through the 1989 offensive remained unchanged.[42]

That plan called for political and military actions designed to undermine and defeat the US-supported effort to create a centrist (Christian Democrat) alternative to the traditional oligarchy and the FMLN, weaken and isolate (both militarily and politically) the Salvadoran armed forces, build a political infrastructure throughout the country that could also be used to gradually amass forces for the military struggle, and combine guerrilla and main-force military actions with increasing political mobilization in an escalating counteroffensive that would finally be combined with urban insurrection to seize power.[43]

Although the failure to provoke an insurrection by the November 1989 offensive did not necessarily invalidate the strategy, it did require a rethinking of the time line and a new assessment of the strategic balance between military and political struggle in the current period. Even though that assessment was only beginning in January and February 1990, all five organizations that constituted the FMLN agreed that the immediate priority was to press for negotiations.

For the Bush administration, US military advisers, and the Salvadoran army and government, the November offensive destroyed whatever illusions existed that the FMLN was fading away as a military threat. Although there was considerable sentiment that the offensive was very costly militarily for the FMLN, there was also growing conviction that continuing to pursue a primarily military strategy to defeat the FMLN would not produce significant results in less than seven or eight more years.[44]

Even prior to the November offensive, the Bush administration had indicated to Salvadoran officials that the decline of the Cold War and the changes taking place in Eastern Europe, together with US budget problems, made it unlikely that Congress would continue indefinitely to provide aid at the level of the 1980s.[45] On top of this, outrage in the United States over the killing of the Jesuits produced strong pressure in Congress to cut off military assistance to El Salvador. All of these factors combined to heighten interest in a negotiated solution by the US government and the government and armed forces of El Salvador.

Thus, for perhaps the first time since at least 1984, all the key actors in the Salvadoran conflict concluded that negotiations were in their short-run interest.[46] A window of opportunity opened in which negotiations mediated by the United Nations replaced the military battlefield as the main theater of operations.

The problem with windows is, of course, that they can close as well as open. Even before the formal agreement to open negotiations was signed on April 4, 1990, the electoral defeat of the Sandinistas in Nicaragua altered the regional context in which the Salvadoran conflict took place and stimulated yet another reassessment of the political and military balance of forces among the parties to the conflict. Such reassessment has been a continuing feature of the past year and a half.

Although there are different ways of characterizing this period during which fighting and negotiations continued simultaneously, the analysis here is divided into five time periods: from the Sandinista defeat through May 1990, May until early September 1990, from September 1990 through mid-January 1991, from mid-January through the March 10 elections, and the period since the elections.

Establishing a Framework (February–May 1990)

For the FMLN, entering into negotiations raised fundamental questions. Was the objective of negotiations to achieve a political settlement of the war or to buy time until conditions were more favorable for a military victory? How to answer that question involved not only an assessment of the likelihood of creating conditions for a military victory but also an estimation of whether the other side was really looking for a political solution. If the Salvadoran government and the United States viewed negotiations primarily as a political trap for the FMLN, the options available to the FMLN were different than otherwise.

The FMLN also had to assess its willingness to enter into elections and its prospects upon doing so. At root this required specifying the kinds of legal, physical, and political guarantees needed to ensure an open and free electoral process, the skills needed to compete effectively, and the time needed to develop those skills.

At a more mundane level, leaders of the five organizations constituting the FMLN also had to assess the potential impact of a negotiated settlement on each organization. Despite talk several years earlier about forming a single Marxist-Leninist party, the different organizations remain politically distinct.[47] Different perspectives on negotiations fostered (and were fostered by) competition between the organizations.[48] In addition, the reassessments necessitated by the offensive and the prospect of negotiations generated intense debates and disagreements *within* each of the five organizations.

These questions and issues were not quickly resolved. Nor did the five organizations reach consensus on a new strategy to replace the one followed since 1986. The result was that FMLN tactics in the negotiations from May through the summer seemed highly ad hoc and reactive. The only real consensus within the FMLN was that, if they were to participate in elections in March 1991, a minimum of six months would be needed after a cease-fire for them to compete effectively. Working backward from the March 10 election date, a deadline of early September for reaching agreement on a cease-fire was set.[49]

The government and the armed forces of El Salvador also had to resolve disagreements within and between their respective spheres. During January, February, and March 1990 the United States, through the military advisory group and State Department officials, pressed hard for changes in the armed forces High Command to remove officers associated with human rights abuses. They also told Salvadoran officials that, although the US government would not try to force the Salvadoran government to negotiate an end to the fighting, US financial assistance was likely to decline in 1991 and thereafter.[50]

The parties agreed to UN-mediated negotiations at a meeting in Geneva that ended April 4, 1990. At a meeting in Caracas May 16–21 they agreed to an agenda for the talks that envisioned three stages to the talks: first, negotiations to reach political accords on key issues sufficient to permit an agreement on a cease-fire; second, renewed negotiations to achieve more permanent accords on the same issues discussed in the first stage, which would lead to the reincorporation of members of the FMLN into civil society; third, final accords to consolidate the results of prior negotiations.

The issues to be negotiated, according to the agenda agreed upon at Caracas, included changes in the armed forces, human rights guarantees, strengthening of the judicial system, reforms of the electoral system, constitutional reforms, a pact over economic and social problems, and

UN verification. These issues were to be taken up in order, though the sequence could be changed by mutual consent.[51] Implicit in this agenda was a notion that limited changes might be sufficient to create conditions for a cease-fire but that more fundamental changes might be needed before the FMLN would renounce armed struggle and participate in a reformed political process.

Tactics in Search of Strategies (June–September 1990)

At meetings in June and July, FMLN and government proposals for dealing with the armed forces were discussed. FMLN proposals called for cleansing the officer corps, prosecuting those officers implicated in four key human rights cases (the killing of Archbishop Oscar Arnulfo Romero, the National Trade Union Federation of Salvadoran Workers [FENASTRAS] bombing, the Jesuit killings, and the kidnapping and murder of Héctor Oquelí Colindres), and abolishing the Atlacatl Battalion, Treasury Police, National Guard, civil defense forces, and the National Intelligence Directorate (DNI), among other things. The government counterproposal called for including notorious FMLN abuses in cases scheduled for exemplary prosecution, amnesty for other cases, and transferring control of security forces to other institutions.[52]

Faced with an impasse in the discussions over the armed forces, the UN mediator suggested that the parties discuss the next agenda item, which dealt with human rights. They did reach agreement and sign an accord on human rights on July 26, 1990, but the agreement was criticized by human rights groups and others within El Salvador as insufficient because UN verification would not become effective until after a cease-fire was in place.[53] The FMLN was anxious to keep the talks alive after the impasse concerning restructuring of the armed forces and apparently was not aware how the human rights agreement would be perceived. It tried, unsuccessfully, to reopen the human rights accord for further modifications at the next meeting, which was in San José in August.[54]

By the time of the August 17–22 round of negotiations it was clear that there would not be accords sufficient to achieve a cease-fire by September.[55] At this round the FMLN presented a revised proposal on the armed forces that considerably expanded the scope and depth of the changes being sought.[56] A further round in September brought no movement on the armed forces issue.

The US role during this period is difficult to discern. The defeat of the Sandinistas apparently reopened an internal debate within the administration over what attitude to take toward the negotiating process.

39

Some favored pressing the Salvadoran government and armed forces to negotiate a political settlement as quickly as possible, whereas others favored prolonging the negotiations in a belief that loss of Sandinista support would weaken the FMLN over time.[57] The role of the United Nations was primarily to facilitate and to gather information. The UN mediator did not offer specific proposals but did try to maintain communication between the parties.

Changing the Correlation of Forces (September 1990–January 1991)

Failure to achieve accords that could lead to a cease-fire by September 1990 brought renewed struggle on the political and military battlefields away from the negotiating table. On September 4, the FMLN released a new political program, the third in eleven years. The new program dropped all references to a coalition or transitional government as a prelude to new elections and instead called for reforms of the existing political framework in line with the negotiating position of the FMLN. The principal difference between the new program and those issued earlier in the war was that the new program was cast in the language and framework of democratic ideology.

On October 27, 1990, the US Congress approved a foreign aid bill that withheld 50 percent of the $85 million in military assistance for fiscal year 1991 to El Salvador. The bill contained provisions designed to pressure both the FMLN and the government of El Salvador to accept active mediation by the UN and to accept a plan by the UN secretary-general for a settlement.[58] President Bush signed the bill into law on November 5. The vote was perceived by Salvadoran military leaders as a message that they must accept significant internal reforms.

At a session in Mexico City that lasted from October 28 to 31, the FMLN and the Salvadoran government agreed to an expanded role for the UN mediator and to maintain strict confidentiality over the timing and substance of future meetings. On October 31 the UN mediator presented to the parties a "working document" dealing with reform of the armed forces. The preamble discussed progressive and complete demilitarization as an interim goal toward ultimate abolition of armies but put it in the context of regional efforts to demilitarize. The substantive proposals called for creating an ad hoc commission to review the records of army officers and to have power to retire officers whose competence or human rights record were wanting. This ad hoc commission was to consist of three persons named by the secretary-general of the United Nations, and it was to complete its work within three months after being named.[59]

The document also called for abolishing the Treasury Police and the National Guard and removing all security functions from a reorganized National Police (which would assume those civil police functions previously assigned to the two forces being abolished). It also called for abolishing the DNI and transferring its intelligence-gathering functions to a new body under civilian control.

The UN working document also described a special commission that would investigate the most well known cases of human rights abuses to discover the truth and to make recommendations for further action. This commission would also be composed of three persons appointed by the UN secretary-general and would complete its work within six months.[60]

While the parties were still assimilating the working document, on November 19 the FMLN launched a new military offensive. Although some attacks were in cities, most of the fighting took place in the countryside. During this offensive, which continued sporadically through the end of the year, the FMLN announced that it was converting its guerrilla forces into a regular army called the National Army for Democracy. It also employed surface-to-air missiles against Salvadoran military aircraft, an escalation of weaponry that significantly altered the military balance of forces. This offensive was more selective and less national in scope than the one a year earlier. The primary military objective was to push Salvadoran government forces completely out of territory traditionally controlled by the FMLN. The political objective apparently was to create conditions on the ground that would back up negotiating demands for a cease-fire in place that would put considerable territory under FMLN control.[61]

The offensive underscored a shift in the focus of FMLN tactical thinking. Prior to September a considerable amount of internal debate centered on what stance to take with respect to the coming elections and how that played into negotiating demands. After September the FMLN gave up any thought of direct participation in elections and began planning for a situation where there would be a prolonged period of armed truce. In this scenario the FMLN would effectively govern large areas in the eastern part of El Salvador and be the only armed presence in those areas. At the same time, it would be waging a political struggle in the rest of the country over a several-year period in preparation for the next elections, which were scheduled for 1994.

For the Salvadoran government, however, the March 10 elections loomed increasingly important in relation to negotiating tactics. Reflecting polls that showed a strong desire for peace, government officials spoke optimistically about prospects for reaching negotiated agreements and asserted their flexibility in terms of making structural changes.[62]

ARENA leaders believed that a cease-fire before the elections would benefit the party because the ARENA government could campaign as the party that brought peace.[63]

The Salvadoran armed forces and US advisers had concluded by November that the FMLN was unlikely to participate directly in the March elections. They were more concerned with countering FMLN tactics to extend and consolidate territory.[64] The FMLN offensive was quite successful in putting the army on the defensive because ground troops had difficulty getting air support after the FMLN introduced surface-to-air missiles. There were several incidents in which large numbers of army troops were forced to flee across the Honduran border after FMLN attacks.

There were several indications in late 1990 that the Salvadoran army High Command was seriously preparing for structural reform of the armed forces. The army was working with the UN to computerize the personnel records of officers, and the High Command was conducting its own internal review of personnel records prior to a decision about how to respond to proposals for an external commission that would conduct such a review. At the same time, the army's social security institute was divesting itself of debt and privatizing some holdings. In spring 1990 the FMLN presented a list of close to thirty high-ranking army officers it was accusing of serious human rights violations; by December a majority of those had been retired or moved out of important positions. All of these actions suggested that the army hierarchy was preparing to make concessions in the negotiations.[65]

The UN working document, which came about in the context of the FMLN offensive and introduction of missiles, the congressional vote to withhold a portion of military aid, US pressure to reform, US preoccupation with activities in the Gulf, and the election campaign became a serious framework for reaching agreement on restructuring the armed forces. A new round of negotiations took place in Mexico on January 3–5, 1991, with this document as the focus of discussion.

During the January meeting, all the parties agreed that the National Guard and Treasury Police should be abolished and that security forces should be removed from a reorganized National Police.[66] There were a number of modifications to the text of the working document, most of which strengthened provisions designed to cleanse the armed forces of units associated with human rights abuses and protect against future abuses. The most lengthy and difficult discussion centered on the composition and procedures for naming the ad hoc commission. The Salvadoran government was concerned that the procedure for selecting the members was humiliating and that it gave the appearance of violating sovereignty. The armed forces insisted that the commission should include armed forces representation; the FMLN was equally insistent that such representation would make potential witnesses afraid to testify before the commission.

The formula that emerged removed specific references to the groups that could nominate persons to the UN secretary-general for possible membership on the ad hoc commission and simply stated that individuals and institutions could suggest names within thirty days of signing the document. The secretary-general would consult with the parties and then name members to the commission who, in his judgment, met the agreed-upon criteria. In addition to these three members named by the secretary-general, the president of El Salvador would name a representative of the armed forces who would consult with and present points of view to the commission, but who would not have a vote or participate in deliberations of the commission.

On January 7 the UN representative prepared and circulated an aide memoire that codified the points of agreement that had emerged as amended text in the working document. There was considerable optimism expressed by all the parties that the February meeting would produce a signed accord dealing with changes in the armed forces.

Pausing to Reassess the Balance of Forces (January–March 1991 Elections)

Prior to the February meeting, the FMLN experienced two profound political setbacks. On January 2, 1991, an FMLN unit shot down a US helicopter in rebel-controlled territory. Two of the three crew members survived the crash and apparently were subsequently executed by FMLN soldiers acting on orders of a district commander.[67] The FMLN at first categorically denied the killings but later admitted that an illegal execution may have occurred. It announced that two FMLN officers had been placed under arrest and would be tried in the presence of international observers. In a second political setback, the FMLN was forced to return eighteen surface-to-air missiles to the Sandinista army after the Soviet Union publicly identified the serial number on a missile used to shoot down a Salvadoran air force plane as one the USSR had supplied to the Sandinista army in 1986.[68]

Although the United States and the Soviet Union issued a joint statement on January 4 supporting the negotiations and the UN's role as mediator, the US attitude noticeably hardened in January. The official US response to the executions was cautious at first. Although the administration stated immediately that it appeared the men had survived the crash and then been killed, it waited until forensic specialists examined the bodies before speaking out more strongly.

On January 15 President George Bush released the $42.5 million in military assistance withheld by Congress, though he suspended delivery for sixty days to encourage a negotiated settlement. On February 1, the same day that a new round of talks began in Mexico, the *New York Times* carried a story citing unnamed top State Department officials as criticizing UN mediator Alvaro de Soto for being too accommodating to the FMLN.[69]

In the Mexico talks, Salvadoran government representatives stepped back from positions they had accepted in January regarding changes in the military. They now insisted that President Cristiani, rather than the UN secretary-general, appoint the ad hoc commission. They also insisted that a member of the armed forces be a full member of the commission. Despite several attempts by the UN mediator to find new formulas, the talks broke off with no results. A subsequent meeting in Caracas in late February produced a further hardening of position, as the government proposed changes to forty-one of the fifty-three paragraphs of the working document. The meeting broke up without setting a date for the next meeting and with much public recrimination.

The deterioration of negotiations reflected several changed circumstances. The shooting down of the helicopter and the killing of the US crew changed the political balance within the United States in that congressional willingness to challenge Bush's restoration of withheld funds dissipated. The incident also strengthened the position of those officials who had been arguing for a tougher US stance in relation to negotiating demands.

The decision to restore funding, along with the criticism of de Soto by a top State Department official, relieved US pressure on the Salvadoran armed forces to accept reforms. ARENA's concerns about the effect of negotiations on the upcoming elections also declined, as polls showed ARENA well ahead and the Democratic Convergence faring little better than in the 1989 elections.[70] Negotiations ground to a halt pending the election results.

Keeping the Negotiations Alive (April–May 1991)

The results of the March 10 elections were ambiguous enough to keep hopes alive for a negotiated settlement. ARENA failed to get an outright majority, but a likely alliance of rightist parties will control the Legislative Assembly.[71] The Christian Democrats got almost as many votes as they received in 1988, but they showed themselves politically weaker, especially in San Salvador. The Democratic Convergence demonstrated significant popular support but a weak organizational apparatus. It had difficulty campaigning and getting candidates and campaign workers in several parts of the country because of intimidation. The elections also demonstrated the need for changes in the legal and constitutional mechanisms for conducting elections in order to guarantee free and fair elections. The electoral campaign was marred by intimidation, particularly against leftist parties, and the counting of ballots produced significant examples of fraud.

The vote may provide some indirect measure of the FMLN's current capacity to influence voting. A poll conducted by the University of Central America (UCA) between February 23 and March 2 asked which party people would vote for if the vote were held that day.[72] Four days before the election, the FMLN urged voters to participate. The actual vote suggests that the PDC, the National Conciliation party (PCN), the Nationalist Democratic Union (UDN), and the Authentic Christian Movement (MAC) all did better than the poll suggested, whereas the CD did about as projected and ARENA did worse.[73] The PDC, PCN, and MAC votes may well be a result of strong organizational apparatus of these parties (and, perhaps, of fraud). The UDN vote is more likely to reflect "hidden left" voters who decided to vote at the last minute.

The FMLN was encouraged by the election results because votes for left parties were higher than polls had projected and because ARENA did not win an outright majority. On March 19 the FMLN proposed a new round of negotiations with an accelerated agenda that would simultaneously discuss the armed forces, constitutional reforms, and a cease-fire. They urged that agreement on constitutional reforms be reached prior to April 30 so that they could be approved by the sitting Legislative Assembly and that the negotiators strive to reach accords on the other two issues by May 30. They suggested that military leaders from both sides participate in the cease-fire discussions and that a way be found to encourage input from political parties and other social forces.

The FMLN proposal was accepted, and on April 4 the new round of talks began in Mexico. The session continued until April 28 with a two-day break to allow Salvadoran government negotiators to confer with President Cristiani. During this round of negotiations, the extreme Right mounted an intense campaign against constitutional reforms and other concessions.[74] At one point, ARENA president Armando Calderon Sol felt compelled to publish a signed declaration in which he denied having signed a secret document with the heads of the PDC and CD dealing with negotiation of the accords.

The United States was also highly visible during the negotiations. Gen. Colin Powell, chairman of the Joint Chiefs of Staff, made a brief stop in El Salvador on April 8 on his way to Honduras. In Honduras he gave an ambiguous answer to a reporter's question that was interpreted by many in El Salvador as a threat to use US military force in El Salvador.[75] On April 12, Bernard Aronson, assistant secretary of state for inter-American affairs, made a surprise visit to President Cristiani. The following week he told a congressional panel that the United States had evidence that the FMLN was responsible for burning down *Diario Latino* and that the administration was preparing to replace the aging helicopter fleet of El Salvador with new helicopters. He also began adding to his comments of support for the negotiations a warning that the United States would "defend the security" of El Salvador.

On the military front, the Salvadoran armed forces began strong operations against FMLN-controlled territory during the negotiations and the FMLN attacked economic targets throughout the country.

The threatening environment was reflected at the negotiating table. From April 12 through 22 there was little if any movement. The FMLN announced that army restructuring and a cease-fire were no longer on the agenda for this round and that the only subject under discussion was constitutional reforms. Although the FMLN proposed a large number of changes, four were considered most important: (1) creating a constitutional mechanism that would permit popular plebiscites on important matters, (2) changing immediately the Supreme Court membership and insuring that the court would not represent only one party, (3) replacing the political party–based Central Elections Council with a Supreme Electoral Tribunal that would be nonpartisan in makeup, and (4) modifying the procedure for reforming the Constitution to make it easier and quicker.

On April 27 the negotiators agreed on a package of constitutional reforms that did include changes to the Supreme Court and Central Elections Council. The Legislative Assembly passed the rest of the packet of reforms on April 29 but altered the text agreed to for these two. At a hastily called session on April 30, the assembly did change the elections council to have five members (instead of the current three) including representatives of the four parties that received the most votes in the last presidential election plus a president appointed by the Supreme Court.

The passage of constitutional reforms kept the negotiating process alive but without much momentum. The FMLN achieved little of its negotiating agenda during the April round. Negotiations on restructuring the armed forces remained deadlocked. In discussions about the conditions of a cease-fire, the Salvadoran government position was that guerrilla-controlled zones were limited to small, remote areas in northern Chalatenango and Morazán. It also insisted that FMLN political activity be restricted to the controlled zones until the insurgents lay down their arms and that FMLN radio stations be shut down.

The FMLN apparently decided to take what it could get in the way of some constitutional reforms in order to keep negotiations over a cease-fire alive.[76] The impression given by the outcome of the April round and statements made afterward by the different parties was that the FMLN was more anxious than the government to achieve a rapid cease-fire and that the government was content simply to prolong the negotiations.

In May the FMLN carried out major attacks against the electrical system, causing the most serious energy crisis of the war to date. The economic impact of this was large, and both the private sector and the government urged an end to the campaign. The FMLN made it clear that the attacks would continue unless there was progress at the negotiating table. The armed forces also were active in attacking the periphery of FMLN-controlled areas, seeking to contest FMLN territorial claims. The FMLN and Salvadoran government agreed to a new round of talks in late May to continue negotiations over the armed forces and a possible cease-fire.

Prospects for an End to the War

All wars end sooner or later. They end in victory, in defeat, or in compromise. Revolutionary civil wars like the one in El Salvador are no exception. The practical problem for combatants is to end them on favorable terms. So long as one side or the other perceives a possibility of outright victory in the near term it is unlikely to settle for less. In such circumstances war continues until the other side surrenders or is defeated. The recent Gulf War ended in this way.

A situation in which neither side perceives a possibility of near-term victory does not necessarily lead to compromise, however. So long as both parties are confident that they have sufficient resources to avoid defeat in the near and medium term, they may opt for long-range strategies, hoping to gradually shift the correlation of forces in their favor. This situation is typical of prolonged revolutionary wars. The nationalist guerrilla war in Eritrea is a recent example (though that war may be coming to a climax).

Wars that end through real political negotiations are actually rather rare.[77] They tend to occur when (1) neither side perceives a possibility of near-term victory, (2) all the combatants perceive high immediate costs to continued fighting, and (3) all the combatants are uncertain that they can maintain sufficient resources to avoid defeat in the medium and long term. Under such circumstances all the parties may settle for minimum, rather than maximum, objectives. Continuing negotiations in Angola and Kampuchea exemplify this situation. The series of negotiated agreements leading up to and following the 1990 Nicaraguan elections between the Sandinistas and their domestic opposition were a version of this type of settlement.

These are not mutually exclusive categories. The changing correlation of political and military forces that defines the course of all wars constantly creates and alters the perceptions (and the actual situation) of combatants.[78] The course of war in El Salvador over the past eleven years demonstrates the ebb and flow of political and military advantage.

The prospects for achieving a negotiated solution to the Salvadoran conflict in the near term will be shaped by how the combatants perceive the current balance of political and military forces and the underlying dynamics affecting that balance. Although outsiders cannot predict with certainty all the factors that will enter into their evaluations, the following considerations seem likely to form part of their thinking:

1. The FMLN is increasingly isolated in terms of external support for continued military struggle. Neither the Soviet Union nor the Sandinistas seem interested in supporting a prolonged revolutionary war by the FMLN, nor does the FMLN have support for such an effort from European or Latin American social democracies. Cuba is the only country still expressing strong solidarity.

2. Despite growing international isolation, the FMLN retains a very solid social base within El Salvador and seems to have sufficient resources to continue military actions at a high level. It retains the military initiative and has the capacity to defend territory and destroy the economy, but it does not have the capacity to defeat the armed forces so long as the latter has the support of the United States.

3. The willingness and ability of the Bush administration to provide continued political and financial assistance to the government and armed forces of El Salvador is greater now than it was a year ago, but that could change rapidly. The helicopter incident and the Gulf victory strengthened the administration's hand vis-à-vis Congress. A cutoff of US aid does not seem imminent.

Yet the Jesuit case remains a time bomb that could explode and lead to renewed demands to cut off funding if a cover-up or complicity by the armed forces high command is demonstrated. The continuing US budget crisis and competing foreign policy priorities also suggest that support at present levels is a short-term fact.

4. The government and the armed forces are internally divided between extreme rightists who oppose any compromise and believe that the FMLN cannot survive without external support and those who believe

that the government's position will deteriorate in the likely event of a decrease in US aid.

5. The medium- and long-term material impact of the loss of Soviet and Sandinista support on FMLN military capacity is unclear. Thus far there is no obvious negative impact.

Taken together, these considerations suggest that the prospects for a negotiated solution remain favorable over the medium term but that the short-term likelihood of a cease-fire is diminishing. The FMLN would evidently accept a cease-fire in place that would give it control of some territory while it continues to organize politically throughout the country: It cannot hope to achieve more than that through increased military activity.

The Salvadoran government and the Bush administration, however, have reasons to prolong negotiations while testing the impact of loss of Soviet and Sandinista support on FMLN military capacity. Continued US support at present levels seems likely for six months to a year, depending on how the Jesuit case proceeds and on other domestic considerations in the United States.

These different time lines suggest that if a cease-fire is not achieved in the next round of negotiations, renewed fighting is likely. The FMLN will be pressed to demonstrate that it retains the capacity to threaten military victory and to destabilize the economy. If the outcome of such a round of fighting fails to indicate any diminution of FMLN military strength, the likelihood of renewed efforts to achieve a negotiated solution will be high. By fall 1991 prospects for renewed US pressure to settle will increase. The record of the negotiations since early 1990 demonstrates that the government and the armed forces are responsive to such pressure.

Negotiating a political settlement to the civil war in El Salvador will not be easier than waging the war has been for the combatants. The hopes, and the illusions, that have thus far sustained a determination by the FMLN, the Salvadoran government and armed forces, and the United States to continue fighting in hopes of achieving "victory" will not easily be replaced by a determination to achieve a negotiated political settlement.

Notes

1. Declaring that "the hour of the Revolution has arrived," the FMLN began a "final offensive" in January 1981 intended to "intitiate the decisive military and insurrectional battles for the seizure of Power by the People" (from the FMLN's

call for a general offensive, January 1981). Despite the failure of that offensive and long periods spent militarily on the defensive, by late 1988 the insurgency once again felt that victory was near: "Bearing in mind the scope of the crisis and the capability of the army, it can be said that the FMLN has achieved the military capacity to convert an insurrectional explosion into victory." This last quote is from Joaquín Villalobos, "Popular Insurrection: Desire or Reality?" in *Latin American Perspectives* issue 62, vol. 16, no. 3 (Summer 1989): 13. This article is an English translation of the first two-thirds of a longer FMLN internal document entitled *Perspectiva de Victoria y Modelo Revolucionario,* which was circulated in December 1988.

2. One of the main "death squads" in the early 1980s was named the Maximiliano Hernández Martínez Anti-Communist Brigade, after the general who ordered the massacre of some 30,000 peasants following a failed Communist-led uprising in the 1930s. The Communist leader of that uprising, who was arrested and executed, was Agustín Farabundo Martí.

3. See, for example, US Department of State, *El Salvador: The Battle for Democracy,* Public Information Series, November 1988, p. 2. Confidence that electoral competition had supplanted armed struggle as the only viable political option for most Salvadorans permeated the document: "In 1988, it is clear that the majority in El Salvador has found the political voice that it lacked in the violent uproar of 1977–81. It exercises that voice through political parties and electoral judgments on issues and performance. The consensus on democratic principles and procedures underscores the political irrelevance of the two extremes, which have only violence with which to resist the democratization of power."

4. In a radio interview on station YSU on April 27, 1991, for example, Joaquín Villalobos asserted that "this is the beginning of irreversible negotiations to end the war." Responding to a key FMLN negotiating demand to demilitarize El Salvador, Minister of Defense René Emilio Ponce declared in an interview with TV Channel 12 on May 6, 1991, that, "if the FMLN wants the Armed Forces to disappear, they will have to do it on the battlefield."

5. The exact number of voters in 1982 has been a matter of dispute. According to the Central Electoral Council (CCE), there were 1,551,687 votes cast in 1982, of which 1,362,339 were valid. The Center of Documentation and Information (CUDI) of the Jesuit-run José Simeón Cañas University of Central America immediately challenged the official results, arguing that it was not possible for that many people to have voted. They concluded that the official totals were inflated by at least 450,000 votes. See Centro Universitario de Documentación e Información (CUDI), "Las elecciones de 1982. Realidades detrás de las apariencias," *ECA: Estudios Centroamericanos* (May–June 1982): 403–404.

6. The first round of presidential elections in 1984 drew 1,419,996 voters and the second round in April of that year brought increased turnout of 1,523,946 voters. By the time of Legislative Assembly elections in 1985, only 1,101,606 Salvadorans went to the polls. The decline continued in Legislative Assembly elections in 1988, which drew 1,092,567 voters. The second presidential election in 1989 witnessed a further decline to 1,003,161 voters. All figures are from official CCE results.

7. There were 1,153,013 votes cast in 1991, according to CCE figures.

8. US Department of State, *El Salvador: The Battle for Democracy.*

9. ARENA got 466,091 votes in 1991 compared with 402,304 in 1982. All rightist parties together got 560,622 in 1991 compared with 702,961 in 1982. The

exact parties contesting elections has varied, but included among rightist parties that have campaigned are the National Conciliation party (PCN), Authentic Institutional Salvadoran party (PAISA), Popular Salvadoran party (PPS), Authentic Revolutionary party (PAR), and Liberation party (PL).

10. The PDC vote was 294,029 in 1991 compared with 546,218 in 1982. In the second round of the 1984 presidential election the PDC received 752,625 votes. All centrist parties together got 304,798 votes in 1991 compared with 659,378 in 1982. Other centrist parties include Democratic Action (AD), Popular Orientation party (POP), the Stable Republican Centrist Movement (MERECEN), and the Authentic Christian Movement (MAC, which grew out of a merger between MERECEN and a breakaway faction of the PDC in 1989).

11. Rightist parties received 546,841 votes in the 1989 presidential election and 560,622 votes in the March 1991 Legislative Assembly election. Centrist parties received 354,551 votes in 1989 and 304,798 votes in 1991.

12. Three social democratic parties allied in the Democratic Convergence (CD) received 127,855 votes, or 12.15 percent of valid votes. The Nationalist Democratic Union (UDN), historically close to the Salvadoran Communist party, got 28,206 votes, representing 2.68 percent of the valid ballots.

13. Karl Marx, *The Eighteenth Brumaire of Louis Bonaparte* (Moscow: Progress Publishers, 1972), p. 14.

14. A good summary of this period can be found in Richard A. Haggerty, ed., *El Salvador: A Country Study* (Washington, D.C.: Library of Congress, 1990). Another excellent account of the period is Tommie Sue Montgomery, *Revolution in El Salvador: Origins and Evolution* (Boulder, Colo.: Westview Press, 1982).

15. For a more detailed analysis of this period see George R. Vickers, *El Salvador 1987: U.S. Policy on the Defensive* (New York: Institute for Central American Studies, 1987).

16. For example, the Legislative Assembly appoints the Supreme Court and attorney general as well as the head of the Central Electoral Council, which oversees elections. The Constitution not only prohibits the president from running for reelection but also specifically charges the armed forces with responsibility to ensure that this prohibition is obeyed.

17. Title 5, for example, effectively blocked implementation of Phase 2 of the agrarian reform program promulgated by the reformist junta in 1981. Article 248 required that any constitutional amendments be approved by two successive legislative assemblies (the second by a two-thirds majority).

18. "Foreign Economic Trends and Their Implications for the United States," statistical abstract prepared by the U.S. Embassy, San Salvador, and published in the International Marketing Information Series (Washington, D.C.: Department of Commerce), November 1986, p. 2.

19. The 1986 inflation estimate is from "FY88 Economic Policy Profile (Kemp Report)," US Embassy cable.

20. "Foreign Economic Trends," p. 5.

21. The estimate for 1986 is from a January 21, 1987, interview with a senior US Embassy official.

22. The estimate of $1 billion in earthquake damage is from an interview with an officer in the US Embassy's economic section in June 1987.

23. "Earthquake Damage: Reconstruction Plans," US Embassy handout.

24. For a detailed discussion of this split and reactions to it by the United States, see Frank Smyth, "Duarte's Secret Friends," *The Nation*, March 14, 1987.

25. As early as June 1984, a US Embassy official told me that it was critical

for Duarte to "mend his fences" with the Right and to take steps that would reassure the business community.

26. It is certainly true that the Salvadoran private sector was dominated by extreme right-wing elements. One newspaper, for example, editorialized against Duarte's proposed war tax on the grounds that "the government says that those who have the most must pay the most. The truth here is quite obvious. The intention is to destroy capitalism in El Salvador and this will be achieved by distributing poverty." The same editorial attacked Duarte's proposal for universal military service, charging that "it is a means of breaking down the social structure of the nation, punishing the young people who have committed the sin of having hard-working parents who want to share with their children the fruits of their work." *El Salvador News-Gazette*, vol. 10, no. 419, January 19–25, 1987.

27. The new FMLN strategy was set forth at a meeting of the FMLN's General Command in June 1984. At a June 1985 meeting of the General Command, the strengths and weaknesses of the new tactics were evaluated and the strategy was expanded and linked to a longer-term aim of initiating a strategic counteroffensive. A General Command document analyzing the objectives and strategy of the United States and the government and armed forces of El Salvador, and laying out the logic and steps of the FMLN response, was adopted at the June 1985 General Command meeting in Morazán.

28. According to Salvadoran armed forces figures.

29. A senior official of the US military group in El Salvador told me in June 1986 that "we have done what we can do" with respect to increasing the size and improving the equipment of the Salvadoran armed forces.

30. In June 1986, US military group officials claimed that the attacks in the west were carried out by guerrilla bands infiltrating from Santa Ana and then returning. One adviser acknowledged that he was not certain of this explanation and said that "we have to keep a close eye on this development." Subsequent actions make it clear that the guerrillas had developed an infrastructure in the west.

31. One of these supermarkets was located directly across the street from the Camino Real Hotel, where most foreign journalists have offices. The attack was, presumably, for their benefit.

32. *Campaña de Contrainsurgencia "Unidos para Reconstruir,"* March 1986.

33. Ibid. The plan called for the formation of a Joint National Coordinating Committee (Comité Nacional Conjunto de Coordinación) to direct the campaign, composed of the chief of staff of the High Command of the armed forces, a delegate of the president of El Salvador, and the director of the National Commission for Restoration of Areas (CONARA), with the committee reporting directly to the president. This structure was to be duplicated at the departmental level. The armed forces chief of staff was named as coordinator of this committee, and the departmental commander of the armed forces headed the corresponding committee at the departmental level.

34. *Fase preparatoria de la contraofensiva estratégica,* document of the FMLN General Command adopted at their meeting in November 1986.

35. The organizational preparation of the FMLN was centered in a tactic of *doble cara* that combined open organizing with a clandestine structure intended to survive repression such as that which took place between 1980 and 1982. *El poder popular de doble cara,* January 1987. This was an internal FMLN document used to train cadres in the organizational strategy.

36. As late as June 1989 US Embassy officials and Salvadoran military officers

assured me that the FMLN was incapable of large-scale military action. I was told by other US officials that internal discussions in the embassy were much less confident but that there was no consensus on an estimation of FMLN military capacity.

37. By early 1986 the FMLN concluded that it had defeated the US strategy of building up the Christian Democrats as a reformist alternative to the FMLN. In a lengthy analysis published in May 1986, Joaquín Villalobos argued that "The social base that was supposed to have been built in support of the Duarte government has vanished. . . . All pretexts of reform or political games aimed at confusing or winning a social base have been abandoned" (translated from the original Spanish). The analysis appeared under the title "El estado actual de la guerra y sus perspectivas" in *ECA: Estudios Centroamericanos*, no. 449 (March 1986). Although the issue was listed as the March issue, it did not appear until May.

38. This interpretation is supported by the analysis contained in *Perspectiva de Victoria y Modelo Revolucionario*, which was still confidential at the time. In that document Villalobos argued that "elections are short-lived and completely incapable of containing discontent, popular violence, and the convergence of those forces favoring a political solution. Elections held at this time will work against, rather than for, the counterinsurgency plan."

39. Joaquín Villalobos, *Perspectiva de Victoria y Modelo Revolucionario (San Salvador: Edición Sistema Radio Venceremos, 1988)*. An English version of the first two-thirds of this analysis appeared under the title "Popular Insurrection: Desire or Reality?" in *Latin American Perspectives*, issue 62, vol. 16, no. 3 (Summer 1989).

40. Ibid., p. 6.

41. The November 1989 offensive resembled the 1968 Tet offensive by Vietnamese revolutionaries in several respects. In both cases the scope and location of initial attacks caught government defenders by surprise despite prior warnings that an offensive was imminent; in both cases the guerrilla forces overestimated the degree of readiness of the urban population to rise up; in both cases the effort to stimulate an insurrection exposed part of the clandestine structure of the guerrillas in urban areas to repression; in both cases the guerrillas took heavier casualties than necessary because they left their forces exposed for too long a time; in both cases the military costs of the guerrilla offensive were more than offset by the political victories the offensive achieved. In the case of the FMLN offensive, the killing of six Jesuit intellectuals by an army unit ensured that the political loss by the Salvadoran government would more than offset any military setbacks for the FMLN.

42. The last third of Villalobos's *Perspectiva de Victoria y Modelo Revolucionario* was an analysis of the changing international context that stressed the pluralistic and nationalist features of FMLN ideology and program and asserted the FMLN's willingness to struggle for fundamental change through genuinely democratic processes. One clear sign that this message was directed at the Bush administration was the publication of an English version of this section under the title "A Democratic Revolution for El Salvador," in *Foreign Policy*, no. 74 (Spring 1989).

43. This strategic plan was similar in many respects to that of Vietnamese revolutionaries during the Vietnam War. I have discussed this elsewhere in "United States Military Strategy and the Vietnam War," in Jayne Werner and Lu'u Doan Huynh, eds., *The Indochina War* (New York: M. E. Sharpe Publishers, 1991). Also see Col. Gen. Tran Van Tra, *Vietnam: History of the Bulwark B2 Theatre, Vol. 5: Concluding the 30-Years War* (Ho Chi Minh City: Van Nghe Publishing House,

1982). This was published in English in *Southeast Asia Report*, no. 1247, JPRS 82783 (February 2, 1983), by Foreign Broadcast Information Service.

44. In mid-February 1990, I interviewed Salvadoran government and armed forces officials and US government representatives in El Salvador. The time projections were obviously arbitrary, but estimates of the time needed for military pressure to produce results ranged from seven years to "never." Perhaps more important, some of those I interviewed had given much more optimistic estimates in prior interviews over the past several years. I should emphasize, however, that the February interviews were conducted prior to the Nicaraguan elections on February 25, 1990. All those I interviewed expected the Sandinistas to win those elections, and several of them believed that Sandinista logistical, political, and material support was very important to the FMLN.

45. During that period, total US financial assistance to El Salvador amounted to $5.35 billion, of which $1.7 billion was military aid.

46. There were two meetings between President Duarte and FMLN representatives in 1984 and 1985 that briefly raised hopes for serious negotiations. Both sides seemed more interested in appearance than substance, however, and no ongoing process emerged from these meetings. In 1987, following the "Esquipulas II" agreement (this is generally called the "Arias Plan" in the United States), two more rounds of talks were held, but these also failed to establish an ongoing process.

47. The General Command document adopted in June 1985 placed the highest priority on integrating the five organizations into one Marxist-Leninist party. That emphasis disappeared in subsequent strategy documents. Despite increased cooperation and coordination, particularly at the military level and in fund-raising and "foreign policy" efforts, the organizations retained their distinct identities.

48. During most of 1990 it appeared that three organizations were solidly supportive of ending the war through negotiations, but there was some dispute about the identity of the three. The National Resistance (RN) and the People's Revolutionary Army (ERP) were two of the three. Some claim that the Salvadoran Communist party (PCS) was the third, whereas others say the third was the Revolutionary Party of Central American Workers (PRTC). It is clear that the Popular Armed Forces for Liberation (FPL) was not solidly committed to negotiations.

49. During negotiations in May 1990 to set the agenda for the substantive negotiations, the FMLN suggested a time frame as follows: from May to September 1990, accords over demilitarization, democratization, and a social-economic pact; from October to December 1990, accords over constitutional reforms and mechanisms of verification; for sometime in fall 1990, depending on how negotiations were proceeding, a cease-fire from January to June 1991, and implementation of verification mechanisms; for July 1991, an end to the war.

50. According to US officials I interviewed in February 1990, this message was conveyed informally and politely. Interviews with Salvadoran government officials at the same time made clear that the message was received.

51. *Agenda General y Calendario del Proceso Completo de Negociación*, Caracas, May 21, 1990.

52. "Proposal of the Government of El Salvador on Agreements Related to the Armed Forces for Arranging a Halt to the Armed Confrontation and Any Act That Infringes Upon the Rights of the Civilian Population" (translated from original Spanish), July 1990.

53. *Acuerdos Sobre Derechos Humanos,* San José, July 26, 1990.

54. The debacle over this accord provides further evidence that the FMLN delegation did not yet have a fully worked out strategy for the negotiations but instead was reacting on a case-by-case basis. Internal FMLN *ayuda memoria* during this period clearly indicate that their negotiating team had not been prepared for the government of El Salvador's tactic at the July meeting. The Salvadoran government negotiators presented no proposals and simply waited for the FMLN to make suggestions.

55. The FMLN apparently concluded that the government was simply trying to prolong the negotiations without seeking accords. A July 30 *ayuda memoria* complained, "El Gobierno está imponiendo un ritmo lento. No pone nunca las cartas sobre la mesa. No presenta propuestas. Se limita a esperar a que el FMLN presente sus planteamientos para luego intentar reducirlos al mínimo. Esta actitud no es congruente con el propósito de alcanzar en Septiembre todos los acuerdos políticos que permitan la concertación del cese del enfrentamiento armado."

56. On April 30, 1990, prior to the actual commencement of negotiations, the FMLN presented its basic negotiating demands in a document entitled "La Solución Negociada a la Guerra en El Salvador." In that document, and in subsequent negotiation sessions, the FMLN called for investigation and punishment of those responsible for the four infamous cases of human rights violations. In the revised proposal presented in August, the list was expanded to include practically every human rights violation since 1980. Entitled "Posición del FMLN para Desmontar El Militarismo, Alcanzar El Cese de Fuego y Avanzar a la Democracia Sin Armas," the document presented eighteen points regarding the armed forces that were preconditions for a cease-fire.

57. The lines of debate were not neatly drawn because some of those who believed that Sandinista support was a significant factor in FMLN strength also believed that continued Sandinista control of the Nicaraguan armed forces would permit a continuation of that support. There was general agreement that negotiations were at least tactically desirable because military escalation by the FMLN while negotiations were under way would be politically difficult and potentially costly.

58. Other provisions permitted the president to restore aid if the FMLN launched an offensive or received significant lethal arms shipments from outside El Salvador and to terminate aid if the government failed to conduct a serious inquiry, with external professional law enforcement assistance from agencies like INTERPOL or Scotland Yard, into the Jesuit killings.

59. The three persons were to be of "recognized independence" and with a reputation for commitment to democracy. They were to be chosen from lists of five names that were submitted by each of the negotiating parties, by the archbishop of San Salvador, and by the Interpartidaria.

60. This proposed commission was quite similar to the Rettig Commission, which was formed in Chile after the transition to civilian rule last year.

61. The claim to have a regular army also supported this objective because it implied that the conflict was a civil war rather than simply armed protest.

62. CID-Gallup, a Costa Rican firm, conducted polls in September 1989 and March 1990. A research institute of the University of Central America (UCA) conducted three polls in September 1989, March 1990, and June-July 1990. In addition, ARENA conducted its own internal polls.

63. One Western official told me in December 1990 that in talks with US

and Salvadoran armed forces and Salvadoran government officials, President Cristiani was the only one who believed there could be a cease-fire before the elections.

64. A Salvadoran armed forces seminar on November 27, 1990, focused on the role of repatriated communities in FMLN strategy. A background paper for that seminar (which may have been prepared by US advisers) presented a lengthy assessment of FMLN strategy with respect to the elections and the negotiating process. That assessment is in line with the analysis of FMLN thinking presented here.

65. The Armed Forces of El Salvador (FAES) prepared a response to the UN working document that included a series of counterproposals yet accepted much of the rationale. The specific counterproposals were called "Nuestro Proyecto de Desmilitarización." They called for regrouping most of the security functions of the National Police, National Guard, and Treasury Police under a new vice-minister of interior security in the Interior Ministry.

66. In the January meeting the parties agreed to rename this group the National Civil Police.

67. It seems extremely unlikely that the action reflected higher-level FMLN policy. The district commander was a hard-liner known to have made threats against US military advisers, and the political cost to the FMLN was enormous. It permitted President Bush to release the military aid that had been withheld and fostered a more negative attitude of the United States toward the negotiating process. The FMLN unit involved was part of the ERP.

68. In December 1990 the Sandinista army arrested four Nicaraguan army officers and eleven Salvadorans in the case. The four Sandinista officers were charged with selling the missiles for money and were sentenced to three years in prison. The accused publicly named Joaquín Villalobos as having been involved in the deal. According to sources in the Nicaraguan army, Humberto Ortega threatened to expel all FMLN cadre from Nicaragua if the missiles were not returned. Although the story that the sale was done for private profit seems dubious, the incident clearly caused a serious rupture in relationships between the FMLN and the Sandinistas. The role of the USSR also provides support for rumors that the United States had obtained Soviet backing to press the FMLN to reach a cease-fire.

69. Clifford Krauss, "U.N. Aide Assailed in Salvadoran Talks," *New York Times*, February 1, 1991, p. A3. The comments apparently were made by Assistant Secretary of State for Latin American Affairs Bernard Aronson. Secretary of State James Baker subsequently told the Senate Subcommittee on Western Hemisphere Affairs that the comments were "not authorized," but he told some members of the subcommittee that he agreed with the substance of the comments. This suggests that the criticism reflected a policy decision to delay any quick accords.

70. A poll by the UCA in January suggested that ARENA had a commanding lead, with 37.3 percent of those polled saying they thought ARENA would win and only 10.7 percent saying they thought the PDC would win. A second UCA poll in late February showed a similar ARENA lead, although the PDC and CD fared somewhat better.

71. ARENA will have 39 deputies (out of a total of 84), the PCN will have 9, and the MAC will have 1.

72. The results appeared in *Proceso*, no. 465, March 6, 1991. The poll was conducted by the Instituto Universitario de Opinión Pública (IUDOP). The poll

found 28.8 percent supporting ARENA, 14.7 percent favoring the PCD, 7.7 percent supporting the CD, 3.2 percent supporting the PCN, 1.1 percent for the UDN, 1.1 percent for other parties, 15 percent who said "none of them," and 27.2 percent who said they did not know or did not answer.

73. This conclusion is based on an assumption that normally the "do not know/no answer" respondents would have voted more or less like those who stated a preference. In fact, it would appear that they voted disproportionately for the PDC, PCN, UDN, and MAC.

74. On March 22, the Cruzada Pro-Paz y Trabajo, associated with Roberto D'Aubuisson, accused the government and army of "falling into a trap." On April 5, they accused the government of "high treason" and of "giving the country to the communists on a gold platter" (ad in *Diario de Hoy*). On April 6, the formation of a National United Front to "defend the sovereignty of the country" was announced. On April 8, the "Frente Femenino" published a full-page ad in *Diario de Hoy* saying, "This space is reserved for the names of the ten traitor deputies who support the reform to Article 248 of the Constitution."

75. What he said was "We are very anxious to see the conflict ended in El Salvador. We are very encouraged by the UN-sponsored talks that are taking place in Mexico City now and we hope that if both sides continue to show flexibility then perhaps during this round of negotiations we will come to an agreement that will lead to a cease-fire and a peaceful settlement. My interest is in peaceful settlements. We believe that in this new world order that President Bush has spoken about the way to resolve conflicts is through negotiation, through discussion among responsible parties, and not through acts of war. What we saw in the Persian Gulf and what was necessary there to deter the aggression of Saddam Hussein we hope is not the model to be followed. But at the same time if it becomes necessary to defend freedom . . . then one must do it."

76. The final constitutional reforms approved by the Legislative Assembly did little to satisfy FMLN concerns that the right wing could manipulate and obstruct a negotiated political settlement and elections through the constitutional and legal framework. The final changes did not differ radically from GOES proposals made during the April round.

77. I am not speaking here of face-saving negotiations that mask the underlying reality of defeat.

78. A few years ago the Eritrean guerrillas struggled to maintain a prolonged revolutionary war against an entrenched and well-financed Ethiopian military regime. Today they seem on the verge of victory. But who can be sure that today's allies will not turn against them once their common foe is defeated? The Eritrean guerrillas' objective is an independent Eritrea. They are allied with two other guerrilla groups that are opposed to the military regime governing Ethiopia. Should these groups succeed in overthrowing the current Ethiopian government, it would not be particularly surprising if they opposed the breakup of Ethiopia.

3

Commentary

John McAward

I want to call attention to a number of important issues, several of which Tom Gibb mentioned. First, is the need to focus on minority rights as being essential in a democracy. Second, polls show that the people of El Salvador are war-exhausted. They do not trust the military and they do not trust the armed opposition. (I continue to marvel at the ability of both of those groups to believe that they have the support of the people, as if anybody who approaches with gun in hand is going to get an honest answer to any question.) The great majority of people in El Salvador are focusing on an end to the war because all sectors realize that the economy and the country will not progress until it ends.

The third point is that the people who will take office broadly reflect the way the people in the country voted on March 10. Fourth, the team with which President Cristani has surrounded himself deserve and are receiving praise, even from World Bank officials who travel through El Salvador. Their economic data are clear and precise and they have a plan of action. El Salvador has become a model that people in the international community can praise.

I would disagree with some of the points that George Vickers made. The first relates to the idea that the US policy on elections is an illusion. I opposed that policy when it began in the early 1980s. I believed that nothing short of the total destruction of the Salvadoran armed forces would be able to bring peace and justice to El Salvador. But, at least with regard to the political sector, I have to admit now that I was wrong. US policy was more farsighted than those of us who at that time were considered to be activists could envision.

John McAward is senior consultant for Freedom House.

But US policymakers did have a vision, and I think that we are now seeing its benefits in the political area. We are also seeing its benefits with regard to the military, albeit certainly with less success. The Jesuit killings illustrate those imperfections clearly. We must recognize the need to get to the bottom of those killings. The people who planned and carried them out have to be prosecuted. The people who were in on the plans but who did not agree with them have to come forth and give public testimony. There are people in the High Command who knew about the plans or who knew afterward who carried out the killings. But they left their president and commander in chief and US policymakers swaying in the wind for five weeks trying to excuse or explain the killings or blame them on the FMLN.

However, never did I think that I would see a sitting Salvadoran president, democratically elected, remove a colonel (Max Leiva) from office a day after he was caught in a visa scam. And this colonel, who was in charge of immigration duties, was a close friend and ally of Maj. Roberto D'Aubuisson. I understand that D'Aubuisson rattled the president's cage, but the colonel remains out of office. He has not been prosecuted—I do not think that is feasible within the present justice system—but the fact that he was removed by President Cristiani shows that the situation inside the country has changed drastically.

I also do not agree that the population is disillusioned with elections. They might be disillusioned with elections being able to bring democracy to the country, but my question is "What else is there?" There is no alternative to elections. I think the people recognize that. As time goes on and elections become more honest, the interparty relationships that are in place in El Salvador today will reform the electoral process and we will continue to see improvement.

I expect that we will see an entirely new civic culture develop among the young people. As part of this culture, they can be trained as poll watchers by the US Agency for International Development (AID). This training would address some of the problems with poll watching that Gibb and Vickers raised. It takes approximately 12,000 people to monitor 6,000 voting tables, yet in the present climate it is difficult for a person on the political left to sign up as an authorized poll watcher or candidate for fear of the consequences afterward. These issues can and must be addressed.

I did not see the elections as a disintegration of the center with a push to the extremes. On the contrary, I saw a reaffirmation of the center. The established parties—the National Conciliation party (PCN), the Christian Democratic party, and ARENA—garnered a great number of votes (more than 80 percent). The Democratic Convergence, which I do not see as radical, emerged as a new party. Some people in the State

Department might disagree, but I consider someone like Rubén Zamora, a leader of the Democratic Convergence, to be well within the mainstream of political action and political thought of the United States.

As the negotiations continue we must keep in mind the reasons why the war started. Regardless of what one thinks of the FMLN and its tactics over the past ten years, El Salvador owes a great debt to the fighters in the FMLN for going to war. The alternative was the annihilation of the poor by a military that was out of control. (In 1979, even its own officers sponsored a coup to bring some of the elements back under control.)

But a number of things have changed in El Salvador and in the world in the past several years. First, George Bush has brought an entirely new attitude, philosophy, and perspective to Washington. His administration has tried to find bipartisan support for its Central American program, and they have had a great deal of success. Second, free and fair elections in Nicaragua were a positive step. I was not surprised by the results. Third, the US invasion of Panama was another signal that right-wing military leaders would not remain in charge of their countries after elections. Fourth, was the fall of communism in Eastern Europe. Finally, there has also been a slight change in the private sector in El Salvador. The majority of leaders in the private sector now see their workers as human capital. And they are treating their human capital as carefully as they treat their dollar capital.

The United States still faces a challenge. We who have been lobbying for El Salvador in the United States will have our work cut out for us in the 1990s. Salvadorans are going to need help reintegrating the armed forces, both the FMLN and the army, into civil society. In some cases, the United States may have to support some military officials with criminal pasts on reserve status (similar to the Spanish model, under which the army was sent home with full pay). If El Salvador can produce the same results as the Spanish government with a life-time salary plan, then the United States should seriously consider the idea. Sensitivity and balance should be shown toward the *commandantes* of the FMLN. Those who cut short their academic careers to carry out this war need to be protected and provided for in some way. Scholarship moneys could help prepare them for future employment, either in the private or public sector.

For now, the United States needs to give a strong signal to the Salvadoran military that a resolution of this conflict has to come now and that the United States will not support any backpedaling on their part. Based on my own talks with Gen. Emilio Ponce and with some of the other officers in El Salvador, postwar planning already has filtered down to the lieutenant level; it is not a mere facade at the top. We must be careful not to give the army the sense that their military careers will end and that they will be turned out. If the officer corps is not treated fairly, serious problems will continue in El Salvador.

Among my worries is Roberto D'Aubuisson's cancer. When he dies, the impact of his death could either cause right-wingers to renew their death squad activity in El Salvador or they could realize that they have taken their last shot and must now look to democratic pluralism to survive. The Bush administration needs to recruit someone who would wield solid political influence to carry a strong message to the far right in El Salvador that the US government is not going to stand by and watch them destroy any peace agreement that is reached. Republican senator Jesse Helms of North Carolina might be a good candidate.

Governing El Salvador presents challenges. There needs to be a decentralization of services. The government must find some way of: (1) raising tax moneys through a land tax at the local level, (2) strengthening the mayors and municipal councils, and (3) giving local people a say in who polices them. Not only must the ruling structure be changed from the top down, but there must also be percolation from below.

4

Discussion

Patrick Morris (Bethesda, Maryland): According to Tom Gibb, there is so much cynicism, at all levels in El Salvador, that what is happening there in terms of negotiations and prospects for changes through the electoral process seems not to register among the populace. Yet I cannot believe that some hope has not been identified in all of this. What is the public's attitude toward the foreign involvement, not only of US and international organizations but also of private organizations from outside the country who are operating there? Do some of these extranational bodies and actors have an influence—a hopeful influence—on the electorate and the people at the local level?

Tom Gibb: I think the degree of cynicism toward politicians and, in part, the lack of hope about the negotiations is a problem with communication more than anything else. Salvadorans do not have the access to see how people's real positions are changing; all they hear is the rhetoric. I stopped at an army checkpoint and mentioned to the soldiers that there might be a cease-fire later this year. They thought I was completely crazy. The realization that the war might end has not filtered down to everyone in El Salvador, and that is a big problem.

The Salvadorans are friendly people, very open in many ways, and in *campesino* communities their values are quite strong. Yet, despite all the discussion about it, Salvadorans are cynical about the war ending. It is a cynicism brought about by the war and the present political situation in El Salvador; it could change if there is a settlement.

The opportunities for aid and development work have been increasing in the past few years and are going to continue to open up considerably, especially if there is some kind of a settlement. That is a big "if"—partly because there is going to be a stage of intense competition between the political Left and government institutions over who will do the best kind of development projects. This competition to win hearts and minds will be very positive.

US influence in helping to bring about the changes we have been discussing is firmly based on the need of the military and the Salvadoran government for US money. This is especially true for the military, which needs money to fight the war. Without US funding, they will be in trouble. The FMLN has not wanted to come to a settlement on a cease-fire until there have been concrete changes, especially within the military. And if over the past eleven years the United States has not been able to produce the changes necessary to bring the military under civilian rule, which is partly because of the war, then it will not be easy to exert pressure after the war is over. After the war, the foundation of US influence is going to be greatly diminished.

Miguel Salaverria (Ambassador of El Salvador to the United States): Those who stayed in El Salvador during the years of armed struggle and who have worked for democracy and an electoral system have a responsibility to improve this system. Unfortunately, the complaints about the electoral system come from those who have stayed away from El Salvador during the struggle and have wanted to take over the government and install a Marxist-Leninist regime. Everyone seems to forget that Fidel Castro put together the FMLN in Nicaragua.

As president of the National Association for Private Enterprise (ANEP) in El Salvador, I was part of the effort to contract with Price Waterhouse to audit the electoral system to see if the law was being complied with; we received a healthy report from them. The suggestions that were made to improve the system were accepted by all the parties in El Salvador. There may be problems, but I do not see who would want to ruin a good system that has cost us years of struggle to try to perfect. People who come to El Salvador now and criticize the system are not being fair; they should have seen how hard it has been over the past eight years.

To say that nothing has changed in El Salvador is to ignore the suffering that we have experienced—the loss of jobs, the collapse of the economy, and the masses of refugees. The cost of this destruction, caused by the FMLN, is over $4 billion. It is unfair to those who have worked to improve things in El Salvador to say that the situation is not better. Coffee and sugar cane production doubled in one year. For the first time since 1974, we are self-sufficient in corn and beans. Even though others try to destroy all that, we continue to reinforce our economy and our democracy. It is true that this government has implemented a strict economic policy. That is bitter medicine, especially for the poor people, and we see the results in the voting. Because the cost of the products they buy is going up faster than their salaries, the people in the cities voted against ARENA. But in the countryside, where there was no work at all until recently and where we are now seeing 100 percent employment, the people are happy, so they voted for ARENA.

Tom Gibb: Things may have improved in comparison with the early 1980s. But the worries this time were expressed by observers who have given previous recent elections in El Salvador a reasonably clean bill of health. These were experienced observers who monitored the elections in Guatemala and Nicaragua and who were there with the Organization of American States [OAS] delegation. British observer David Browning, who has observed elections and has studied El Salvador since the 1970s, was worried by the discrepancies, the irregularities in the registration process, and by other events that happened on the day of the election. To be fair, one has to seriously address those problems; otherwise, one must criticize them. If one just accepts it openly, the situation will not improve.

There were important, positive aspects to the election. Whether those positive aspects can ultimately result in relatively fair elections depends entirely on the negotiating process. The promise that was there will dissipate quickly if there is not substantive progress in the negotiations. Those negotiations are going to go on for some time. My fear is that if there is not significant progress soon, the talks will continue indefinitely.

PART 2

THE UNITED STATES AND DEMOCRACY IN EL SALVADOR

5

The Role of US Policy

—————— *Bernard W. Aronson* ——————

There have been many conferences about Central America and El Salvador over the past several years, but probably none is more timely than this one. As we sit here and discuss these issues, the parties to the conflict in El Salvador are meeting in Mexico City, trying to negotiate peace. So what we are talking about is not a theoretical proposition, but a live and present challenge.

When the presidents of the Central American countries signed the Esquipulas II Accord in 1987, President Oscar Arias Sánchez said: "Without democracy, there can be no peace in Central America." That is a profound and important statement. We saw in Nicaragua that the process of ending a civil war was also a process of democratization, of opening up the political system and creating political space for all who were willing to live within a democratic system and compete for power through a political process. That is also the process under way in El Salvador.

In 1972, José Napoleón Duarte ran for president in El Salvador. By all accounts, he and his coalition won that election, but their victory was thwarted. At one point in that process, Duarte and his supporters appealed to the international community, including the United States, to throw its political and moral support behind his democratic forces, but the international community failed to do so. In many ways, the revolution was born in that failed electoral process. President John Kennedy was right when he said, "Those who make peaceful revolution impossible make violent revolution inevitable."

In the early 1980s I talked with the late President Duarte about the

Bernard W. Aronson is assistant secretary of state for inter-American affairs with the United States Department of State.

years he spent in exile, including years he came to the United States to seek support for democratic forces in El Salvador but found little interest. He said: "I came to your country carrying a lighted bomb in my hands, begging you to cut the fuse and you did not; now the bomb has gone off and you want us to put all the pieces back together again very neatly and easily, and we cannot." There are lessons to be learned from El Salvador, and one of them is that it is important for the international community to defend democracy early when it is threatened and at risk.

It is also important to be honest about the profound changes that have taken place in El Salvador over the past decade, particularly in the past several years. It is difficult to have an honest discussion about change in El Salvador because the subject is so politicized: One side will not credit the changes that have taken place, and the other asserts that no further change is needed. Neither position is tenable.

When President Cristiani took office, the critics of El Salvador argued that he would usher in a wave of repression and the closing of political space and that the chances for dialogue and peace would be diminished. In fact, his efforts opened up political space, certainly during the early period of his tenure in 1989. He said in his inaugural address that he was prepared to negotiate at any time and at any place to end the war.

In the past year we have seen more progress than many had hoped. The elections were a major achievement and one of the most profound changes; it is important to note how that was brought about. The parties agreed to create an interparty commission in which every political party in the country was represented. Each party was given an equal vote on the commission: for example, ARENA, which had won 52 percent of the electoral vote, and the Nationalist Democratic Union (UDN), which had not even competed, were given the same vote. The members of the commission came up with a consensus package that added twenty-four at-large seats to the National Assembly and carried out a reform of the voter registration process.

When the process by which the votes are tallied in El Salvador is examined, one can see that the smaller parties actually were given an advantage in gaining seats. As a result of that, and also because the OAS oversaw the election and offered added security, the Left entered the elections. For the first time, the FMLN did not attack the elections. The Democratic Convergence won eight seats; the Nationalist Democratic Union won another seat. Charges of fraud were levied, but as the charges were being made, the ruling parties' vote margin was going down and the margin of the opposition parties was going up. That is not usually the pattern when there has been fraud. The OAS, though noting some inefficiencies, ruled that the elections were carried out in a proper manner.

In the negotiations themselves, again it is important to note that much more has been achieved and agreed upon than is reported or acknowledged. The parties agreed last year on a new commission, to be appointed by the secretary-general of the United Nations, to oversee and defend human rights in El Salvador. On what the FMLN has always said is the key to ending the war—reform of the armed forces—the parties have agreed on 80 to 90 percent of the toughest issues on the table. In the current round of negotiations, the following three issues were put forth with the hope that a comprehensive agreement could be reached: constitutional reforms, reform of the armed forces, and a cease-fire. Unfortunately, that package has been broken up and the issue of a cease-fire has been taken off the table for this session. Nevertheless, in that arena of negotiations, which is distinct from the political negotiations, a fair amount of work has been done and the United Nations mediator deserves great credit for his efforts.

One may have read that the political parties reached a consensus on a series of fundamental constitutional reforms. They talked to the FMLN in Mexico City and took the guerillas' views into account. The clock is ticking because the current assembly dissolves at the end of April. In order to pass constitutional reforms to implement political agreements, the first vote has to take place before May 1. All of the political parties in the current assembly are committed to introduce and vote on the specific constitutional reforms. The question that is still open is whether the FMLN will participate in the consensus behind those specific reforms. The FMLN believes, not entirely correctly, that once a cease-fire is in place the chances for reform are over. My own view is that reducing the threat of violence and the level of hostilities creates an atmosphere in which it is easier to carry out reforms.

Not long after the Japanese attacked Pearl Harbor, Americans had a kind of hysteria and enormous fears for US internal security. Without any due process or without any grounds, we rounded up American citizens of Japanese descent and forced them to live in camps where they were detained and deprived of all their civil liberties. Any society that is threatened at the fundamental level of its security and survival reacts. In the middle of a war, while the FMLN continues to roam through the country, attack government officials, blow up power lines, and promote violent demonstrations, the government of El Salvador is negotiating the reduction of its armed forces, the composition of its officer core, the nature of its combat units, and the opening up of political space to the very guerrilla group that is attacking it. The government deserves credit for carrying out that kind of effort.

If over the past two years we had listened to the voices of pessimism and gloom, we never would have supported elections in Haiti or Nicaragua. We would have accommodated Manuel Noriega. We would have accepted the inevitability of an economic crisis in Mexico and many other parts of the world. Instead, we have chosen to act on our hopes and not on our fears; in every case where we have done so, the optimists have been proven correct. I am an optimist about El Salvador.

There is a broad consensus that unites decent people from the democratic left to the democratic right on the point that this war must end and that fundamental reforms are needed to strengthen and consolidate and expand democracy in El Salvador. The people there have had their fill of violence from both sides, and anyone who advocates violence or uses it does not have the support of the Salvadoran people. But ending the war will not be easy. In some ways, the closer they get to agreement, the harder it gets. But progress has been made and many issues that would have been untouchable in view of the history of this war have already been resolved. People who used to be on death lists now travel freely and safely in El Salvador and participate in the political process. Although there are some danger signs and there is always a possibility that extremists on both sides will try to undermine the process, this war will come to an end through negotiations.

The United States fully and unequivocally supports the negotiating process. We are not going to change that commitment. We do not want to see a military solution to this war. But we are also unequivocally committed to the defense of the security of the government of El Salvador, and we are not going to shrink from that responsibility either. Hopefully, there will not be a need to demonstrate that, and the process of negotiations will accelerate and begin a new era in the history of El Salvador.

Despite all of the violence, loss, and destruction of the past ten years, El Salvador's economy is growing today. The people of El Salvador are hardworking, productive, and industrious. If peace can come with reform, El Salvador will recover much more quickly than other countries in the region that have undergone these kinds of struggles. We still have the opportunity, under the legislation voted by the Congress, to use a portion of our military assistance for fiscal year 1991 to support a cease-fire and the peaceful reintroduction into civic life of combatants on both sides. We would be happy to use it for those purposes, once a cease-fire has been established. That is another reason why quick progress is a positive development—it frees up resources to devote to peace and to national reconciliation and reconstruction.

This process will succeed. Something may happen to threaten it, or there may be a setback. There are many dangers. In some ways, the closer it gets, the more the forces that are not reconciled to a settlement redouble their efforts to prevent one. But if the will of the Salvadoran people is listened to and respected, then this war will end quickly.

6

Commentary

Shortly before I began work on El Salvador at the Washington Office on Latin America in the late 1970s, there was testimony on Capitol Hill about police units using radio communications and talking about numbers of *tamales*. The tamales referred to ballots that needed to be stuffed in ballot boxes. There is no doubt that there have been many, many changes in El Salvador since then and that El Salvador looks extremely different today. But optimism and differences must not replace analytic clarity or gloss over basic issues lying behind the elections.

Today, certainly in the context of the March 1991 elections, it is still important to examine the political power of the armed forces as an institution and their responsiveness to civilian authorities, especially in judicial investigations. This has been a core issue over the decades since the "tamales" period. As regards the past few months, there is a need to distinguish between the real irregularities in the recent March elections and the gains for political pluralism that clearly came out of that process, for example, the seats that were gained by the leftist and center-left parties. Those gains for political pluralism do not make the irregularities any less important, particularly because the key test for the Salvadoran social fabric—the transformation of the FMLN into a political force—will be affected by perceptions of fair play in the electoral process and of fair chances for participation in electoral politics.

On Capitol Hill, attention has been given to the broader political representation in the newly elected legislature, not to new consensus on the need for additional electoral reform or to the relation of the elections to negotiations or, much less, to the 1994 elections. These latter issues

Heather Foote is the Washington representative for the Unitarian Universalist Service Committee.

are relevant to a core process that Tom Gibb noted: the transformation of the conflict from the military to the political battlefield. To what extent do Washington and Capitol Hill understand the 1991 March elections in that context?

In the March 1991 elections, the Bush administration shifted its past policies toward one that had long been advocated by Congress. The biggest difference of the 1991 elections in comparison to prior elections is that the administration did not argue that these elections were an *alternative* to face-to-face negotiations between the FMLN and the government. We have not heard the refrain of past years: "What is there to negotiate?" Therefore, the administration did effectively send the message that elections are not the sole path to conflict resolution. This message that negotiation has to be a part of conflict resolution is partly responsible for a strong far right reaction that has emerged in El Salvador as we get closer and closer in the negotiation process to some of the core issues related to the military.

The Bush administration's message on the need for both negotiations and elections has been fairly clear. Other administration messages have not been so clear or—and this is a difficult problem in US policy—the administration has not been able to calibrate its private diplomacy with public actions or statements that leave a far different public perception of that diplomacy in the United States and in El Salvador. Several examples demonstrated these problems of lack of clarity or perhaps in the sending of mixed messages.

The first relates to the administration's January 1991 decision to release the military aid that Congress required to be withheld. The administration wants to hold all the policy cards in its own hand; therefore it said that it had the right to release the aid. But the aid has not yet actually been released. Nevertheless, it is clear from my recent visits to El Salvador that the public perception there is that the Salvadoran military already has received the aid.

Second, an ongoing question is the US administration's position on the role of the United Nations in the negotiations. A *New York Times* article of February 1, 1991, quoting unnamed administration sources, detailed some fairly sharp criticisms of the chief UN intermediary in the negotiations. About the same time, administration officials at various levels were expressing total support for the UN process in their public statements. This is one of the most important areas of mixed messages.

Third is Colin Powell's trip to the region. I do not yet have enough precise information as to what he said; I am prepared to believe that his remarks in Honduras were misquoted or misunderstood. Nevertheless, for a variety of reasons, some of which perhaps may or may not be controllable by the administration, a few comments have set off quite a reaction in terms of what US military intentions are for El Salvador.

The fourth example is the dialogue in the third week of April 1991 in the Senate Foreign Relations Subcommittee, where the representative from the Pentagon and Sen. Christopher Dodd engaged in a delicate exchange—for the first time in public—about the issue of El Salvador's aging helicopter fleet. The issue was replacement of the aircraft and how the administration's diplomatic line of support for negotiations coincides—or does not coincide—with its military line of planning for helicopter replacement, with both the Salvadoran and US militaries believing that the FMLN is escalating its firepower.

Finally, in terms of mixed messages, is the "love feast" in which the Bush administration, the Salvadoran government, and the FMLN have all participated, raising expectations tremendously for this latest round of negotiations. They talk of an imminent cease-fire, perhaps just a few weeks away. At the same time, however, the Bush administration is laying the groundwork—should the warfare escalate—for the next political battle over who is to blame for the failure to come to agreement. I mention these factors because of their effect on perception, especially in El Salvador, among mass mobilization organizations, the Salvadoran military, and the most conservative elements of society, which may or may not be in the ARENA party.

As the negotiations move ahead on the most controversial issues (and the talks must do more to tackle the difficult problems of military reform), there is a need to see which Salvadorans are inside the tent of elections plus negotiations for a settlement and which remain outside that tent. Second, we need to ensure that all key US policy interlocutors are inside that tent of elections plus negotiations. Negotiations do involve power sharing and power divisions, decisionmaking that is different from that which exists in Salvadoran society today. Third, US policy needs to take into account that public perceptions, especially those created by the United States, which is a powerful factor in the success of the negotiations, are as vital a part of reality as private diplomacy.

I want to underscore the remarks that have been made about the shift from the military to the political battlefield. The question is whether the likely repolarization of society predicted by one of the speakers is going to break that shift or transformation or whether, on the contrary, what we are seeing is simply an inevitable emergence of vitriol as the negotiations get closer and closer to the core issues that need to be addressed to achieve a settlement.

Salvadoran army colonel Mauricio Vargas, who met with the congressional group the Unitarian Universalist Service Committee, which visited El Salvador in mid-February 1991, was correct when he said that the negotiations in El Salvador were unlike those in Colombia and Nicaragua because the military as an institution is being negotiated.

I take slight exception to the point that a political settlement is possible only when *all* parties believe this is more in their interest than not pursuing negotiations. I would quote another government negotiator, David Escobar Galindo, who said that obstacles to the negotiations will not disappear; the question is whether the negotiations process can get around those obstacles.

Given the very strident language being used by some parties in El Salvador and the inevitable setbacks ahead, it is only over time that we will be able to better answer the question of whether the March elections can be understood as one step in the overarching negotiations process and as a shift in political battlefields that will lead to much wider political pluralism in Salvadoran society.

7

Discussion

Heather Foote (Unitarian Universalist Service Committee): Could you expand on how you see the difference between legislative reform initiatives coming from some of the political parties that are in Mexico and a reform package that would come out of the UN negotiating process on constitutional reforms?

Bernard Aronson: The political parties in the assembly have the legal and political responsibility to pass any constitutional reforms. They have been elected by the people of El Salvador to carry out that responsibility, so their involvement is both appropriate and positive. It would not be useful for the parties to reach agreement at the negotiating table in isolation from the political parties that have to vote on it in the assembly. And, clearly, a consensus that includes the Christian Democrats and ARENA is relatively broadly reflective. The Democratic Convergence was invited to join that process and at one point they were a part of it. I do not know if, in the end, they will agree to be part of this consensus or not.

It was positive that the parties went to Mexico City and met with the government, particularly with the FMLN, whom they had not talked to about the specifics. The issues on which they are prepared to carry out specific reforms are the issues that the parties at the bargaining table are addressing. The hope is to implement some of the more important reforms, particularly those that require constitutional action, before the assembly expires.

In the original accords in Geneva and Caracas, it was spelled out by both the government and the FMLN that other sectors in El Salvador should participate in the process. Clearly the elected political leadership is one of the more important of these sectors. The parties have discussed these ideas with the FMLN and tried to take its views into account. A consensus that unites all the parties would be another important step forward. But it is important not to lose the opportunity to have the most important reforms passed in the current assembly before it expires.

Terry Allen (Gemini News Service): It has been reported that the United States is going to be sending Cobra helicopters to El Salvador. Do you advocate such a step? Do you feel it will be a destabilizing influence on what seems to be military parity existing between the FMLN and the army of El Salvador?

Bernard Aronson: I discussed this issue in my recent testimony before the Senate Foreign Relations Committee. We hope that there will be peace in El Salvador well before we have to make that decision and that the issue will not have to be joined. I think there is a good likelihood of that.

The helicopters that the Salvadoran air force and armed forces currently use are a model that is no longer in the US inventory. Spare parts are increasingly unavailable, and simply because of attrition they have to be replaced. The replacement is not an increase in firepower. The suggestion that this is an escalation is incorrect. But there is a relatively long lead time in preparing for a replacement model, and that lead time is long enough so that if there is seriousness at the bargaining table the replacements may not need to be sent because there will be a cease-fire.

It is also worth noting that the only major escalation in fighting capability that has taken place in the past year has been by the FMLN, by introducing successively more sophisticated generations of surface-to-air missiles—starting with SA-7s in November 1989, SA-14s last year, and now SA-16s.

Gilbert P. Richardson (American Association for the Study of the United States in World Affairs): Would you comment on some of the underlying causes of the exacerbation of relations between the army and the Roman Catholic church? Is it because the church is influencing the decisions that are made in Congress?

Bernard Aronson: The vast majority of churches in El Salvador have no problems with the army or the government. The group of churches that have been most involved in political activity from time to time have had problems, sometimes serious problems. One has to take each case and argue whether their problems are legitimate or a result of political harassment. There have been instances of both. Clearly the killing of the

Jesuits was cold-blooded murder. There is no justification for it. But there was a case, during the FMLN offensive, in which the guerrillas brought some homemade mortars onto church property. There was an army raid to go after those mortars. It is important to discuss this issue using specifics as opposed to generalizations.

Ellen Brown (New Channels Communications): You stated that if the security of the Salvadoran government were threatened, the United States would have to take other actions. Could you be more explicit about what these actions would be? Does that hold the door open for military intervention or escalated funding of the Salvadoran military?

Bernard Aronson: The United States is fully committed to a negotiated settlement to end the war and we are using all of our influence and resources to try to make that succeed. We are are committed to the defense of the security of the government of El Salvador. How and in what manner we might have to or would choose to exercise that second responsibility is something about which I am not going to speculate. We ought to be speculating about peace and making efforts to ensure that the negotiations succeed.

Charles Nelson (United States Institute of Peace): Would you comment on the past and future respective roles of the UN and OAS in contributing to the peace process?

Bernard Aronson: We have seen some unique and historic new roles for multilateral institutions in Central America, particularly the UN and the OAS, in contributing to regional peace and ending regional conflicts. In many ways, Nicaragua was a model for a successful end to a regional conflict, despite the problems; this model is being applied not just elsewhere in Central America but also in other parts of the world, such as Angola, and possibly in Afghanistan and Cambodia.

When a conflict is extremely polarized and bitter, when the gulf between the sides and the lack of trust are enormous, and when there has been killing and death and suffering on both sides, it is important to have institutions that can be trusted by both sides and yet have the resources to have an active presence on the ground that can make a difference.

In Nicaragua, the UN and the OAS monitored the elections. They were there throughout the registration and electoral period. They were in remote rural areas. They gave voters and candidates a sense of security so that political space could be opened up, and anybody who wanted to close that space knew that they would pay a price internationally—because the international community was present and watching and would point a finger at the guilty parties.

In Nicaragua since the elections, the OAS has managed the International Verification and Follow-up Commission (CIVS), which oversaw the demobilization of the resistance. The OAS has continued to play a role in helping the resistance resettle in remote areas and in attempting to guarantee their security there. A UN peacekeeping force was brought into Nicaragua to oversee the cease-fire, the separation of forces, and, eventually, the demobilization of the resistance.

The same institutions are playing somewhat similar roles in El Salvador. The difference is that the UN is also playing the crucial role of mediator in the negotiations. In El Salvador the two sides have been killing each other for at least eleven years. Just the ability to begin a dialogue and establish a process through which trust can be built is very, very difficult. When the parties were unable to bridge their differences, the UN offered formulas to try to bring them together or at least to set out a menu of options that the parties should address.

The creation of mechanisms such as these that can help resolve long-standing regional conflicts is an important component of our attempt to define a new world order in which the rule of law is established more firmly. El Salvador will be another fundamental step forward if this effort is successful.

Tom Gibb: The timetable for a peaceful settlement in Nicaragua was first the achievement of political agreements, followed by a long period of cease-fire. Next, there was an election in which everyone participated and accepted the results. Finally, the military issue was addressed. The demobilization of the *contras* (the Nicaraguan resistance) did not occur until after the elections. In El Salvador, it seems that events are occurring the other way around. Do you think that this is realistic in light of the Nicaraguan experience? Or is it likely that the peace process will have to last until the 1994 elections, the next opportunity for everyone to compete for power?

Bernard Aronson: If we have to wait until 1994, then we do not have a peace process—we have a war for three more years. The sequence of events in Nicaragua was a little different because there was not a cease-fire that both parties abided by until after the elections. The government of Nicaragua unilaterally abrogated the cease-fire in October 1989. That was another reason why the OAS and UN presence was so important in that period. But the sequence in Nicaragua was dictated by the reality of the situation and internal events. It is not a formula that will be exactly duplicated in El Salvador, but many of the elements will be duplicated.

If the political space for the elections in El Salvador had not been opened up, if the results had not been respected, if they had not been free of fraud, then a more pessimistic outlook might be more warranted. But, in fact, all the parties that wished to participate did so. In Nicaragua, the *contras* did not participate in the elections, but everybody understood that the process was open to any legal political party that wanted to participate. This was also the case in El Salvador.

The Democratic Convergence was able to win about 14 percent of the vote in the election, which was more than most predicted. Except for a few incidents, especially considering the number of new participants, the campaign was relatively free of violence and intimidation. It went more smoothly and more peacefully than it might have. Hopefully, if elements in the FMLN so choose, they will have constituted themselves as legal political parties by 1994 and they will have a chance to run in the elections. However, the Democratic Convergence and Nationalist Democratic Union (UDN) have clear, traditional ties to the FMLN, so it is incorrect to suggest that anybody was not represented in the last vote.

Cheryl Morden (Church World Service and Lutheran World Relief): One of the conditions Congress cited for releasing the aid had to do with injury to civilians, a condition that applied to both parties. Yet according to the report that accompanied the presidential determination, there were no injuries attributable to the government during the recording period. Documentation from human rights organizations in El Salvador shows that there are numerous examples of injury to civilians, including deaths, that are attributable to the government. There is concern that the failure to report them may reflect a certain lack of evenhandedness in the implementation of the policy framework. Could you comment on whether you think that this is a useful approach?

Bernard Aronson: It is important that we have a bipartisan approach to El Salvador. Not until we were able to speak on behalf of a broad, principled policy that has united both parties in Congress and the executive branch could we play a constructive and decisive role in Nicaragua. The same is true for El Salvador. In general, the idea behind the legislation passed by Congress to create pressures for peace and negotiations is a good one. We had some differences with some members of Congress about how to accomplish that goal, but I think that basic principle is sound.

It is unfortunate that President Bush's determination that the FMLN violated the legislation, which they did flagrantly, is seen somehow as a signal sent by the United States. The FMLN fully had the power to respect the standards that Congress had laid out, specifically that they must not import significant shipments of weapons or target civilians. If the FMLN had respected those criteria, there would not have been any need to make that determination. In fact, the report did mention instances of government violence against civilians, in particular an air force bombing of a small village that killed a number of civilians. When we made the determination that the FMLN had violated the criteria, President Bush voluntarily held back the release of the money for sixty additional days. He said that if a cease-fire were reached in that time period, the money would not be committed for military purposes.

In weighing how and whether to commit those funds, which we are now free to do, we are going to take into account three criteria. First is the security of El Salvador. Again, the FMLN has an open opportunity: It can reduce or halt offensive activity and it can agree to a cease-fire. Second is progress in the negotiations toward a cease-fire. We hope that the parties agree to a cease-fire quickly. Third is progress in the Jesuit case. It will not be easy to balance all three of those issues, though the security of the country will override the others if necessary.

We would much prefer to use those funds for peace than for military purposes. If the parties can reach a cease-fire, that is what the funds will be used for. That money could go a long way not just toward enforcing a cease-fire, which is an interim goal, but also toward helping combatants on both sides return to civilian life, find new livelihoods, and support their families. The funds would help in the process of restructuring and reducing the armed forces. In sum, the opportunity is there—and I hope the parties to the negotiations seize it.

PART 3

THE TRANSITION TO DEMOCRATIC GOVERNMENT: THREE KEY ISSUES

8

Human Rights:
Has There Been Progress?

——————— *Cynthia J. Arnson* ———————

The subject of human rights in El Salvador has, for the past decade, stood at the center of the US policy debate over the wisdom of supporting the government of El Salvador in its war against rebels of the Left. Key issues in that debate have been whether US assistance, particularly military assistance, helps or hinders progress in the human rights situation and the extent to which other policy interests ought to take precedence over a concern for human rights. The Reagan administration at first tried to underplay and deny those abuses that were occurring, but ultimately there has been consensus—first among the public and in Congress, belatedly in the Reagan administration, and now in the Bush administration—that Salvadoran government forces have been responsible for widespread abuses against Salvadoran civilians. These abuses have included torture, disappearance, assassination, and wholesale massacre. There is also widespread recognition that these abuses both gave rise to the current conflict and have continued to fuel it. Moreover, there is consensus that the FMLN guerrillas have been responsible for serious violations of the laws of war including, most notoriously, assassination and kidnapping.

The question, in the early years of the debate and now, has been how to end those atrocities and carry out the institutional changes necessary to see that they are not repeated. I would like to provide a brief overview of some of the recent developments in the human rights situation in El Salvador and then look at those questions of military reform and impunity that are central to the ongoing negotiations between the Salvadoran government and the FMLN.

Cynthia J. Arnson is associate director of Americas Watch.

The last six months of 1990 were relatively hopeful. The FMLN and the Salvadoran government signed a human rights accord in July 1990 that represented the first concrete achievement of the dialogue process.[1] In the wake of the accord, but perhaps only in part because of it, reported human rights violations, including disappearances, death squad killings, and deaths, that were attributed to the army and security forces declined, sometimes by as much as half. Violations committed by the guerrillas remained at a relatively constant level throughout 1990 but were fewer in number than in 1989.

It is entirely possible that both sides in the conflict moderated their behavior because of the UN-mediated peace talks. They did not want to be accused by the other side of carrying out actions that sabotaged the negotiations and poisoned the climate in which they were to take place. The actions of the US Congress, which reduced military aid by 50 percent in 1990 out of anger over the Jesuit murders and the lack of progress in prosecuting those responsible, also appear to have had an effect on Salvadoran government behavior: For the first time, Congress demonstrated that there were costs associated with carrying out acts of political murder. Unfortunately, the positive developments of the second half of 1990 did not continue into 1991:

- Preelectoral political violence before the March 10, 1991, legislative elections was greater than before the March 1989 presidential elections, despite the fact that the FMLN pledged to refrain from military actions that would disrupt the vote.

- At the beginning of the year, FMLN guerrillas shot down a US helicopter flying over eastern El Salvador and then executed in cold blood two US servicemen who had survived the crash. The FMLN pledged to conduct a trial of those responsible, although its right to do so has been challenged by the Salvadoran government and the Bush administration. (Both the FMLN and the Salvadoran government have executed prisoners and those placed out of combat by their wounds—a clear violation of the laws of war.)

- In January 1991, fifteen men, women, and children were killed, most of them stabbed to death, by several armed men in the hamlet of El Zapote near San Salvador. Although the government's insistence that the motive may not have been political but instead was personal in nature may be true, there are serious reasons to doubt the thoroughness of the government's investigation, especially with regards to possible military involvement in the murders.[2]

- The first months of 1991 also saw the return of a kidnapping-for-profit ring of the sort that operated in El Salvador in the early to mid-1980s. Then, as now, criminals acting with the apparent cooperation, if not participation, of the military have kidnapped members of the private sector and then ransomed them back to their families for substantial sums of money. In the mid-1980s, because the victims were members of the conservative Salvadoran elite, there was optimism that the kidnapping-for-profit case could be cracked and ultimately solved. Instead, suspects and judges were bribed, intimidated, and killed while the investigation went nowhere.

Several of those implicated in the original scheme have been spotted recently in San Salvador and are suspected to be behind the current spate of kidnappings.[3] The resurgence of the kidnapping-for-profit enterprise is only one example of what happens when some in the military commit crimes in El Salvador and are not prosecuted. It is rather astonishing to point out in 1991 that although thousands of cases of political killings, torture, and disappearance of civilians at the hands of government forces have been documented, no officer has been convicted of a politically motivated human rights abuse in El Salvador.

The case of the six murdered Jesuit priests and their housekeeper and her daughter may go to trial later this year (1991), and there is every indication that it will. But the investigation has been impeded by a lack of cooperation by senior officers and tainted by allegations that senior officers had prior knowledge of the murder plot and conspired to cover up the crime. Many of those following the case closely also find it inconceivable that the one colonel under indictment could have planned a crime of such magnitude on his own.[4]

Even when the United States has made a human rights case a high priority, as the Bush administration did with the 1988 massacre of ten peasants in the town of San Sebastián, San Vicente, the Salvadoran judicial system has failed to respond. Although twelve military suspects were detained in the case as a result of US pressure, the courts dismissed charges against all but one of the accused. In early 1991, the State Department described the case as "virtually collapsed."[5]

It is no surprise, given these examples, that the question of military impunity for human rights crimes remains one of the most difficult issues dividing Salvadoran government and FMLN delegations in the current peace talks. As one who works in human rights, I would like to offer my perspective on the question of accountability. It is crucial to note that human rights abuses of the scale and duration of those in El Salvador have been possible only because those who ordered and carried out such abuses have enjoyed a total impunity guaranteed by the state. Laws and practices that shield those who have committed human rights violations from exposure, investigation, and prosecution are, therefore, likely to reproduce a new cycle of abuses.

The declaration of an amnesty for the ostensible purpose of national reconciliation may, in fact, only guarantee that new crimes are committed. Wiping the slate clean and pretending that human rights abuses did not take place is not the same as ensuring that they will not happen again. I do not want to oversimplify a complex situation in Nicaragua, but some instances of political violence since President Violeta Chamorro took office in 1990 have erupted precisely because those who abused power and authority in the past continue to occupy positions of responsibility.

It may be that at some point in the peace talks the different sides in the Salvadoran conflict agree to an amnesty except in several significant human rights cases agreed to by both sides. Such an agreement would represent a truly Pyrrhic victory. It would prevent the deep wounds of the past from healing, allow resentments to continue to burn, and ultimately endanger the hopes for true social reconciliation.

* * *

In the nine months since this presentation was given in April 1991, El Salvador has traversed a political universe. The peace talks that were so carefully nurtured by the United Nations and by Secretary-General Pérez de Cuéllar himself culminated in the January 16, 1992, signing of a peace accord between the Salvadoran government and the FMLN. The peace plan envisioned a cease-fire by February 1, 1992, and the complete demobilization of the FMLN as a fighting force by October 31, 1992. In exchange for their demobilization, the FMLN negotiated basic changes in Salvadoran society, perhaps none so radical as the restructuring of the armed forces and a redefinition of their role in society. Just as human rights abuses helped give rise to and sustain the Salvadoran conflict, so any settlement of the war needed to address the principal source of human rights violations: the armed forces. The peace accord sets forth the dissolution of the internal security forces most notorious for their brutality, which were the Treasury Police, the National Guard, and the civil defense. The existing National Police is also to be disbanded, and in its place a new National Civil Police is to be created under close international supervision. The new police force gives preference in recruitment to those without prior military service but is, in theory, open to FMLN combatants as well as to former members of the disbanded National Police.

Also to be dismantled are all the army rapid-reaction infantry battalions, one of which, the Atlacatl, was associated with some of the most horrendous massacres of the war. The Atlacatl's mark on Salvadoran society includes the murder of almost 800 peasants in and around the town of El Mozote in December 1981, the murder of approximately fifty peasants on the bank of the Gualsinga River in 1984, and the 1989 assassination of six Jesuit priests and their housekeeper and her daughter.

The agreement to reduce the army by approximately half, to revise the curriculum of the Military Academy, and to remove the army from any responsibility for internal security marked a further recognition that not only abusive practices but also the structures of repression had to be altered in order to bring the conflict to an end.

Perhaps the most dangerous aspect of postwar El Salvador is the potential for political violence by those opposed to the provisions of the peace accord. Within hours of the breakthrough in the negotiations on New Year's Eve, 1991, for example, a bomb destroyed the vehicle of the Reuters correspondent in a parking lot of the Camino Real Hotel and a group calling itself the Salvadoran Anti-Communist Front (FAS) issued death threats against several journalists. Six days later, a death squad calling itself the Secret Army of National Salvation threatened eleven prominent members of the Salvadoran Protestant National Council of Churches, accusing them of active collaboration with the FMLN. In a January 12, 1991, homily, Auxiliary Bishop Gregorio Rosa y Chávez warned of renewed violence by extremist groups trying to block the peace accord.[6] Precisely because acts of political violence, most notably assassination, could cause the transition process to unravel, those opposed to the restructuring of Salvadoran society have every incentive to stage violent provocations.[7]

Even before the final signing of the peace agreement on January 16, 1992, the negotiations process yielded several positive developments in the human rights field. In July 1991, a year after the Salvadoran government and the FMLN signed a comprehensive human rights accord, which was itself an important stepping stone toward the wider peace agreement, the United Nations Observer Mission in El Salvador (ONUSAL) began monitoring the human rights situation inside the country. This involved the UN in an unprecedented monitoring effort inside a member state, even while the civil conflict continued to rage. With over 100 observers (including thirty-one military and police advisers) and six regional and subregional offices, ONUSAL had an impact on the observance of human rights that was felt within months of its establishment.

Part of the deterrent that ONUSAL was able to exercise was directly related to its power to deploy personnel anywhere in the country without prior notice and, perhaps more important, to visit prisons unannounced. It remains to be seen, however, to what extent ONUSAL's presence can spur Salvadoran governmental institutions, including the courts, to perform their central role in human rights protection. There are limits, after all, to how much international organizations can substitute for, and not just encourage, local institutional development.

Before the final peace accord was signed, the Salvadoran government and the FMLN had also agreed to changes in the judicial system. The accord signed in Mexico on April 27, 1991, provided for direct election by two-thirds majority of the Legislative Assembly of Supreme Court magistrates, the attorney general, and a newly-created human rights ombudsman, thus making it more difficult for the ruling party to politicize and dominate the appointments process. The accord also envisioned the creation of a National Council for the Judiciary, to oversee the training of magistrates and other judicial personnel. Better preparation, along with the dedication of at least six percent of the national budget to the judiciary, was intended to raise the standard of competence and professionalism within El Salvador's notoriously non-functioning judicial system.

The peace agreement prescribes sweeping changes for the future and provides two important mechanisms for coming to grips with the past. In April 1991, the Salvadoran negotiating teams agreed to create a nonjudicial Commission on Truth to investigate major human rights crimes of the past decade.[8] With only six months to complete its work, it is clear that the Commission on Truth will not function as did the Chilean National Commission on Truth and Reconciliation (the Rettig Commission), which spent nine months interviewing survivors of persecution during the Pinochet regime and documenting over 2,200 cases of execution, disappearance, and torture resulting in death. Rather, the Salvadoran Commission on Truth will most likely focus on a handful of prominent cases,[9] gathering what is known (and, hopefully, what has not yet come to light) about the abuses and giving an official imprimatur to widely held suspicions about ultimate responsibility. The commission can issue recommendations based on its findings, including recommendations that perpetrators of abuses be prosecuted by the courts.[10]

Because the Commission on Truth will probably deal with a small number of the most infamous human rights cases, the broader work of weeding out corrupt, brutal officers from the military falls to an ad hoc commission of three Salvadoran civilians. This ad hoc commission will review the records of military officers with an eye toward purging those guilty of serious human rights abuses. Because the peace accord does not envision widespread prosecution for human rights offenses (but speaks, rather, of "exemplary action in the tribunals of justice"),[11] the work of the ad hoc commission—and the extent to which its recommendations are enforced—will potentially have the most lasting impact on the future observance of human rights.

Virtually all processes of democratic transition in Latin America, including those accompanying a negotiated settlement to civil conflict, have involved some form of amnesty for crimes committed during the previous regime. Amnesties have been promulgated in the name of social reconciliation, in which victims and their relatives are asked to forgive and forget, setting aside any desire for revenge. They also emerge in situations where civilian power is circumscribed, at times severely, by the ongoing power wielded by the military.

The amnesty adopted by the Salvadoran Legislative Assembly on January 23, 1992, represents a compromise between those, primarily in the governing ARENA party, who wanted a total amnesty, and those in the FMLN and opposition parties who wanted to exclude those guilty of war crimes or grave abuses of human rights. (The positions provide an interesting commentary on who in Salvadoran society fear accountability.)

The compromise, worked out by the National Commission for Consolidation of Peace (COPAZ) and created to monitor compliance with the peace agreement,[12] exempted from the amnesty those who had been tried and convicted by civilian courts[13] and exempted those cases for which the Commission on Truth recommended prosecution. The compromise thus allows the vast majority of murderers and torturers to go free yet preserves the principle of accountability in some of the most notorious cases.[14]

The end of the military conflict in El Salvador will bring about an immediate improvement in certain aspects of the human rights situation by ending war-related violations such as indiscriminate attacks on the civilian population and summary executions of wounded combatants. However, human rights abuses in El Salvador have only partly been related to the rhythm of the war. They predate the outbreak of civil conflict and helped give rise to it. To the extent that the peace agreement actually succeeds in abolishing those forces most responsible for abuses, and restructures and reduces what remains of the armed forces, the prospects for improved human rights observance increase dramatically. The lack of prosecutions, however, will continue to burden Salvadoran society with unrepentant criminals who may or may not be purged from the military and, if purged, may continue to act outside the law even if they no longer enjoy positions of authority.[15]

The most immediate test of human rights in postwar El Salvador will be the treatment afforded ex-combatants of the FMLN as they turn in their weapons and return to civilian life. Indeed, it is difficult to separate the question of their personal security after a cease-fire from the broader questions of human rights reform in El Salvador because concerns for the former produced the imperative for the latter. The presence of 1,000 UN observers to oversee the process of disarmament will no doubt reduce the risk to ex-fighters. If the security of ex-combatants can be guaranteed while the military reforms envisioned in the peace agreement are implemented, then there is hope for the broader, participatory democracy based on respect for human rights that is the utmost goal of the end of the war.

Ultimately, the guarantee of human rights will have to expand beyond questions of sheer physical survival for former enemies if democracy is to exist as other than a mere formality. The creation of a functioning judicial system that would sanction authorities of the state as swiftly as members of popular social movements is essential if the rule of law is to have meaning. Human rights abuses flourished in the past because of the impunity enjoyed by those who committed them. It may be that the judiciary can begin to exercise a more independent role now that the pervasive influence of the armed forces stands to be curtailed by the peace agreement.

Notes

1. The Agreement on Human Rights, also known as the San José accord, committed the Salvadoran government and the FMLN to take "all necessary steps and measures . . . to avoid any act or practice which constitutes an attempt upon the life, integrity, security or freedom of the individual. Similarly, all necessary steps and measures shall be taken to eliminate any practice involving enforced disappearances and abductions."

The accord envisioned the establishment of a human rights verification mission "to investigate the human rights situation in El Salvador . . . and to take any steps it deems appropriate to promote and defend such rights." See Americas Watch, *El Salvador and Human Rights: The Challenge of Reform* (New York: Human Rights Watch, March 1991), Appendix I.

2. All of the above phenomena are discussed in Americas Watch, *El Salvador and Human Rights*.

3. See Human Rights Watch, *World Report 1991* (New York: Human Rights Watch, 1992), pp. 216–217.

4. The Jesuit case did go to trial in 1991. On September 28, 1991, a five-person jury convicted Col. Guillermo Alfredo Benavides of murder; Lieut. Yusshy René Mendoza Vallecillos, who oversaw the operation on the campus of the University of Central America, was convicted solely of the murder of fifteen-year-old Celina Mariceth Ramos. All seven other defendants were acquitted; of the seven, two lieutenants were given three-year sentences in January 1992 for the lesser charge of conspiracy to commit acts of terrorism. (A lieutenant colonel was also given a three-year sentence for destruction of evidence.) The jury verdict on September 28 was the first to convict a senior Salvadoran officer of a human rights crime. However, the jury's decision to let triggermen go free sent the dangerous message to troops that they could kill with impunity as long as they claimed to be following higher orders.

Following the verdict, Rep. Joe Moakley, chair of the Speaker's Task Force on El Salvador, cited "experienced, respected, and serious" sources in the military as having told him that "the decision to murder the Jesuits was made at a small meeting of officers held at the Salvadoran Military School on the afternoon prior to the murders." Those present included the current minister and vice-minister of defense, the head of the army First Brigade, and the former head of the air force. See Human Rights Watch, *World Report 1991*, pp. 223–225.

5. US Department of State, *Country Reports on Human Rights Practices for 1990* (Washington, D.C.: US Government Printing Office, February 1991), p. 615.

6. Reuters, "Catholic Church in El Salvador Fears Renewal of Violence Despite Peace Pact," *Miami Herald,* January 13, 1991.

7. The greatest threat to peace in early 1992 appears to emanate from the extreme Right and their allies in the Salvadoran army. This is not to rule out opposition to the peace treaty by members of the FMLN, though evidence of their resistance to the peace accord has yet to surface.

8. The formation of the commission is spelled out in the *Acuerdos de México,* April 27, 1991, p. 5. See also *La Prensa Gráfica,* "'Second Part' of 'Mexico Declaration' Annex," in *Foreign Broadcast Information Service,* May 3, 1991, pp. 5–6.

9. These will include abuses by both government forces and the FMLN. As of this writing, there is no indication of which cases the Commission on Truth will consider.

10. In mid-December 1991, UN secretary-general Javier Pérez de Cuéllar named three prominent non-Salvadorans to the commission: former Colombian president Belisario Betancur, former Venezuelan foreign minister Reinaldo Figueredo, and Thomas Buergenthal, president of the Inter-American Institute for Human Rights.

11. Text, Gobierno de El Salvador y Frente Farabundo Martí para la Liberación Nacional, *Acuerdo de Paz,* p. 10.

12. COPAZ is composed of members of the Salvadoran government and military, the FMLN, and representatives of political parties currently in the Legislative Assembly.

13. This exemption covers the handful of human rights cases that have been brought to court and resulted in convictions: the 1989 Jesuit case and the case of the four US churchwomen killed by National Guardsmen in December 1980; the 1985 Zona Rosa case in which FMLN guerrillas assassinated thirteen people, including four off-duty US marines, at a sidewalk café (three members of the FMLN were sentenced in May 1991 for their participation in the attack); and the 1987 case of murdered human rights activist Herbert Anaya. In October 1991, a jury convicted a young member of the FMLN for the Anaya murder. All of these cases have been marked by serious anomalies in the judicial process. In the churchwomen's and Jesuits' cases, there is serious doubt that all those in the military who were involved were prosecuted. In the Zona Rosa and Anaya cases, there is serious doubt that the members of the FMLN who were convicted were, in fact, those responsible for the murders. See Human Rights Watch, *World Report 1992*, pp. 222–223.

14. It is unclear whether the exemplary cases selected by the Commission on Truth will also be subject to amnesty sometime in the future. The amnesty law provides an opportunity for the Legislative Assembly to extend the amnesty after the Commission on Truth finishes its work.

15. In a sobering reminder of the dangers of failing to prosecute, high-ranking Argentine federal police officers arrested in late 1991 for their role in a kidnapping ring included many who were accused of serious abuses during the military junta's "dirty war."

9

The Tanda System and
Institutional Autonomy of the Military

—————— *José Z. García* ——————

The Salvadoran Polytechnic Institute, a military academy, was closed in 1922 by a shaken civilian president, Jorge Meléndez, as a punitive, cost-saving, and precautionary measure after cadets there participated in a failed coup attempt against him earlier that year. For the next few years officers were selected from the ranks of enlisted troops and promoted by ad hoc practices that caused widespread suspicion that professional criteria were not as important to a military career as favoritism. Partly in response to this criticism, a new military school, the Gerardo Barrios Military School, was organized in 1927; it commissioned forty-three officers three years later. Graduates from the class of 1930 are known in Salvadoran military history as the first *tanda* (turn, or rotation) of the modern period of the armed forces.[1]

The first graduating cadets had reason to feel confident in their future prospects. Eight years had passed since the last professional officers had been commissioned from a military academy. Rapid acquisition of responsibility and rank seemed possible. New military codes were strict in rank-in-grade requirements, and training was far more extensive and up to date. By the late 1930s, however, disillusionment had set in among new graduates. Personal favoritism and political loyalty still counted, and officers in the higher ranks tended to band together against the new cadets. A dangerous conflict between young and older officers developed.

The new military academy was only five years old when Gen. Maximilian H. Martínez came to power in 1932, following the civil strife that ended with the *matanza* of that year. Martínez, desiring to build a loyal army to support

José Z. García is professor of government at New Mexico State University.

95

his regime, rewarded favored officers with prestigious civilian posts. Three generals were placed in the cabinet, a captain was named treasury minister, and a colonel was placed in charge of the government printing house. Many other agencies were staffed by officers thought to be loyal to Martínez. All of this caused a good deal of resentment among officers overlooked for such prestigious assignments. In October 1935, a general out of favor with Martínez was arrested with twenty-five fellow officers and charged with plotting against the government. In November 1936, a similar conspiracy was uncovered and the implicated officers were summarily shot. In January 1939, another plot was uncovered involving twenty-five captains and lieutenants and two generals.

This latter conspiracy involved large numbers of graduates from the new military academy and was motivated in great part by discontent with Martínez among junior officers. By the end of 1939, 203 officers had graduated from the new academy, outnumbering all other active officers. Aware of these problems, senior officers thereafter reduced the number of academy graduates for a few years. But by 1943, 245 officers had graduated, out of an officer corps of about 375.

In 1944, a major insurrection headed by two colonels and a general nearly succeeded in overthrowing Martínez with the support of sizable numbers of junior officers who took command of the First, Second, and Fifth Infantry Regiments, the artillery regiment, the communications building, and the airport. The coup failed when key senior conspirators inexplicably capitulated; this resulted in the execution of twelve officers. But a civilian uprising that accompanied it succeeded in getting General Martínez to resign, leaving the government in the hands of Gen. Andrés I. Menéndez. Menéndez, contemplating several incidents in which junior officer discontent resulted in coup plotting, tried to satisfy some of the professional demands of junior officers. He was overthrown a few months later by a clique of older officers who organized hasty elections in 1945 in which only an aging general, Castaneda Castro, became a candidate.

Castaneda, in turn, tried to reduce the chances of junior officer threats to his rule by reducing the quota for second lieutenants, lieutenants, and captains from the 352 authorized in 1936 down to 280 in 1945. But junior officers tried to overthrow him within weeks of his coming to power and a second conspiracy of junior officers in 1948 succeeded in ousting him. The junior officers who engaged in this conspiracy, many of them of the rank of major and from the class of 1931, decapitated the senior officer corps.

It should be noted that the conspiracies of this period were associated with more than the professional grievances of junior officers. They also involved constitutional issues of succession, and ideological and policy disputes, and civilian groups participated in virtually all plotting. But it is significant that surviving officers of that period in recalling these matters tend strongly to impute careerist motives over any other in ascribing their own or others' reasons for joining or not joining a conspiracy. This suggests strongly that these grievances were fundamental in shaping perceptions and responses to other motivators.

The present tanda system dates from the coup of 1948. The officer who emerged from the coup as leader of the armed forces, Oscar Osorio (class of 1931), served as president of the country from 1948 to 1956.[2] Aware of the troubles of the past, Osorio tried to prevent generational grievances from surfacing by creating a set of informal rules, which still constitute the tanda system. Most important, an officer graduating from the military academy is assured eventual promotion to colonel barring serious disciplinary action or separation from active duty. Officers in a tanda move up the military hierarchy more or less simultaneously and eventually get a turn at top jobs in the armed forces. Continual movement of classes upward lessens the chances that intergenerational strife, such as that which marked the armed forces during the 1930s and 1940s, will get out of hand, because collective and individual patience will inevitably lead to rewards. Moreover, simultaneous tanda mobility tends to lead to a high degree of cohesion within each rank simply because most officers at every rank have known each other for many years. The hierarchical structure of military command, however, assures obedience from the top down. Although the tanda system greatly reduced generational conflict within the officer corps, it did not entirely remove it, and though it virtually guarantees an officer the rank of colonel, it does not necessarily guarantee good position.

The tendency of presidents to keep a defense minister and troop commanders in place for several years often produces a certain amount of tension in junior ranks. A dominant tanda remains in power long enough to sour the chances of a younger tanda, which may find itself in semiexile with attaché jobs until retirement, when a younger group takes over the top jobs. This compression has at times resulted in the displacement of nearly a decade of tandas, as was the case in the late 1950s, when the tandas of the 1930s finally yielded their positions to the tandas of the early 1940s. And it was not until the late 1970s that the tandas of the early 1950s began to rise to prominence.

The Tandona

Over time a pattern has emerged: Every so often tensions arise as the top leadership in the armed forces, usually represented by two or three dominant tandas, maneuver to remain in positions of power as long as possible and junior tandas try to oust them. As time goes on, the junior tandas voice increasingly public complaints about their leaders. Stories of corruption and ineptitude at high levels circulate in military and civilian circles. Government officials grow concerned about potential intramilitary strife. And eventually a displacement occurs. When this happens, a scramble takes place to determine which of the succeeding tandas will be dominant. In some cases several tandas are bypassed in favor of a younger set of tandas.

The last such power shift occurred in the late 1980s after several years of rule by the tandas of the late 1950s, dominated by generals Vides Casanova and Rafael Bustillo of the 1957 tandas and by Gen. Adolfo Blandón of the 1960 tanda. The transition was accompanied by all sorts of internal strife driven essentially by career concerns but almost always, in the context of a difficult guerrilla conflict, disguised as conflict over military policy. There was no doubt about which tanda would dominate, because it had been clear for many years that the large forty-six–man *tandona* (class of 1966, also known sometimes as the *sinfónica* tanda) would come to power. As the largest graduating class ever assembled (there was no class of 1965; two classes were joined in 1966), the tandona prepared from the very beginning for eventual command. One member of a junior tanda (who did not graduate and later joined the FMLN guerrillas) recalls that even at the academy tandona members were highly cohesive and dominant. The acknowledged leader of the tandona is Gen. René Emilio Ponce.

Gen. Vides Casanova was minister of defense from 1981 to 1989. As his period came to an end he opted to favor the tandona, a class whose members distinguished themselves by their anti-American nationalism, close connections with the right wing, business acumen, and, with Vides's support, their near-monopoly of batallion-sized troop command positions. They skillfully exercised a moral edge, which they claimed to enjoy over senior tandas because of their greater combat experience and because they had pushed an anti-US bias to an audience of junior officers (who in fact had acquired more combat experience than the tandona). By the late 1980s tandona members dominated virtually all troop command positions, including all six brigades, the military detachments, and even the rapid deployment infantry battalions (BIRIs). Never before had any single tanda dominated as thoroughly.

The period of tandona rule, however, was not entirely auspicious. Members were widely accused of human rights violations. There were highly publicized accusations of corruption. Tandona-managed military operations were frequently criticized and the tandona was collectively blamed for not being able to defeat the guerrillas. By 1990, after the Jesuit and other human rights cases and after Gen. Maxwell Thurman, Commander-in-Chief of the US Southern Command in Panama, told them they could not win the war militarily, junior tandas were complaining, sometimes bitterly, about military leadership under the tandona. It is difficult to sort out how much of this criticism has been driven by bureaucratic fear and how much has been driven by policy concern.

Whatever the case, this negative publicity has almost certainly shortened tandona control. The guerrillas have taken to denouncing them and may yet hold out for massive resignations as a price for a cease-fire. The next likely dominant tandas are the 1972 and 1973 classes, but until they have more experience, an interim set of tandas (possibly the 1970–1971 group, which is known for its talent) may take control in the next year or two if there is a change.

Peace talks during 1990 and 1991 almost certainly were affected by widespread sentiment against the excesses that have occurred under tandona leadership. Guerrillas have pressed with some success to purge military officers, and a final cease-fire arrangement may well include a provision whereby the remaining tandona leaders will retire and make room for younger officers. In this sense both the guerrillas and junior officers have an interest in such an arrangement—for very different reasons. But if the tandona proves to have staying power with President Cristiani, the few remaining members may supervise the institution for the next three years, until presidential elections in 1994.

Many US policymakers and human rights advocates criticize the tanda system as embodying many of the evils that the US government professed to be trying to eliminate. If the foregoing analysis is correct, however, the tanda system should be viewed in historical context as a largely successful effort by the military to create internal stability and continuity. That evil still occurs within the institution is without doubt. But that the tanda system itself is somehow responsible is questionable. Corruption and human rights abuse within a military institution is symptomatic of extreme weakness in civilian democratic institutions.[3]

The Issue of Autonomy

As an institution, the Salvadoran armed forces faced severe challenges arising from the civil war. Their enemies, of course, were hoping to destroy them altogether. Their allies, interested for various reasons in preserving them, pulled and tugged at them, often in different directions. And a Greek chorus of outside onlookers never tired of bemoaning their discovered sins. Consider, for example, some of the changes they either made or were asked to make as an institution during the 1980s:

1. Concerning domestic political relations, the armed forces were asked to unravel relations with the officialist PCN, a party created in 1962 expressly as a vehicle for a military presidential candidate and governing with military presidents until 1979; to ally themselves with the PDC, a party that the armed forces had rejected a decade earlier; and to accept and indeed help administer an agrarian reform stronger than one the armed forces had rejected a decade earlier.

2. Regarding internal changes as a military force, they were asked to improve human rights performance with civilian groups and guerrilla combatants and to learn counterinsurgency doctrine and adapt it to local conditions.

That the armed forces were able to survive the civil war and navigate successfully through a rapidly changing political environment is testimony to extraordinary institutional resilience and an ability to make autonomous decisions. Although it is too early to tell which direction the armed forces will take during the postwar period, in general three major factors are discernible today: (1) the leverage the United States exercises over the military has decreased, (2) cooperation between armed forces and government has increased, and (3) the overall autonomy of the armed forces in its relations with other domestic actors has increased, at least in the short run.

As the guerrilla threat diminished, the armed forces tended to grow increasingly independent of the US Embassy. This was especially true after Congress made it clear in 1990 and then in 1991 that funding levels would continue at reasonably high levels. For a long period during the 1980s, latent anti-US sentiment had been brewing within the armed forces over various issues but was not allowed to surface because of the exigencies of the moment, which were believed to require high levels of funding. When these were assured, anti-US sentiment increased.

Relations between the government and the armed forces improved markedly after the election of President Alfredo Cristiani. During the Duarte years the armed forces and the PDC maintained a studied cooperation but it often seemed as though the two institutions were pursuing parallel but not coordinated policies. For example, coordination of military and bureaucratic assets were required for the success of Municipalities in Action, a program designed to win over populations in conflictive zones. As military commanders gained effective control over a region, the plan was for a package of AID-funded government services—restoration of electricity and water, medical care, and so on—to be made available to local authorities. The program was a dismal failure during the Duarte period, among other reasons because of widespread government corruption. With the election of Cristiani, the armed forces and government began to cooperate much more intimately in Municipalities in Action, so by 1991 it was perhaps the most successful program that AID could point to in its entire scope of action. As cooperation has increased, it has led to some suspicion that the old alliance between right-wing oligarchy and military would be revived, a suspicion that was fueled by the wave of violence against some labor unions in 1989 and 1990.

Whether this cooperation will continue when US funding levels decrease and the armed forces must lobby in a postwar setting for its share of scarce resources is unknown. So far, President Cristiani has seemed to most observers to be cautious with the armed forces, rarely exerting his power as commander-in-chief, at least in public.

The evidence, though very sketchy, would suggest that the armed forces are emerging from the war with a greater sense of autonomy vis-à-vis other political and social forces in Salvadoran society. Ten years of civil war have created military perspectives on the nation that are not shared by any other groups. Military officers now have a far more cosmopolitan understanding of their about-to-be concluded experience in combat than they ever had before. Relative success against an insurgency has brought about a new self-confidence, but the need to negotiate a settlement after ten years of war has taught increased respect for the adversary.

Perhaps the most interesting question relates to the connection between the military and the nation's agrarian elite. For over a century the armed forces of El Salvador have acted as often violent protectors of a peculiar political economy dominated by coffee and, in more recent times, cotton and sugar cane growers, who controlled a highly exclusive banking system to which many social groups did not have access except at usurious interest rates. Indeed, most analysts agree that a major cause of the insurgency was widespread popular resentment against the rapaciousness of the traditional oligarchy and the brutality of sectors of the armed forces acting on their behalf. And a good deal of US policy toward El Salvador and many policies of the Salvadoran government during the 1980s were predicated on the assumption that political tranquility in the long run could be achieved only by reducing the power of the oligarchy and the closeness of the relationship between the oligarchy and the armed forces.

A major difficulty in assessing the extent of change in the autonomy of the armed forces is that after years of civil war and numerous changes in the policies and goals of government, the structure and composition of the oligarchy has probably changed, but in as yet largely unstudied ways and degrees. In addition, the attitude of government elites toward the oligarchy may have undergone some change as well. It is difficult to know what impact privatization may have on the oligarchy's political clout.

Although it is too early to offer much more than speculation, it appears that the old coffee oligarchy has diminished overall financial capacity in comparison with government. At the start of the conflict, coffee revenues were roughly double those of total government expenditures; today coffee revenues are roughly half of total government revenues, largely as a result of various increases in noncoffee sources of funding. The actual contribution that coffee makes to the national budget has also declined, down to about 20 to 30 percent from the more normal 40 to 60 percent (the rates vary according to the international price of coffee). This decline would suggest the makings of a more pluralistic government. And though there is some evidence that the traditional "fourteen families" are making a concerted bid to repurchase the banks that were nationalized as part of the reform effort a decade ago, it is also true that many military officers have used the relative wealth that members of the institution have enjoyed during the war to invest in a wide variety of enterprises, including banks. The armed forces are in the process of putting together a military bank for officers and enlisted men. They are unlikely to want to return to the days when banks charged exorbitant interest rates and were controlled by only a few.[4]

The International Connection

This war has been extremely international, with both sides supplied amply from foreign powers and private groups. On the human rights issue, international assistance on both sides played a role in making violations costly. The US government has invested over $4 billion in an enterprise in which the long-term democratic role of the armed forces was a stated goal. The Left was able to use human rights violations by the armed forces as a justification for funding the war. It is almost certain that international actors on both sides of the civil war helped restrain the armed forces from less democratic behavior and it seems likely that continued international monitoring of human rights and democratic practices may be useful in the future.

Ultimately, whether a new civil-military relationship will develop will depend far more upon the creation of a consensus and understanding among major political actors regarding the limits of military intervention and the continued active monitoring of international groups interested in democratic and human rights practices than it will upon events taking place within the armed forces. At the present time, officers have been indoctrinated with the need for the armed forces to remain apolitical and to respect human rights. But experience suggests that the doctrine is less likely to be violated when institutional actors are aware that the tangible potential costs—to the institution and individuals in it—of violation are high. If the armed forces as a whole are more autonomous vis-à-vis other actors today than they were before, they have also demonstrated great political flexibility over the span of more than a decade. Their capacity to act and the legitimacy that they enjoy as political actors are far greater than they were a decade ago.

It is ironic that in some ways the armed forces, of all the major actors in the Salvadoran civil war, have had the least coherent idea of for what they were fighting. In great part this is because exigencies in 1979 forced officers to choose between their own vision of reality—under severe domestic and international attack—and that of their allies and benefactors. That they were humble enough to accept political views inimical to their own is the major distinguishing feature between themselves and the Nicaraguan National Guard of the Somoza regime. But if this flexibility saved them from destruction it also placed them at a disadvantage because they were forced to learn from others not only how to fight a war but also to accept on faith the ultimate purposes for which the war was fought, because these were not generated within the institution.

Many US officials working with the armed forces understood overall strategic imperatives only dimly or incompletely. Sometimes Salvadoran officers' fears of communism—encouraged openly by US officials only a few years earlier—were now characterized as rabid. But other times US officials and some of the private guests of the government quietly sympathized with anticommunism as an ultimate end. For still others the struggle was ultimately about human rights or even more abstract geopolitical or democratic goals. A similar confusion plagued many US policymakers in Washington. And given that the Salvadoran armed forces had little inclination and less time or resources to forge a common ideology of the war, it is little wonder that some of the best minds would find themselves confused and frustrated with policy imperatives they did not understand and that sometimes reversed original intentions.[5]

At the present time the evidence suggests that the Salvadoran armed forces have not yet engaged in much collective introspection about their wartime experience. What was the war really all about? Was it about democracy or human rights or fighting communism, or simply survival? What was the impact of the war on the institution? What were the various impacts of US assistance on the institution? What did the war do to Salvadoran society at large? How did it affect civil-military relations?

The Salvadoran military is an institution that has survived a difficult and bloody war. Its future behavior, for better or worse, depends in part on its updated notions about itself and its relations to others. It would seem useful for academics and other interested groups to encourage the armed forces of El Salvador to tell their story, as they see it. They should be encouraged to make some meaning out of their experience in war and share this with others who may have differing perceptions.

Notes

1. Details of this period of Salvadoran military institutional history can be found in Rafael Meza Gallont, *El Ejército de El Salvador (Breve Boceto Histórico)* (San Salvador: Imprenta Nacional, 1964).

2. The intramilitary strife that led to the Osorio coup is explored in some detail in José Z. García, "Origins and Consequences of Factionalism Within the Salvadoran Armed Forces," unpublished manuscript (1983), available from author.

3. A highly critical account of the tanda system can be found in Joel Millman, "A Force unto Itself," *New York Times Magazine,* December 10, 1989.

4. The best single source for examining empirical evidence of social inequality in El Salvador remains Eduardo Colindres, *Fundamentos Económicos de la Burguesía Salvadoreña,* (San Salvador: UCA editores, 1979).

5. This argument is elaborated more fully by the author in "Democratic Consolidation in El Salvador?" *Current History,* December 1988, p. 437. Two excellent sources for understanding the Salvadoran armed forces are Raúl Benítez Manaut, *Le teoría militar y la guerra civil en El Salvador,* UCA editores (San Salvador: 1989); and Max Manwaring and Court Prisk, *El Salvador at War: An Oral History,* (Washington, D.C.: National Defense University, 1989).

10

The State of the Economy

Roberto Murray Meza

The 1980s: A Decade of Economic Decline and Stagnation

After more than twenty-five years of uninterrupted growth (at an average annual rate of 5 percent in real terms), the economy of El Salvador entered the 1980s in a virtual free-fall. From 1979 to 1982 real GDP dropped 22 percent and fell well below the overall level of output achieved in 1974. During the same period, real income per capita declined 27 percent; this pushed average incomes lower than levels achieved in 1964. Over the rest of the decade, the economy limped along, growing at an average annual rate of only 1.5 percent. El Salvador ended the decade with a GDP 13 percent below its high point eleven years earlier.

One area that epitomizes the overall economic decline in the 1980s is export performance. From 1977 through 1980 exports averaged $1 billion per year and exceeded imports in three of those four years. After 1980, however, exports dropped almost steadily to less than $500 million in 1989. Even with the remarkable 17 percent surge in 1990, the value of export revenue is still only about one-half of that registered in 1979, El Salvador's peak year for exports.

Not only did the Salvadoran economy suffer the consequences of a major drop in export earnings, but it also missed out on the potential benefits of what could have been a major expansion of exports to world markets. After the downturn at the beginning of the decade, the world economy experienced one of its longest periods of continuous growth in history. Several of El Salvador's Central American neighbors, includ-

Roberto Murray Meza is president of Cervecería La Constancia, S.A., in San Salvador.

ing Costa Rica, Guatemela, and Honduras, were able to increase substantially their exports to the United States. Lacking an economic policy framework providing sufficient incentives for exporters and faced with extremely low levels of investor confidence, El Salvador was unable to capitalize on this opportunity. Over the same period, its exports to the United States fell by one third.

The reasons for El Salvador's economic troubles during the 1980s are many. First, global economic conditions at the beginning of the decade caused serious difficulties for most Third World nations. The effects of the second oil price shock (1979–1980) were especially hard on small open economies completely dependent on oil imports. Following in the wake of this oil price increase was the 1981–1982 global economic recession, the impact of which was amplified into actual depressions for most Third World countries. Export volumes nosedived and export prices fell precipitously. World interest rates soared while credit and investment capital dried up. Therefore even without its civil war, El Salvador would have suffered serious economic setbacks at the beginning of the decade.

Compounding these unfavorable global economic trends was the marked increase in political instability, insurrections, and civil war throughout Central America, not only in El Salvador but also in Nicaragua and Guatemala. These developments further depressed the already low levels of investor confidence in the area and contributed to massive capital flight from the region. The additional stress placed on the individual Central American economies by this political turmoil exacerbated that already existing from the world recession and contributed to the collapse of the Central American Common Market (CACM). The formation of the CACM had been a major impetus to the high economic growth rates achieved by El Salvador and Central America in the 1960s and 1970s. Its demise further hurt export performance, especially for El Salvador, whose manufacturing sector had prospered greatly from increased sales to regional markets.

Adding to these problems was the 1986 earthquake, which left more than 300,000 people homeless and resulted in $1 billion in material damages to the capital city of San Salvador alone.

In discussing the factors contributing to El Salvador's economic performance in the 1980s, poor policies and economic mismanagement also have to be mentioned. Early in the decade the country's private banks were expropriated and run into the ground by the state. Throughout most of the decade a highly overvalued exchange rate was maintained that penalized exports and distorted domestic prices. Excessively high effective rates of tariff protection contributed to an import substitution model of development that, though providing limited gains during the expansion of the CACM, discouraged the formation of efficient productive activities able to compete in world markets. Fiscal and monetary policies were erratic, and the government expanded its control of the economy by setting prices and monopolizing the domestic and international marketing of key products.

The Cost of War

The most devastating impact on the economy of El Salvador has been the civil war. The cost of the war has been extremely high: More than 75,000 lives have been lost; hundreds of thousands have been injured and maimed; 0.5 million people have been displaced from their homes in El Salvador; and about 1 million people have been forced to flee the country and live as refugees. For those remaining in El Salvador, damage from the war has resulted in a substantially lower quality of life. The cost of the war to the economy between 1981 and 1990 has been estimated to be more than $2 billion.

Since the war started in 1979, one of the prime objectives of the guerrillas has been to cause the collapse of the economy in the hope that this would stir public discontent with the country's fledgling democratic system and lead to the fall of the government. One of the guerrilla strategies to achieve that objective included systematic attacks on, and the eventual destruction of, physical infrastructure such as bridges, the power grid, and communications equipment. Interruptions in electric service results in factories producing less, the destruction of bridges interrupts transportation services, and the disruption of telecommunications hinders business activities. This destruction has required that financial resources previously allocated to other activities be diverted to the restoration of services, either through repair or replacement (over $1.1 billion between 1979 and 1990).

Agricultural production for export, which traditionally has consisted of coffee, cotton, and sugar, has declined about 22 percent over the course of the war. Major causes of this decline, according to farmers, were uncertainty over government agricultural policies and low world prices. In the eastern region of the country significant damage to agriculture was attributable directly to the war: Coffee mills were destroyed, crop dusters were shot down, and coffee trucks loaded with harvest were routinely burned and pickers harassed.

Stagnation in the production of basic domestic food crops can also be directly linked to the war. Thousands of rural peasants were recruited to fight on both sides of the conflict, and many thousands more were displaced from their homes. The result is that large areas of land that

107

once produced food crops are fallow. Food crop production is now at about the prewar level; however, total population has grown approximately 18 percent during this time period.

The industrial sector, which experienced a 21 percent decline in output over the 1979–1985 period, was particularly hard hit by the war. Between 1979 and 1983, the then-growing assembly industry was attacked directly. Industrialists were kidnapped for ransom or killed. Factories were invaded by guerrillas and their supporters. As a result, foreign industrialists fled and the assembly industry all but collapsed. Power interruptions hurt the capacity to produce; migration reduced the availability of skilled labor; government social and economic policies, such as the agrarian reform and the nationalization of the banking system, contributed to loss of investor confidence; and the foreign exchange shortages associated with capital flight reduced the availability of raw materials, spare parts, and intermediate goods needed for production.

The transportation sector has been a direct target of guerrilla attacks, particularly during their declared transportation stoppages. Cargoes were dumped, trucks were burned, and buses were machine-gunned. Between 1979 and 1990, well over 2,000 trucks and 30,000 buses were damaged or destroyed. One transportation cooperative estimated that over $56 million is needed to replace its damaged equipment.

The war has been especially detrimental to El Salvador's educational system. Before 1979 the Ministry of Education was increasing access to primary schools through school construction and by hiring new teachers. Since the outbreak of armed conflict, more than one-half of the nation's schools have had to be closed and approximately 800 schools have been destroyed. With a greater portion of fiscal expenditures required for security-related activities, less money has been available for social programs in general and education in particular. Declining budgets have resulted in shortages of textbooks, inadequate teacher training, and insufficient educational material for teachers and students. Although donor assistance has been instrumental in preventing any major declines in the country's educational level, any gains that may have been made in the absence of war did not materialize.[1]

Economic Adjustment Under Cristiani

When Alfredo Cristiani became president in June 1989, his top priorities were the achievement of peace, economic recovery, and the eradication of poverty. His government's representatives immediately engaged the

FMLN in serious negotiations to end the war. At President Cristiani's request, United Nations general-secretary Javier Pérez de Cuéllar agreed to mediate the negotiations. Although the talks have had their ups and downs, their overall impact has been to raise hopes that the conflict may finally be nearing an end. But stopping the war would not by itself bring sustained improvement in economic performance or the alleviation of poverty. Given the crisis state of the economy at the end of the decade and the pressing needs of the poor, efforts to get the economy moving again could not wait for eventual success at the negotiating table.

It can be argued that improved economic prospects might facilitate reaching a peace agreement. It is easier to lay down a rifle and pick up a shovel in a growing economy than in a stagnant one. A healthy economy would also ease the transition of large numbers of the military back to civilian life. Therefore the Cristiani government moved to reform and stimulate the economy. In contrast to the state interventionist policies of previous administrations, the Cristiani government adopted a free market, laissez-faire philosophy to guide its economic program. It was confident that under more liberal market conditions the private sector could stimulate improved conditions on both economic and social fronts and that such improvements would be dispersed throughout the country to benefit the majority of Salvadorans. Reflecting this outlook, in July 1989 the Cristiani government initiated the most far-reaching economic adjustment program in the history of El Salvador.

Trade Liberalization

The government initially moved away from the fixed exchange rate, progressively passing more foreign transactions to the free market. By June 1990, it had adopted a fully flexible exchange rate system. The banking sector now competes with the newly legalized foreign exchange houses in the foreign exchange market. The Central Bank still participates in the market, but the rate at which it buys and sells foreign exchange is based on the free market rate. This new regime, which is more flexible and responsive to domestic and international economic conditions, has halted the growing overvaluation of the *colón* and achieved an estimated 21 percent depreciation of the real exchange rate during 1990.

The government reduced the distorting effects of import tariffs and nontariff barriers (NTBs), such as quotas, import prohibitions, and prior deposits for foreign exchange permits. The elimination of most NTBs, the reduction in coffee export taxes, the elimination of export taxes on sugar and shrimp, and the adjustment of import tariff rates all supported

109

the new exchange rate regime. It is estimated that with the new 5 to 35 percent range of nominal import tariff rates and the abolition of many NTBs, the average effective rate of protection (that is, the protection given to value added in the production process) has fallen from 47 to 33 percent. These changes have not only exposed domestic production to the healthy effects of international competition but have also significantly reduced disincentives for investment in a wide range of profitable export activities.

Reducing the Economic Role of the State

The administration swept away a host of price controls and monopolies that posed serious constraints to increased investment in the productive sectors of the Salvadoran economy. Price controls were removed for 230 items and left on only a few essential items. The operation of the government basic grains marketing board ceased in late 1989, and a system of price bands for corn, linking domestic to world prices, was introduced to maintain producer and consumer price stability for corn.

The government completed titling of most of the agrarian reform properties and introduced long–sought-after beneficiary rights legislation into the Legislative Assembly. A secure title increases a farmer's propensity to make production and conservation investments in the land. The beneficiary rights legislation, when passed, will grant Phase 1 land reform beneficiaries freedom to choose their own land tenure arrangements and permit them to reorganize factors of production. The government has developed a mechanism to finance the voluntary transfer of land to small farmers.

As a result of a government study of petroleum policies, the importation of crude petroleum was removed from the state-owned electricity company and privatized. Finally, legislation permitting private competition in the marketing of coffee was passed by the Legislative Assembly.

Fiscal Sector Reform

The administration also streamlined the tax rate structure and eliminated exemptions on indirect taxes to improve the efficiency of the tax system and set the stage for greater tax collections in the near term. The continued need to finance the war and to provide necessary public services limited the possibility of reductions in current expenditures, which were already low. Accordingly, late in 1989 the Legislative Assembly passed a comprehensive package of tax reform measures focusing on the stamp tax, the income tax, the wealth tax, and several excise taxes.[2]

Reform and Restructuring of the Financial Sector

Interest rates—both on deposits and loans in the banking system—were raised to positive real levels in order to stimulate savings, improve profitability in the banking system, and allocate credit in a more rational manner. Lending was reduced to three categories plus housing. In a separate measure, the Central Reserve Bank of El Salvador contracted for an audit of all nine state-owned commercial banks to determine the extent of nonperforming assets. As a result of this and other analyses, three of the nine commercial banks were affected. The government then secured passage in November 1990 of key legislation to implement reform measures and to reprivatize the banking system—the Portfolio Clean-Up and Strengthening of the Commercial Banks and Savings and Loan Associations Law, the Commercial Banks and Savings and Loan Associations Privatization Law, and the Financial System Superintendency Law. These laws provide the basis for a private financial system and strengthen supervision and regulation.

Internal and External Financial Balance

The Cristiani administration has begun to implement measures to close the fiscal and balance-of-payments deficits and has implemented strict monetary programming to control inflation and enforce stability in domestic financial markets during this adjustment period. Domestic credit expansion has been held to levels consistent with reducing pressure on prices and the balance of payments while allowing real growth targets to be achieved. Of the domestic credit made available under the government economic program, strict limits have been placed on credit to the public sector to reserve as much credit as possible to finance private-sector investment and production.

Enhanced International Standing

The improved economic policy of the Cristiani government enabled it to enhance its standing in the international financial community. In August 1990, El Salvador signed a standby arrangement with the International Monetary Fund (IMF). An IMF review at the end of 1990 rated the government's performance very favorably. Although the standby permits El Salvador access to a 35-million SDR (special drawing right, about $48 million) medium-term loan facility, the much higher than expected foreign exchange inflow resulting from the government's policy reform successes have made such drawings unnecessary for the time being.

A Paris Club debt rescheduling agreement was completed in November 1990. More than $138 million in interest and principal payments to the United States, Japan, France, Spain, and Canada, originally due through September 1991, were rescheduled on favorable terms over a twenty-year period.

In February 1991, El Salvador signed a $75 million structural adjustment loan (SAL) with the World Bank that will support, inter alia, fiscal reforms and privatization of El Salvador's commercial banks. The World Bank and the government are also designing a social sector rehabilitation program. As part of the program, the government has committed itself to increasing the proportions of the national budget allocated to the social sectors.

In December 1990, the Inter-American Development Bank approved a $60 million loan for El Salvador to support government efforts to reactivate domestic production and to strengthen, modernize, and privatize the financial system. The program will fund multisectoral credits to promote private-sector investment in the installation, expansion, modernization, and diversification of production operations.

El Salvador successfully negotiated accession to the General Agreement on Tariffs and Trade (GATT) in December 1990. El Salvador's trade regime is considered one of the most liberal of any Third World nation now in GATT and has become the model for other nations seeking to join. Once the accession agreement is ratified by the Salvadoran Legislative Assembly, El Salvador's exporters will benefit from most-favored–nation treatment in world markets. In addition, membership will give El Salvador a voice at the GATT table, where it can work with other Third World nations on trade issues of particular importance to El Salvador.

Economic Adjustment with a Human Face

The economic adjustment process that is under way in El Salvador is creating a macroeconomic environment with incentives and support for lower-income groups to become more productive in the medium and long term. In fact, marginal groups have already benefited from the effects of the adjustment program. For instance, contributing about 50 percent of the increase in GDP in 1990 was a 7.4 percent surge in output originating in the agricultural sector. The elimination of government marketing monopolies resulted in substantial increases in prices received by farmers directly for the sale of their farm products. Many of these farmers are considered to be in the lowest income groups. There is also evidence that many agricultural workers were paid wages considerably above the legal minimum wage in 1990 because farmers had trouble finding available labor. Although this difficulty can be partially explained by irregular weather patterns, which altered harvest schedules for some crops, the jump in agricultural output is a factor as well. Higher agricultural production also has helped to hold food prices down, which has especially benefited the urban poor.

Notwithstanding this progress, there are still vulnerable groups that require special attention to prevent undue hardship during the adjustment process. These include those currently living in extreme poverty and employed in non–agricultural-related fields. They are largely urban residents who are unable to purchase a nutritionally adequate food basket. As part of its economic adjustment program, the Cristiani administration has developed a strategy to create higher-paying job opportunities for the poor through economic growth that stimulates an efficient use of labor. It is also engaging in activities designed to improve the educational status and health conditions of the poor and hence their capacity to respond to increased opportunities for productive employment. These activities are being complemented by the establishment of a social safety net for those poor groups that do not benefit immediately from the new opportunities resulting from the economic adjustment program.

The implementation of a number of current donor-funded projects has been accelerated, bolstered with new funds, and expanded geographically to create as many new, albeit temporary, jobs as possible during the adjustment period. These include earthquake reconstruction activities to rebuild and rehabilitate schools, hospitals, roads, and bridges; expansion of urban water and sanitation facilities; installation of rural water systems; and the construction of small-scale infrastructure in rural townships. These jobs will provide badly needed additional sources of income for poor families. Also, society at large will benefit from the economic and social infrastructure that will be put in place through these programs.

In order to promote activities specifically designed to cushion the impact of adjustment on vulnerable groups, the government has created the Salvadoran Social Investment Fund (FISS). The fund will channel an estimated $30 to $60 million in donor resources annually to projects primarily designed to benefit low-income groups. The projects will be implemented by private nonprofit organizations and municipalities. They will be targeted to the poorest areas of the country and will help low-income groups meet their basic education, health, and nutritional needs. The fund will also finance activities designed to promote domestic production, including local investments in infrastructure and occupational training.

On October 31, 1990, the Salvadoran Legislative Assembly approved (by a substantial majority) legislation creating the FISS and providing the equivalent of about $3.5 million for its initial funding. The law passed by the assembly established the FISS as a truly unique organization in El Salvador. The FISS was created as an autonomous institution with its own administration and thus can operate free from government interference. Special procedures were approved to facilitate its operations and prevent excessive bureaucratic complications. Personnel to run the FISS are being selected on a competitive basis. Also, to ensure the highest standards of financial accountability, the FISS will be subject to audits by independent and internationally renowned accounting firms.

Results of Policy Reform

Real Sector Performance

Reflecting especially strong performance in the agricultural sector and substantially better than expected results in manufacturing, real gross domestic product rose 3.4 percent in 1990, well above the program target range of 2 to 3 percent. This increase represents an improvement over the 1.1 percent growth rate achieved last year and the 1.5 percent average annual rate over 1983–1989. Benefiting from an improved system of incentives as well as favorable weather conditions, real GDP originating in the agricultural sector grew 7.4 percent. The removal of price controls, the elimination of government monopolies on coffee and sugar, and sharp depreciation of the real exchange rate sharply boosted prices in the sector and led to increased plantings. Major gains were registered in nearly all agricultural categories.

Coffee output is estimated to have increased by about 19 percent in calendar year 1990. This increase, however, resulted primarily from a strong 1989–1990 harvest, which showed an almost 80 percent increase over the previous crop year. The 1990–1991 coffee crop is expected to show a 15 to 20 percent drop because of irregular rains and heavier than normal winds during November and December along with the effects of the normal cyclical downturn on average coffee tree yields.[3]

Sugar output rose 24 percent in 1990. Higher domestic sugar prices sparked increases in the area under cultivation for both the 1989–1990 and 1990–1991 seasons. Factors contributing to higher prices for producers included a major increase in El Salvador's quota for the US market, higher world prices for nonquota sugar, and continued domestic price supports.

Favorable weather conditions and the elimination of the government monopoly on basic grain marketing enabled Salvadoran farmers to achieve a record harvest in 1990. Overall basic grain production increased 4.5 percent to 19.2 million quintals and surpassed the previous record harvest of 1988 by nearly 0.5 million quintals. Record harvests were registered for corn and beans, the two most important staples for domestic consumption and an important source of income for small farmers. With both improved yields and greater areas under cultivation, bean production rose more than 30 percent, sorghum 11 percent, and the corn harvest, though showing only 2.4 percent growth, bettered its earlier record. Also having a positive influence on corn production was the imposition of a new flexible tariff rate system in which the tariff rate is adjusted within a specific range based on fluctuations in world prices.[4]

The manufacturing sector showed substantially lower real growth than agriculture, increasing 3 percent in 1990. The reforms in the trade and exchange regime hit hard at import substitution industries. Construction activity dropped 13 percent in 1990 after five consecutive years of strong positive growth. Major factors depressing the construction sector include the slower than expected implementation of the public-sector investment program and a reduced demand for private-sector housing construction. Real GDP originating in the services sector grew 2.8 percent in 1990.

Price Trends

Strict adherence to a sound monetary program was instrumental in bringing inflationary pressures under control in 1990. Without the sudden jump in prices after the start of the Gulf crisis, inflation would have been well within the 15 to 18 percent target range for the year (on an end-of-period basis). With the impact of higher oil prices in the last quarter, the actual inflation rate for 1990, as measured by the consumer price index (CPI), was only a bit above the high end of the target range at 19.3 percent. This rate was noticeably lower than the 23.5 percent rate for 1989. Although this point drop represents a significant achievement in itself, the true measure of the government's success over inflation is not clearly evident in this yearly comparison.

At the beginning of 1990, El Salvador was experiencing a major inflation. Part of the reason was the impact of the Cristiani administration's own economic program. Higher prices were the natural and anticipated result of price liberalization, exchange rate, and tariff reforms designed to increase the relative prices of tradable goods and make the Salvadoran economy more competitive internationally. This influence was felt primarily at the end of 1989 but was also a factor in early 1990. Second, particularly strong inflationary pressure occurred during the first few months of 1990 after substantial credit was injected to bolster the financial system immediately following the November 1989 FMLN offensive. Over the first four months of 1990, the CPI rose at an annual rate of 33 percent. Without decisive action to restore monetary discipline, the government's economic program could easily have been derailed.

Once the domestic security situation improved, the Central Reserve Bank moved to absorb the excess liquidity previously pumped into the banking system. Central Bank credit to commercial banks, which was permitted to climb by 42 percent during the month of December 1989 alone, was cut 21 percent by the end of April 1990. Moreover, the Central Reserve Bank obliged commercial banks to purchase over 600 million *colones* worth of "stabilization bonds" (Central Bank liabilities) over the first eight months of 1990, an amount equal to about one-third of outstanding Central Bank credit to commercial banks as of August. This tightening led to a sharp fall in inflation; over the last six months of 1990 the CPI rose at an annual rate of 11.2 percent, about one-third the rate registered earlier in the year.[5]

Another factor helping to hold domestic prices down was an increase in foreign exchange inflows, largely from private remittances. As a direct result of the liberalized exchange rate (and full legalization of the foreign exchange houses), tight monetary policy, and increased confidence in the Salvadoran economy, higher foreign exchange inflows provided additional financing for imports. This financing resulted in less pressure on the exchange rate during the last half of the year and thus helped keep the domestic currency cost of imports down.

The External Sector

The reforms in the trade sector and improved monetary discipline, along with a Paris Club rescheduling of bilateral debt made possible by increased lender confidence in the government's economic program, have contributed to major improvements in the balance of payments in 1990.

The current account deficit in the balance of payments fell from the equivalent of 9.5 percent of GDP in 1989 to 6.6 percent of GDP in 1990. A 17 percent jump in exports combined with a 46 percent increase in recorded remittances were key factors. Higher remittances were the result of the combination of continued tight monetary policy and the April 1990 legalization of the foreign exchange houses. Reduced availability of domestic credit and legal access to a market-determined exchange rate has encouraged substantial foreign exchange inflows. Also contributing to the narrowing of the current account deficit was an improvement in net services as drawback exports rose almost 50 percent. In addition, nontraditional exports to extraregional markets grew 34 percent in 1990.

The merchandise trade deficit also narrowed in 1990 to 12.7 percent of GDP from 13.4 percent in 1989. In absolute terms, however, the deficit widened 2.8 percent as the $83 million improvement in exports was more than offset by a $101 million jump in imports. A widening trade deficit can be expected for an economy under a liberalization program. Indeed, the nearly 9 percent growth in imports in 1990 reflected higher real growth in the economy supported by a substantially more liberal foreign trade regime.

Although overall merchandise imports rose 9 percent in 1990, there was wide variance among the different import categories. Nondurable consumer goods imports surged 40 percent. This increase primarily reflects the continuing impact of lower tariff rates for most consumer imports as well as increased reporting of import transactions after the legalization of the foreign exchange houses and an increase in import demand associated with the marked increase in overall economic activity. The 11 percent growth in imported agricultural inputs is in line with the strong positive real growth in the sector. Nonoil intermediate good imports for industrial purposes grew by only 1.4 percent in 1990. This seems inconsistent with the 3 percent real growth reported in the manufacturing sector. However, manufacturers were able to draw from huge inventories built up in late 1989 prior to the increase in tariff rates for most intermediate goods.

Net private capital inflows bounced from a negative $17 million in 1989 to a positive $161 million in 1990. This swing is most likely the result of increased short-term capital inflows that resulted from higher nominal interest rates—which became positive in real terms during the last half of 1990—and greater exchange rate stability. This increase, combined with a $36 million net inflow recorded in the official and financial sector accounts, pushed the capital account balance to nearly $200 million from the $86 million recorded in 1989.

As a result of the improved performance in both the current and capital accounts of the balance of payments, El Salvador's international reserve position was greatly strengthened in 1990. Net international reserves of the Central Bank increased by $117 million, nearly three times the original $40 million target contained in the IMF standby arrangement and about double the $60 million target as revised in November. This reserve increase provides El Salvador with a much needed cushion.[6]

The real effective exchange rate registered a 21 percent depreciation during 1990. Most of this movement occurred during the first half of the year when the nominal exchange rate depreciated over 20 percent from 6.5 *colones* per one US dollar to 7.85 *colones* per dollar. Over the second half of 1990, the nominal rate further depreciated to 8.14 *colones* per dollar.

Fiscal Performance

Strong performance regarding both expenditure and revenue trends in 1990 resulted in a sharp decline in the deficit of the consolidated nonfinancial public sector. Before grants, the public sector deficit declined to 2.5 percent of GDP from the 5.8 percent recorded in 1989. Total expenditures rose 5.4 percent in nominal terms; as a percent of GDP, they dropped from 16.6 percent in 1989 to 13.7 percent in 1990. Current expenditures grew 18.5 percent in 1990, but when adjusted for inflation they showed a moderate decline in real terms. Public-sector capital expenditures, which declined 23 percent, were substantially below programmed amounts for 1990. A number of factors caused this, including the reallocation of public investment funds as a result of a reprioritization conducted by the Cristiani administration, the initiation of new administrative procedures reflecting tighter auditing requirements, and delays in the initiation of projects in early 1990 because of the November 1989 FMLN offensive. Led by a 36 percent rise in tax collections, public-sector revenues showed a gain to 11.2 percent of GDP in 1990 from 10.8 percent in 1989. Although this represents a relatively small increase, it does reverse the negative trend of prior years as public revenues fell from 16.8 percent of GDP in 1986 by the equivalent of two percentage points of GDP in each year through 1989. The fiscal deficit of the central government was reduced from 4.9 percent of GDP in 1989 to 3.1 percent in 1990.

Money and Credit Trends

Overall domestic credit expansion was contained to 8 percent with net credit to the consolidated nonfinancial public sector held to almost zero growth at 0.2 percent. Credit to the private sector grew by 11 percent and accounted for over 99 percent of the increase in net domestic credit for the year. Exchange rate stability and higher real rates of interest on deposits in the banking system have led to an increase in the demand for money, that is, the willingness of the nonbank public to hold monetary assets in domestic financial instruments. The desire of the public to hold more *colones* (and not trade them for dollars or speculative assets) has given the authorities more flexibility over monetary programming and taken the pressure off the balance of payments and inflation. Banking-sector liabilities to the private sector, however, surged by nearly 29 percent. The consequence of these financial developments was overall broad money growth of 27 percent.

Prospects for 1991 and Beyond

Macroeconomic Management

The Cristiani administration program aims to achieve a continued high rate of growth and lower inflation in 1991. Supported by the IMF upper-tranche standby arrangement, the government will attempt to further reduce inflation to the 10 to 14 percent range and to strengthen the balance of payments so as to create favorable conditions for real GDP growth of 3 percent or higher in 1991. To achieve these two objectives, the government has targeted a reduction in the overall deficit of the nonfinancial public sector to a level that can be supported by external grants and concessional loans from bilateral and multilateral creditors without recourse to additional financing from the banking system.

The government will also proceed with the continuation of a monetary program designed to contain pressures on domestic prices and the balance of payments while simultaneously permitting growth targets to be achieved. As such, domestic credit expansion will be limited to 6 percent growth during 1991. With net banking system credit to the public sector programmed to be substantially reduced during 1991, credit will be amply available for private-sector production, commerce, and investment. Consistent with growth and inflation targets and balance-of-payments projections, the broad money supply is programmed to grow 14 percent in 1991.

Regarding external performance, the aim will be to narrow the current account deficit of the balance of payments (before grants) from the equivalent of 6.6 percent of GDP in 1990 to the equivalent of 5.5 percent of GDP in 1991. This target envisages a 15 percent increase in exports combined with 5 percent growth in imports. Private remittances are projected to grow by 9 percent. This will contribute to an increase in the net international reserve position of the Central Reserve Bank of $13 million, which is consistent with a programmed increase in gross reserves to a level equal to 4.8 months of imports, close to El Salvador's near-term goal of five months of imports.

Structural Adjustment

The 1991 economic program also includes the continuation and deepening of the structural adjustments begun in 1989. The government is now outlining a further two-year program of comprehensive structural reform that includes the continued liberalization of the exchange and trade regimes. The government will maintain the unified and flexible exchange rate regime, adjusting nominal rates as domestic and world conditions change. The range of nominal import tariffs will be further compressed to 5 to 30 percent in 1991 with the goal of 10 to 20 percent by 1993. The remaining nontariff barriers, such as import authorizations for certain categories of food imports, will be abolished.

Public-sector finances will be further strengthened. Following on the adjustment and rationalization of tax rates in 1989, the government will initiate a multiyear program to improve the administration of tax collections and strengthen the process of budgeting and expenditure control.

Following on the adjustment of interest rates in 1989, the Cristiani administration has agreed with the World Bank to implement a flexible interest rate regime in which the loan and deposit rates will adjust to market conditions in 1991. Now that the legal basis for a private financial system has been established, the government will begin to restructure the portfolios of problem banks and savings and loans (S&Ls), divest itself of ownership in these institutions, and develop a strong and independent financial system supervisory and regulatory body.

In 1991, the system of price bands will be extended from corn to include rice and possibly sorghum. The government will also continue its program to privatize the assets of the state trading boards for sugar and coffee and the now defunct state agency for basic grains. In addition, the government will obtain passage of the beneficiary rights legislation that was introduced to the Legislative Assembly as part of the 1990 program mentioned earlier.

In addition to economic and financial measures, progress on the political front is essential and the democratic process has to be further strengthened. A major effort is needed by both sides at the peace talks. Specific areas for future emphasis include judicial reform, strengthening the operations and processes of the legislature, and encouraging further development of municipal governments.

When Peace Breaks Out

Once peace breaks out in El Salvador, approximately 20,000 to 30,000 ex-combatants will have to be reintegrated into the Salvadoran economy. This will be a major challenge. However, a number of factors suggest that this process may not be as difficult as previously thought. First, the economy is already showing signs of a strong recovery. From 1988 to 1990, almost 170,000 new jobs were created. With economic growth projected to reach 3 to 4 percent in real terms over the next two years, absorption of the ex-combatants will be greatly facilitated.

Second, once the war is over, some people can be put to work rebuilding the country. For example, when the war-related sabotage of the country's infrastructure is stopped, public utilities will mount a major effort to permanently repair and modernize the nation's electric, water and sewage, and telecommunication facilities. Although some of these facilities were fixed in the interim, most of the repairs consisted of temporary patchwork. Also, hundreds of schools will have to be reconstructed and roads rebuilt throughout the country.

A large portion of El Salvador's productive resources currently unavailable because of the conflict will be able to be tapped and will thus contribute to a faster-growing economy. This is particularly true with respect to additional land that will be made accessible for cultivation. Moreover, programs designed to diversify agriculture and improve productivity, which currently operate in the more conflict-free areas, will be expanded to the rest of the country.

Business confidence is already improving. The end of the conflict should result in substantially greater levels of private investment in both urban and rural areas. This expansion will provide numerous productive employment opportunities.

Finally, many of the government's current programs designed to mitigate the impact of economic adjustment on vulnerable groups and reduce poverty will also provide additional employment opportunities for some of the ex-combatants. The Salvadoran Social Investment Fund (FISS) is a good example. Among other activities, it will channel donor funds into small-scale, labor-intensive projects to build local infrastructure and promote productive activities.

Concluding Remarks

There have been dramatic improvements in the business and economic policy climate in the past two years, and, as expected, business and economic performance have shown strong positive results. Moreover, the Cristiani administration has shown that economic liberalization can have a major impact on the economy even during a period of continuing hostilities.

The decade of the 1980s is behind us. More important, the economic policy framework of the 1980s, based on excessive government intervention in the economy, is also behind us. Prospects for the 1990s are brighter. The economy is starting to grow—and in an efficient way. Opportunities are being created for low-income groups. Also, safety net programs have been created for those not immediately benefiting from the current economic growth and for those adversely affected by adjustment in the near term.

El Salvador missed a golden opportunity to modernize its economy and take full advantage of one of the longest world economic expansions in history. In sharp contrast, the 1990s promise to be substantially different. Should present trends continue, the 1990s should see continued major gains in broad-based economic, social, and political development in El Salvador.

Notes

Note: Sections of this chapter are drawn from documents provided by the Social Security Investment Fund (FISS), the government of El Salvador, and multilateral and bilateral lending agencies providing assistance to El Salvador. However, the opinions are mine.

1. Thus El Salvador's educational situation is about the same as it was twelve years ago. Illiteracy remains high, at about 25 percent for men and 31 percent for women. School enrollment and attendance is still low, with approximately 35 percent of school-aged children out of school. Repetition rates continue at relatively high levels, at about 60 percent. This, combined with high drop-out rates, has prevented any significant gains in educational efficiency. Now, as before the war, about eleven years of education are required to produce one sixth-grade graduate.

2. The stamp tax was greatly simplified: A uniform rate of 5 percent was levied, and most exemptions were eliminated. The income tax for individuals and corporations was modified. For individuals, the top marginal rate was lowered from 60 to 50 percent, and the number of tax brackets was reduced from twenty-four to seven. For corporations, the top marginal rate was lowered from 35 to 30 percent, and the number of brackets was lowered from five to three. Furthermore, corporate income tax payments are now based on estimates of current rather than on previous year revenues. The maximum rate for the wealth tax was also reduced from 2.5 to 2 percent. The wealth tax exemption for individuals was raised from 150,000 to 300,000 *colones* (as of April 15, 1991, one US dollar = 8 *colones*) and for corporations from 300,000 to 500,000 *colones*. Several excise taxes (on public shows, distribution of films, matches, and so on), whose yields were low relative to the costs of administration, were eliminated.

3. The poor weather conditions in late 1990 also adversely affected the quality of a portion of the crop and triggered an earlier than normal start of the 1990–1991 harvest. This caused difficulties in recruiting sufficient numbers of coffee pickers, as workers were employed in the harvest of other crops such as sugar cane. In addition, schools were still in session. As a result, several coffee producers were forced to pay wages substantially in excess of the established minimum wage for coffee pickers.

4. Although not in effect until May 1990, the system was announced several months before and in time to encourage greater plantings for the 1990 season. The elimination of corn imports under donor-funded food assistance programs also helped. However, this was not the case for rice, where food assistance donations depressed domestic prices and contributed to a 10 percent decline in area under cultivation and a 9.4 percent drop in production.

5. Also contributing to the drop in the overall inflation rate over the last half of 1990 were slower increases in food prices. Improved policies and good weather contributed to a bumper 1990 harvest in basic grains. This helped keep the food component of the CPI below a 13 percent annual rate for the last half of 1990, a major improvement compared to the 25 percent annual rate recorded during the first half of the year and a 32 percent annual rate during the last half of 1989.

6. Gross reserves increased to a level equivalent to 3.8 months of imports as of the end of 1990. However, El Salvador is still about $120 million short of its near-term goal of achieving and maintaining gross reserves at a level equal to five months of imports, a prudent figure given El Salvador's excessive reliance on coffee exports, its relatively high vulnerability to adverse global shocks, and the ever-present possibility (although it is hoped that the possibility is reduced) of further setbacks on the political front, which could disrupt net foreign exchange inflows.

11

Commentary

Enrique Baloyra

To analyze El Salvador over the past eleven years, one must simultaneously consider political transition and civil war. Describe it as one may, the bottom line is that there was some kind of obnoxious recursiveness. Events would look good, bad, or indifferent with regard to the war, but that did not necessarily mean that the political transition was moving at the same pace or in the same direction. As a matter of fact, we may not have a theory of transition but, rather, just some primitive understanding of the process. During the war in El Salvador, there have been a number of inflection points (or, in the more technical jargon of the profession, "in-game opportunities") that were just thrown out, or the resilience of and the diffusion of power that had occurred in the society was such that those who held the initiative at that point could not take advantage of it to neutralize the adversary totally.

A few examples, some of which have been mentioned already, may help illustrate the obnoxious recursiveness of the situation. To alleviate the suffering or living conditions of the people, there were at one point fairly successful programs, such as CONARA and Municipalities in Action, which were interpreted and may have been conceived as well within the counterinsurgency framework. From the standpoint of alleviating harsh conditions of life, they were undoubtedly benefiting people. They became, however, a focus and object of conflict and violence.

Second, unlike other processes of transition in Central and Mediterranean Europe and in South America, there was a duality of power. This means that there have been double official interlocutors. It was not just a matter of a set of military extricating themselves from power; there was

Enrique Baloyra is associate dean of the Graduate School of International Studies at the University of Miami.

also a set of civilian authorities trying, at the same time, to recover political space and the decisionmaking power from those military who were standing between them and their adversaries. So it was not just a two-sided game but, rather, a four-sided game.

Also, one cannot understand what is going on in El Salvador without putting this transition process in comparative perspective. At times, observers do not know what to make of a particular development at a certain point because they do not know what the standards of reference are. Peru and Colombia, for example, were simply democracies under seige or, to use Cynthia Arnson's term, weak democracies without peace. Is El Salvador such a case? Or is it more akin to its neighbor Guatemala, where there was almost a total disintegration of state power at one point and there was really no valid set of actors from whom to request responsibility and accountability?

I am going to be optimistic by predicting that the cease-fire is going to be successfully negotiated and that it is going to stick. (I am not going to tell you when, however—I am not that brave.) But I see positive developments pointing in that direction. If one analyzes Radio Veneceremos, which broadcasts the declarations of the FMLN, of two years ago, the discourse was "We will continue to fight until there is no longer poverty and inequality and injustice in El Salvador and until all the cases of abuse are accounted for." That meant fighting until the year 3000, because there is no such thing as a perfect society. If one looks comparatively at the countries of Latin America, only in the case of Argentina was there anything resembling accountability and justice approaching the standards that we regard as universal. Yet even in the case of Argentina the process of accountability and justice was effective only to a point. In all other cases, the process also has required a political, pragmatic solution. One cannot spend 100 additonal years ventilating the human rights situation in the media. Some kind of political settlement will have to be reached in El Salvador.

Also, there is a prevalence of democratic discourse. I have attended many briefings by Salvadoran military. The language of the current minister of defense, Gen. René Emilio Ponce, is much different from that of former defense minister Carlos Vides Casanova, which is fairly intermediate, or the language of José Guillermo García, minister of defense in the early 1980s who was a very entertaining person and gave excellent briefings, but who did not say anything.

Upon close examination, one can see at each level of Salvadoran society a process of replacement and substitution of elites that points to a qualitative improvement. The process of replacement that José García was referring to with regard to the military sphere is similar in other sectors of society, though perhaps less so in the business community and in universities. But in terms of the political class, the political leadership, the military, and diplomacy, the Salvadorans are getting their act together.

I also see the elections as positive and contributing to a better environment for a peaceful settlement. We could call it a bimodal electoral sphere. I disagree that there has been polarization. There has been the emergence of a democratic government versus a democratic opposition, and that is what the system is turning on now. It is no longer the case of a group in the assembly trying to operate more or less by democratic norms and another group that perhaps controlled the security of the assembly and turned off the switchboard so that some of the legislators on the opposite side received threatening phone calls from within the assembly. I think those days are over.

The FMLN did truly go to war in the early 1980s for defensive purposes. If one was going to get killed in the cities for trying to organize or do radical things, one might as well pick up a rifle and be more effective in putting down one's adversaries and defending oneself. Later on, beginning about 1985, and this was possibly an inflection point in the transition, there could have been a reevaluation of that fact. When the FMLN started to implement urban terrorist tactics in particular, their second motivation—which was not to be ruled out of the game, not to be rendered obsolete, but, rather, to remain a force to be reckoned with—may have become more prevalent. Today, both concerns seem to coincide.

Among the claims made by the FMLN, their concern about safety—about being massacred if they rejoin the political process—remains valid. And here I see more conflict between civilians and the military on the government's side than between the armies of both sides. The military men are going to be able to agree on technical terms, as fighting men, and are going to understand each other's concerns.

Recent statements by Vice-Minister of Security Colonel Alberto Montano, Defense Minister Ponce, and others were that they understand that the rebels must be able to stay in their areas. Then the problem becomes whether those areas are going to be reservations from which they cannot come out or be simply safe areas where they will be able, for a time anyway, to be armed and to ensure their own safety until the level of trust increases and until the judiciary strengthens to a point where more effective guarantees are in place. In this sense, with regard to the technical questions about a cease-fire, I would be willing to wager that they have been taken care of already and that the problem is on the civilian side. The civilian allies of both sides are probably asking, "Are you sure you want to settle on those terms?" and "Should you be more demanding?"

Also favorable to an environment more conducive to the cease-fire is precisely the data that were cited in Parts 1 and 2. It is clear, from the experience of the civil wars in England and the United States, that a country can build from disaster, not just from success. In the history of the more successful democracies in South America, for example, Chile and particularly Uruguay, civil war was one of the events that launched these countries on the path first of oligarchic republics and later of quasi-polyarchies.

A country can develop viable, livable political systems from disaster. In this sense, the Salvadorans have something that they, at least at the level of the general public, may not have had before: They know what they do not want. They do not want, for the most part, one side moving into a village and being bombed into oblivion by the other. They want, in a way, to be left alone. They want a settlement. They do not want to be heros; they have produced enough heroes as it is. They want peace and quiet.

However, there are elements that point in the negative direction, mostly stemming from the substance of what all transitions are about: uncertainty. There is no guarantee what the rate of inflation is going to be, though, to be sure, it is very low at this point. And who would have thought that Salvadorans would have increased exports? More remarkable, who would have thought, ten years ago, that a candidate from the ARENA party would run for president vowing to conduct dialogue, which used to be a bad word? It was the president who could have profited the most from eschewing dialogue. And who would have thought that several commanders of the FMLN would declare themselves Social Democrats? Time will tell whether they are or not.

Uncertainty will play on the negative because there are no guarantees. We know the shortcomings of the judiciary system. But unless we want to underestimate the political Right, we must anticipate that they are going to throw a monkey wrench into the process again. Previous "monkey wrenches" included Archbishop Romero and the nuns and Jesuit priests; there were some other instances in which there was at least the intention of disgracing the process to a degree that it was deprived of substance. Should this happen again, the retribution has to be swift, clear, unequivocal, and effective.

As for the future, I would not be surprised to see a cease-fire by early 1992. I also would expect a lot of brouhaha around that cease-fire and acts of provocation directed against the armed forces and against the patience of all democratic Salvadorans, which, fortunately, increase in number every day.

12

Discussion

John McAward: How do you view, over the next couple of years, the introduction into the assembly of the labor leaders from the National Union of Workers and Farmers (UNOC), and how do you see the relationship between the private sector and labor? How is each side going to better understand each other so that some of the battles that were fought in the 1970s and early 1980s do not repeat themselves? What are some of the changes that have taken place inside the country that might make us more optimistic about this relationship? Finally, are there any labor unions or business executives who could have resolved some of these problems, in light of the experiences elsewhere, such as in the United States, Argentina, or Chile? The one famous case might even be Coca-Cola in Guatemala.

Roberto Murray Meza: I will start with the last question. I do not know of any case where a labor leader promoted this type of a solution. But the case of Mexico, I think, is a good example. President Salinas de Gortari established a three-party pact among labor, the private sector, and the government that tied increases in salaries and improvement in benefits to certain levels of inflation, and those levels were tied, of course, to certain monetary, fiscal, and government policies. The pact was established for an eighteen-month period, after which it was to be renewed, providing there was proof of its success. That was an interesting experiment and something like it will have to happen in El Salvador.

With regard to your first question, two considerations are in order. It is an error to confuse labor activities with political activities. It is an error for labor leaders to become political activists in a party. Labor unions and labor leaders should be able to deal and negotiate with any political party. Their function is more permanent than that of the political term of any party in power.

In the case of El Salvador, there may be something of an exception

129

to that situation. It might be good for some of these political leaders to come from the labor unions because they can become better versed in the democratic and legislative process and in the negotiations that will be required with the other parties. We would benefit from their participation in that they will now have a way to articulate their views and their requests and their demands. The leaders and their positions, now as members of the National Assembly, will receive national attention from the media that they did not receive before.

There has been a change in the relationship between the private sector and the labor sector. All have learned from this crisis and this terrible twelve-year period. There have been fewer serious conflicts from within private-sector labor than there have been from within the government labor force. Government workers have held many more strikes and work disruptions than workers in the private sector. The reason is obvious: The private sector has greater flexibility, imagination, and initiative to respond to and accommodate the concerns of labor. The government is more tied down by its budgetary constraints, its bureaucratic procedures, and its real lack of leadership at that level, and it has not been able to deal with the increasing and changing demands of the labor sector. There has been, therefore, a climate of greater harmony and common interest between labor and the private sector, and that has been manifested in the lack of serious strikes.

Robert White (Former ambassador of the United States to El Salvador): In the ongoing negotiations, Article 248 of the Constitution was under consideration and there was a move to amend the Constitution. Then there appeared in *Diario de Hoy* a paid advertisement. It was a death threat to the ten deputies who started this process moving. I would, in this sense, question the optimism of Roberto Murray Meza and Enrique Baloyra about the future of El Salvador. It is nonsense to argue that this advertisement had anything to do with freedom of the press or that the threat was not serious. In any society where there is hope for a future, for accommodation and reconciliation, the editor of the newspaper who published such an ad would be held accountable to the law. Moreover, the people who were behind the advertisement would also be summoned and subjected to legal proceedings.

The executive power and the military, which is part of the executive power, at least in some way, were willing to let this serious threat stand. What message does that send to the moderates in the ARENA party and to the moderates in every sector? At this point, I am not so much concerned about the FMLN because there will be a long period of transition in which they will, in effect, have retaliatory power. But what does this particular incident portend for those who are trying to make the system work?

Edwin Corr (Former ambassador of the United States to El Salvador): I once asked a group of North Americans who had been observing El Salvador for the past decade or more if they had changed fundamentally their original view of the military, the FMLN, and the government. None had. Yet we who are observing the country are asking for very fundamental changes in the attitudes and behavior and ideas of the people involved in that engagement, whether they be in the FMLN, the government, or the military.

Fundamental changes have occurred in the attitudes and the behavior of important sectors of the leadership, across all those institutions and different contenders for power in the society. For the most part, these changes in looking at the world and in the kind of society that they envision for El Salvador are important and are the basis for what progress has been made and will continue to be made.

El Salvador has moved closer to democracy. Salvadorans are moving closer to peace. They are moving closer to economic development, which really cannot take place in a meaningful way until there is peace, with greater equity and distribution. I have doubts about the trickle-down theory; in small countries particularly, it too often is the trickle-out theory. Programs are designed for, but they do not ever seem to reach, the poor.

But having said that, I would also say that all of us who have been following El Salvador for a long time have had unreasonable expectations about the pace of change. It takes a minimum of twenty years to change a military institution. We do not have a good model for making a developing world justice system a just justice system. The truth is that these justice systems since World War II in many cases have deteriorated, not improved. What we are trying to achieve in these countries is difficult. We know how long it takes for economic development. So part of the disappointment and frustration that all of us have experienced relates to unreasonable expectations about how fast change can be achieved.

The major responsibility is now in the hands of the FMLN and also, to a lesser degree, the military. It was reasonable for the guerrillas to take up arms in 1979 and 1980. One could have chosen a different path, as President Duarte did, but, nevertheless, there were reasons why people could strongly justify resorting to war. Since at least 1985, the situation has changed: Whereas in the early days the FMLN could argue that they offset the violence that came from the Right, they have now contributed to the strength of that violence from the Right. The FMLN has enabled an armed force to be built up to 60,000 members, as opposed to a much smaller army. It would have been much better had the rebels returned to achieving the goals and objectives that they said they set out to achieve.

The onus now is on the guerrillas to show that they can go back to those original goals and return to and work within society. An equal onus is on the military to let justice be done, particularly in punishing military officers through the judicial system. Great progress has been made and will continue to be made. Salvadorans will not reach nirvana—development is the exchange of one set of opportunities and problems for another—but they have come a long way.

Enrique Baloyra: There is a point at which, whether in the Soviet Union or Cuba or El Salvador, one must start to act as if one is already in a democracy, if that is what one wants to build. I have seen this in other situations where there were similar death threats, for example, in Brazil. A Brazilian president, who had come to power from within the so-called security community, wanted to deepen the *abertura* (opening) his predecessor had launched, and his former colleagues from the security community launched a campaign of bombings against him. He knew perfectly well who they were. As a matter of fact, a couple of the conspirators blew up in a car because one of the devices they planned to detonate at a rock concert went off accidentally.

Within the conundrum that is created by all of the formal and informal links between military and paramilitary forces, it is difficult to put an end to it suddenly. For example (and it is not that I regard him as a friend), Rubén Zamora, a leader of the leftist Democratic Convergence party, is one of the bravest persons I have ever met. He has been visited closely by tragedy, but he returned to El Salvador a few years ago and was recently elected vice-president of the National Assemby. Another brave person, Roberto Murray Meza, is sitting next to me. Being a businessman in El Salvador is not the same as being a businessman in Baltimore.

So one has to live as if one were living in a democracy, and some people have begun to do that in El Salvador. It is going to be a long while and we may see a few more ghastly things before the judicial system and human rights protection begin to improve. But where Salvadorans are today is light years away from where they were in the early 1980s.

Roberto Murray Meza: With regard to Ambassador White's comment about punishing the people responsible for the death threat, that depends on how significant it is. The significance of the threat has more to do with who published it than with which newspaper published it. Newspapers publish pronouncements from guerrilla commanders as well as from the extreme Right. It certainly would have been different had one of the major political parties published the advertisement. But I do not think it was a group whose opinion is significant with respect to the Salvadoran dialogue and debate.

132

Moreover, the very nature of the media in El Salvador has changed. In El Salvador one can turn on the television and see Rubén Zamora one morning, a labor leader the next, and a videotape of a guerrilla commander after that. I doubt if any other country in Central America has as open a press as El Salvador does today. The *Diario de Hoy* obviously is aligned with a conservative line of thinking. But *Diario Latino,* once owned by the very prominent Pinta family, is now owned by a group of workers and people aligned with an ideology of the Left. So the significance of the threat is questionable. It is deplorable, but I do not think that type of attitude represents a large constituency.

Alberto Harth (The World Bank): I was minister of planning in one of the rightist governments of 1979 and 1980 to which Roberto Murray Meza alluded. I was the only independent and nonpolitical appointee in that cabinet in 1979. When one considers the military, economic, and political situation, one sees a positive future and also the yardsticks by which to measure El Salvador's progress. Where there does not seem to be a yardstick is in the area of human rights. Against what yardstick would you like to measure El Salvador in the future? I am working now in Côte d'Ivoire, and I worked in Bangladesh for four years when it was ruled by a brutal regime. My yardstick of human rights has changed somewhat since I left El Salvador as a result of my experiences.

Cynthia Arnson: I am confused by the question. Do you mean to imply that because there are human rights violations in the Ivory Coast or Bangladesh that somehow it is all right for there to be human rights violations in El Salvador? It is a point of view that I simply cannot embrace.

I sense from your question a desire to know whether I believe that there has been progress in El Salvador or whether there is some absolute standard to which countries can be held. There is an absolute standard, but there are very few governments that meet that standard, including the United States. I do not question the desire of having principles to which we should adhere. Those principles are embodied in conventions and a body of normative international law, which all of us here would subscribe to and support.

I do not think a little bit of torture is okay. I do not think prisoners should be abused. When those kinds of acts occur in the United States, as they have recently in Los Angeles, there is a tremendous repudiation and sense of disgust at what has taken place, and that is appropriate.

There has been progress in El Salvador. The kind of killing that took place from 1979 to 1981 is obviously not the case in the early 1990s. However, at various times when the military has felt a lot of pressure, as it did during the November 1989 offensive, there is a tendency to revert to the practices of the past. I am referring specifically to the Jesuit massacre. The military may, for certain reasons, have found it convenient to kill fewer people, to lower the debate in Congress, and to ensure that aid flowed, but there had not been a basic change of attitudes, and that is what allowed this kind of killing to take place.

The handling of the case is also a cause for concern. It raises doubts as to whether fundamental attitudes and senses of institutional responsibility have actually changed in a major way. Unless those attitudes do change, there is very little hope over the long term for El Salvador. I would place myself, at best, in the guarded optimist category. There has to be a real demonstration that an ethic has changed in El Salvador, and I have not yet found sufficient evidence to support that.

Terry Allen (Gemini News Service): I note Roberto Murray Meza's presentation of the Salvadoran press as the most free and fair in Central America and his dismissal of Ambassador White's mention of the advertisement by saying that it was not a serious death threat because it represented a small constituency. My question is: How many men does it take to pull a trigger?

Second, Roberto Murray Meza mentioned the *Diario Latino* as if it were a beacon of free press in El Salvador. He noted that it is owned by its workers and presents an alternative point of view. It was, in fact, blown up by the government, according to all reports, and completely destroyed less than a month ago.

Roberto Murray Meza: With regard to the free press, I hold to my position. Any newspaper is accessible to paid ads from unions, political parties, combatant groups, and so on. If one listens to the radio between 6:00 and 7:30 in the evening, one will find that there is no group or political constituency that is not heard from. And, as I mentioned, television viewers get an excellent version of the complete political spectrum in El Salvador.

With respect to *Diario Latino,* it is my understanding that Assistant Secretary Aronson made a statement recently that it was blown up by a group affiliated with the FMLN. But regardless of who blew it up, it is continuing to print. It publishes every day and its number of pages and ads is growing.

José García: It is not fair to ask an institution or group of people to change their attitudes toward something out of the clear blue sky. That approach is unlikely to work. Human rights conditions will improve in El Salvador when institutional developments force them to, which means reform of the justice system. In that sense, US policy, at least as it is stated overtly, is correct. A country must have a justice code and it has to be enforced so that when an unfortunate incident takes place there will be swift and certain retribution. Until that happens, attitudinal changes are not likely to take place at the level they are needed—at the behavioral level. The problem is not the attitude; the problem is the behavior.

Cynthia Arnson: I would disagree on the question of how reform of the judicial system is to take place. Is judicial reform a technical issue or, rather, a question of political will? The United States, over the past decade, has poured a fairly substantial amount of money into reform of the judicial system to no avail, because there has not been the change in attitude or in ethic. There has not been an attitude that reflects the conviction that certain kinds of crimes ought not to happen and that people, both in the military and in the political system, will exert significant pressures so that they do not happen. The number of instances of direct military interference in the proceedings or the conduct of the judicial system demonstrates that the problem is not as José García has suggested but, rather, the reverse.

José García: But would you agree with me that at least we do have a ladder that will lead to change against which performance can be judged when obstacles to institutional reform of the judicial system are no longer there?

Cynthia Arnson: A country can have the most beautiful judicial code in the world, but unless there is the political will to enforce it, it really means nothing. The San José Accord has an extensive set of requirements for both the government and the FMLN in terms of the treatment of prisoners, respect for the right to life, and arrest and detainment procedures. But in fact those terms are observed in the breach. It is not a question of elaborating a judicial structure; it is, rather, a question of creating the consensus in society that those norms are to prevail.

PART 4

THE PROSPECTS FOR PEACE

13

The Negotiations Following the New York Agreement

Alvaro de Soto

The presidents of Central America agreed to involve the United Nations in the verification of any accords made by the governments involved in the search for peace and democratization in the region—the two touchstones of the Esquipulas II Accord of 1987. The concept got off to a somewhat shaky start because the corollaries of bringing in outsiders took some time to sink in. An offshoot of this was that the Central American countries requested the United Nations to set up an on-site verification mechanism for compliance with the Esquipulas commitments, which were to prevent their territories from being used to destabilize neighbors and to prevent military aid from reaching irregular movements or insurgent forces in the region. In late 1989, the United Nations Observer Group in Central America (ONUCA) was established.

Also in late 1989, President Cristiani, with the strong backing of his four colleagues in the Central American region, approached the secretary-general of the United Nations to ask his help to bring together the parties in the Salvadoran conflict (the government of El Salvador and the FMLN). A peace effort, started by Cristiani when he took power in June 1989, had been interrupted by the decision of the FMLN to walk away from the negotiating table after the attack against the headquarters of FENASTRAS (National Trade Union Federation of Salvadoran Workers), a labor federation in San Salvador. This attack was followed by the November 1989 offensive by the FMLN.

However, the FMLN also approached the United Nations in late 1989. This action was followed by a personal request for UN assistance from President Cristiani, who went to New York to see the secretary-general on January 31, 1990. The secretary-general acceded to these requests, which was surprising, perhaps even unprecedented, on two

Alvaro de Soto is personal representative of the secretary-general for the Central American Peace Process at the United Nations.

counts. The first is that the United Nations does not usually get involved in internal conflicts. There were, of course, certain aspects that distinguished this particular internal conflict from run-of-the-mill ones—there was clearly an international dimension, to the extent that President Cristiani had received the support of his four Central American colleagues to come to the secretary-general with this request, and because an item on the agenda was assistance for the guerrilla forces of the FMLN from outside El Salvador.

Neither has it been the habit of the United Nations to become involved in either internal or international conflicts related to Latin America. There had always been a tendency to deflect any requests for UN involvement in hemisphere matters to the Organization of American States. Perhaps it was thought, because Secretary-General Pérez de Cuéllar was a Latin American and because regional efforts had failed, that it was time for this last resort.

The secretary-general launched an effort through his representative (me) to try to put together a framework for a peaceful settlement. After two months of my shuttling between President Cristiani and the FMLN General Command an agreement was signed in Geneva on April 4, 1990. In this signing, presided over by the secretary-general, both parties undertook to carry out a negotiating process. This process consisted of both direct meetings with the participation of the secretary-general's representatives as well as intermediation between the parties by either the secretary-general or his representative. It also provided for an indirect involvement of local political parties and social organizations and governments from outside the region that were in a position to assist in the process.

The involvement of political parties and social organizations in the country was particularly important because it aided in achieving the four goals of the negotiations: to put an end to the conflict, to broaden democracy in El Salvador, to guarantee respect for human rights, and to bring about the reconciliation of Salvadoran society. These goals could not be undertaken with just the participation of the two warring parties.

The parties got together for their first direct meeting in late May 1990 and agreed to an agenda for the talks, which laid out as subjects for negotiation political agreements on the armed forces, human rights, the electoral system, the judicial system, economic and social questions, and constitutional reform. Moreover, the parties agreed to verification by the United Nations because this had already been accepted in principle in Geneva. The May 21, 1990, Caracas agreement on the agenda also provided for a two-stage negotiation. The first stage was meant to be political agreements leading to a "cessation of armed conflict," something of a euphemism because the term "cease-fire" is usually utilized in conflicts between states. The second stage of the negotiations would touch on the subjects enumerated previously: political agreements to establish guarantees and conditions for the integration or the reintegration of the members of the FMLN into the civil, institutional, and political society of El Salvador within a fully legal framework.

Under this agenda, negotiations began in earnest on the substance of the issues in June 1990. The first issue to be addressed was that of the armed forces; fifteen months later, this subject is still very much on the table. Progress has been made, but it is not yet a closed chapter. We have run into all the difficulties that necessarily derive from having chosen to address the most difficult issue as the first item on the agenda. Certain determinations were made early on because of the framework that was drawn up for the two-stage negotiation. The first was that there would be no attempt by either side during the first phase of negotiations to put forward draft agreements to reduce the military capability of the other. Progress on the armed forces issue was slow and extremely difficult. The negotiators concentrated on what has now been rendered into English as the "purification of the armed forces"—the question of the impunity of the armed forces; the question of security bodies, particularly the existing Treasury Police, National Police, and National Guard; the question of reforms geared to subordinating the military to civilian control; and a number of other specific measures destined to ensure that there would be a comprehensive reform of the armed forces following the establishment of peace.

From the beginning, the negotiations were haunted by what was referred to as "the future of the armed forces." The FMLN insisted that there should be nothing stated in any document agreed to between the two sides that would prejudge the question of the future existence of the armed forces as such. The FMLN's thesis, since the early 1980s, had been that there was no need for armed forces in a country such as El Salvador and that the way to deal with the problem was to rethink the whole question of the existence of the armed forces. Originally they had suggested that their army and that of the government should be merged. Later on, particularly late last year and the beginning of this year, they were talking about the solution being the dissolution of the two armies, the abolition of both military apparatuses.

Following two frustrated attempts to make sufficient progress to reach agreement on the question of the armed forces, the delegations decided, somewhat abruptly, to switch to the second item on the agenda, that of human rights. Benefiting to some extent from input provided by the United Nations, at the request of the parties to the negotiation, they agreed to a number of stipulations regarding human rights that, in effect, constitute a reiteration of human rights instruments of international law as well as of national law to which the government of El Salvador is a party. They decided as part of this agreement, which was signed in San José, Costa Rica, on July 26, 1990, to ask the United Nations to monitor compliance with the agreements reached. The Security Council established the United Nations Observer Mission in El Salvador (ONUSAL), which will in due course have as its task to verify all agreements reached between the government and the FMLN. For the present, ONUSAL is equipped only with its human rights component. We have fielded a mission of over 100 people who monitor all areas of the country, including those over which the FMLN claims control, for compliance with the San José agreements.

Work proceeded on the armed forces issue without much success. The negotiations entered into a fairly serious crisis and had to be revitalized toward the end of 1990, spurred by the proximity of the date set for legislative and municipal elections in early 1991. The FMLN did not formally agree to respect the results of those elections. However, their attitude toward them was considerably different from that of previous years: They encouraged people sympathetic to the FMLN to actually participate in the election. In essence, the FMLN was trying to get out the vote in favor of the opposition parties. The government approached the United Nations about monitoring the elections, something that the United Nations does not usually do but had done in Nicaragua. But the Geneva agreement had established that the United Nations would verify only agreements between the government and the FMLN, and on this issue there was no agreement. The FMLN did not accept that the United Nations should be involved in monitoring the election. So we stood, as it were, on the sidelines.

However, another factor proved a spur to the negotiations, an item that was low on the agenda—the expiration of the term in office of the outgoing Legislative Assembly. The negotiators viewed this as the last opportunity to introduce constitutional reforms under the existing constitution. But in El Salvador, reform of the Constitution has to be done in two stages: The first requires the support of a simple majority in the Legislative Assembly; and the second requires ratification by two-thirds of the members of a subsequent legislature. (A legislature is measured by the term of office of the legislators rather than by year, as in the United States). If the constitutional reform was not agreed upon before April 30, 1991, which was the last day in office of the legislators, it would have put off constitutional reform until 1994, the year of expiration of the legislature that entered into office on May 1, 1991. So both sides raced to try to carry out reforms in time for approval by the legislature that would leave office on April 30 and thus open the way for ratification by the legislature to be inaugurated on the next day, May 1.

This race for reforms led to a marathon session in April 1991 in Mexico City; it lasted about twenty-six days, virtually nonstop. It was quite dramatic and was a highly debated matter in El Salvador. The very fact that the government was negotiating constitutional reforms with the FMLN was highly controversial, and Salvadoran public opinion was focused on a proposal put forward by the FMLN regarding Article 248 of the Constitution, which referred to the mechanism for constitutional reform. The case they were making is that it would not be possible, indeed it was not even advisable, to carry out in such a short time an exercise as important to the political life of the country as reforming the constitution. Therefore, they argued, an amendment should be introduced that would be ratified immediately by the incoming legislature to relax the procedures for reform, at least for a given period. This became the focus of a very strident internal debate. The idea of revising the constitutional reform mechanism encountered the most severe opposition, particularly from the far Right in El Salvador, which felt that national institutions were being tampered with in a totally unacceptable way. President Cristiani came under heavy pressure internally on this particular matter.

As it turned out, there was no agreement on reform of the constitutional amendment procedure. There was, however, agreement on constitutional reforms that went extremely deep and involved several key areas, the most important being those related to the armed forces. The Constitution, which is still in force, provides for the armed forces to be a permanent institution. The armed forces have responsibilities not only for the defense of territorial integrity and national sovereignty but also for the maintenance of internal order and the defense of laws and the Constitution. These responsibilities include jurisdiction over the existing security bodies, the police among others.

In the reforms pending ratification, the latter provisions have been removed from the armed forces chapter of the Constitution. The armed forces today have responsibilities only in the defense of sovereignty and territorial integrity. In certain "exceptional" (the term used in the constitutional reform) cases the armed forces may be used to maintain public order, but this is subject to a recall by the Legislative Assembly. This is a rather unusual encroachment upon the power of the executive in such a heavily presidentialist system as in El Salvador and, indeed, in most Latin American countries. Once the constitutional reforms are ratified, the armed forces will no longer have any jurisdiction over the police, which will be under a separate and civilian ministry. The armed forces will no longer have any role in the maintenance of internal order or any role or say in the defense of laws or the Constitution. There will no longer be the potential for it to act as an ultimate arbiter of internal politics in

El Salvador (though it has played a very prominent role in this area throughout its history).

There are also important constitutional reforms regarding the judiciary. The system for choosing the body of justices, all the way down to justices of the peace, allowed for a heavy role of the executive, first in the appointment of supreme court justices and, through them, in the appointment of all judges. This has now been changed. A qualified majority is required for the election of Supreme Court justices, and the system for appointments of the remainder of the justices in the judicial system has been professionalized and depoliticized. There is a provision for 6 percent of the budget to be automatically assigned for the judiciary and a provision for the creation of a new prosecutor general and a national prosecutor for human rights who would have broad powers.

The electoral system has also been modified to ensure pluralist control by more political parties than heretofore in the new electoral tribunal that is to be created and to ensure the participation of independents in the control of electoral processes. At the same time, as part of the package of agreements that were reached in Mexico in April 1991, secondary legislation to implement all of these agreements on constitutional reform would have to be approved and, in some way, negotiated with the FMLN or at least discussed with them.

As a final element in the package, the government and the FMLN agreed to the creation of a new body whose members would be appointed by the secretary-general after having heard the views of the parties. The new body would be called the Commission on Truth and would examine and bring to light the truth regarding the more egregious violations of human rights in the past decade. The philosophy behind this is that in order to put behind them the trauma of the past, the Salvadorans must go through the process of facing the truth about some of the more blatant misdeeds of the past decade.

The constitutional reforms were truly a watershed in this negotiation—a symbol of the political determination on both sides to see this process through until its end. President Cristiani, who heads a constitutionally elected government, took the bold political step not only of negotiating with guerrillas but also of negotiating constitutional reforms with them and of actively promoting those reforms for approval in the Legislative Assembly. These constitutional reforms were agreed to on April 27, 1991. There was a last-minute effort that would have had the effect of distorting some of the agreements reached, and Cristiani himself ensured that nothing was changed in the essence of the reforms agreed to between the government and the FMLN. He did so at considerable political risk and, I would say, cost to himself within his own party. He was head of at least certain sectors of his own party that were perhaps not particularly attached to the idea of a negotiated political solution to this conflict.

The FMLN for its part had agreed to reform the Constitution in accordance with the rules of the constitution itself. This action is also a considerable move forward for the FMLN because they consider this constitution part of the counterinsurgency project that was used against them and, from their point of view, against the Salvadoran people. This constitution, after all, was adopted in wartime in 1983, and it was adopted under the presidency of a Legislative Assembly headed by Major Roberto d'Aubuisson, who is the lifetime leader of ARENA and who has traditionally been a mortal enemy of the FMLN.

Despite these demonstrations of significant political will on both sides, the negotiations have seen considerable ups and downs. A month or two following the constitutional reform agreement, the negotiations had reached practically the limit of what they could possibly do within the framework that had been agreed to for a two-stage negotiation. On this point, let me return to an issue that was relevant to what occurred in New York during the last week of September 1991. It proved virtually impossible to reach an agreement on the terms for a cease-fire within the two-stage negotiating framework that had been adumbrated in the Geneva agreements and confirmed in the Caracas agreement. This was the case because some of the core issues of the negotiation, at least from the point of view of the FMLN—the future of the government's army and the future of their own army—were put off until the second stage of the negotiation. Because they were not in a position to know what their future was going to be as an armed apparatus, they needed to take all the necessary precautions at cease-fire time in order to guard against the possibility that the negotiations during the second stage and following the cease-fire might fail.

So the FMLN insisted on terms of a cease-fire that would assure their military capability during that cease-fire. Those terms included freedom of movement, freedom to carry out military maneuvers, freedom to recruit and train combatants, and to continue to supply themselves both in terms of logistics and military supplies—and all this for an indefinite period of time, however long the negotiations lasted and in large swatches of Salvadoran territory. These terms proved quite unacceptable to the government, even though they flowed naturally from the logic of a two-stage negotiation in which the end result was by no means guaranteed or assured.

So the two sides agreed to reconsider the structure of the agenda and to think about compressing it into a single stage. That effort has taken up the time of the negotiators, of myself, and of Secretary-General Pérez de Cuéllar over the past three months or so. The problem became

145

how to put together a package of guarantees and conditions for the reintegration into society of the FMLN: how both sides could go to the mountaintop, as it were, and look at the valley on the other side and decide whether the outline that might emerge from the negotiations would satisfy the basic concerns and allow the FMLN to take the leap into society.

The main issue (and perhaps the most controversial issue) arising in the negotiations was participation in the armed forces by the FMLN. In the early 1980s, the FMLN talked about the merger of the two armies. Later, particularly at the end of last year and early this year, they talked about dissolution of the two armies. They then recognized that neither of those two goals was possible to achieve within the negotiations with the government. The FMLN needed at least some guarantees that they were not going to be done in and that there would be no repression of Salvadoran society. They needed guarantees that society would change within the framework of the Geneva and Caracas agreements and that there would indeed be compliance with whatever agreements were reached. The FMLN suggested that one way to do this was for members of their forces, ex-combatants, to join the officer corps of the army. This concept also proved to be an explosive issue. There were difficulties in the negotiations because the principals were not always fully active in the talks. There reached a stage, toward August, when it was determined that the only way to settle these problems was to address them at the highest decision-making level: the secretary-general of the United Nations.

In late August, Secretary-General Pérez de Cuéllar issued an invitation to President Cristiani and the General Command of the FMLN to join him in New York for consultations to address the set of issues that came under the umbrella of guarantees and conditions for the reintegration of the FMLN into society. As is well known, a summit normally convenes with adequate preparation, absolute certainty that the principals will indeed accept the invitation and attend, some certainty as to the outcome of the negotiation, and some certainty that no one will go home until a predetermined date and, if possible, a predetermined hour, by which time everyone has been able to sign on the dotted line.

What occurred in New York between September 16 and 25, 1991, defies all those established practices of international relations. When Secretary-General Pérez de Cuéllar invited President Cristiani and the General Command of the FMLN, he had no certainty whatever that they would accept his invitation. He gambled that they would, and the gamble paid off. He had no certainty that the members of the General Command of the FMLN would be allowed into the United States and would be given the visas to attend. Again, the gamble paid off. Pérez de Cuéllar originally invited them to New York for two days. He assumed that the political cost of the two parties returning empty-handed would be so high that they would be flexible and prepared to reach agreements where agreements had not been possible at lower negotiating levels. That gamble also paid off. The result was a package of agreements on guarantees and conditions for the FMLN's reintegration into society that were signed under the title "New York Agreement" on September 25, 1991.

There is no provision in the package for participation by the FMLN or members of the FMLN in the armed forces. Nor is there any trace of what I might call the father and grandfather of that particular proposal, which is the plan to dissolve both armed apparatuses or to merge them. Instead, the package affects not only the armed forces but also the political area and certain agreements regarding economic and social questions. This package, which was cobbled together over ten days of very intense negotiations in New York in which President Cristiani never met face-to-face with the FMLN but was very much present in the broader sense, now constitutes the critical mass that can give the FMLN enough assurance for its safety so as not to require the preservation of its military capability.

The main elements of the agreements are what could fairly be described not only as nondiscrimination but probably as a certain degree of affirmative action regarding the participation of members of the FMLN in the new national civilian police that is to be created. The other leg on which the package of agreements stands is the creation of the National Commission for Consolidation of Peace, known by its acronym in Spanish as COPAZ, which is to provide for the participation of civilian society in the implementation of agreements and in ensuring the transition to peace. Thus there is provision not only for participation of the government but also of the FMLN as well as political parties. A UN observer as well as the archbishop of El Salvador are also allowed to participate in its work.

COPAZ is a broad-based political body that, in a more formal way than heretofore, really brings together all of the political establishment of El Salvador with the FMLN, which is certainly a part of the political picture, in looking toward the future. COPAZ will only begin to function as such and be brought into being formally and legally in Salvadoran terms once there is a cease-fire, though the prospective members of COPAZ could informally begin to plow through the huge workload they have in advance of the cease-fire.

All of this does not mean that we are out of the woods. There is work still to be done. But this does remove the roadblocks that were hindering the negotiations process. This is not to say that problems, indeed some fairly important ones, cannot or will not arise. But it is doubtful whether the problems that will arise will be of the magnitude or intractablity of those that have now been sorted out. We now have an idea of what the final package will be.

From the agenda that was also agreed to in New York, it may seem as if everything is still on the table. This is not the case. Under the armed forces chapter, the only virgin territory is the reduction issue. On everything else, much groundwork has been done. There are still the extremely sensitive economic and social questions, which are often referred to by the FMLN as the cause of the war, particularly those that are related to land tenure. There are the issues regarding implementation legislation, the secondary legislation flowing from the constitutional reforms. Last, but not least, there is the question of the terms of the cease-fire.

We do not have everything written out for a peace-by-Christmas scenario. But if there are no major humps, this negotiation should flow relatively smoothly. And the possibility always exists for the secretary-general to gamble on another invitation at the highest decisionmaking level to break deadlocks if the need arises.

14

Discussion

Richard Oulahan (American Institute for Free Labor Development): Is one reason that there has been progress in the negotiations that both sides have started to realize that this is a no-win situation militarily or that the situation has become so stalemated?

Alvaro de Soto: I believe that both sides have come to recognize that military victory is not possible or, if it is possible, that it is only possible at an unbearable cost. This is an intimate belief that I hold, but it is not something that the two sides will necessarily bear me out on. I do not think they will go on record saying that they cannot achieve military victory. But I am convinced that they cannot, and I am convinced that this realization has been an important factor in making the negotiations possible.

Patricia Weiss (Office of the United Nations High Commissioner for Refugees [UNHCR], San Salvador): Given the progress on peace up to this point, could you say something more about how you foresee the modification or evolution of the role of ONUSAL, as it will be undertaking new tasks in the near future?

De Soto: ONUSAL was conceived as an integrated operation responsible for monitoring whatever agreements the parties ask the UN to monitor. It is headed by a civilian and member of the UN staff, Iqbal Riza of Pakistan. As of now, ONUSAL has only a small office under his direction and the Division on Human Rights, which is the mission for verification of human rights that is referred to in the San José agreement; it was established last year.

The Security Council has expressly provided for the possibility of additional components being assigned to ONUSAL as the need may arise. An obvious one is the component that will be needed to monitor the separation of forces between the two sides as well as compliance with the terms of the cease-fire. This is not even at the drawing-board stage yet. It will have to be designed on an ad hoc basis once we get there, and I hope that will be soon.

Juan Señor (MacNeil/Lehrer News Hour): I am curious about how you broker a deal like this. Could you tell us as personally as you can how you get these people to talk? How do you bring the message to the two parties? How do you come up with ideas? Has the United Nations itself been able to find some common ground?

De Soto: Perhaps I should define the terms under which we participate. We call this our "good offices." We are not arbiters and we are not even, formally speaking, mediators. Whatever an arbiter says goes. A mediator is expressly authorized to present proposals that the two sides must consider. Good offices is a broad term that can comprise as much or as little as the parties in a negotiation will tolerate. What is provided under the Geneva agreement is active participation by the secretary-general's representative in any direct meetings as well as his acting as go-between between the two sides when they are not meeting directly. What we have is a combination of the two.

The mistrust between the two sides is extremely acute, to the extent that any proposal presented by one side is immediately worthy of suspicion by the other side. Over the eighteen or so months of this negotiation, we developed an unwritten rule that if either side wants a proposal to have any chance of success, the last thing it should do is label it as its own proposal because that will immediately reduce its chances of being well received by the other side.

During the negotiations we have frequently seen the need, with the consent of the parties, to put forward what we call working papers, which they have been kind enough to consider, amend, and sometimes tear to bits. But, in any case, they have been the basis of most of the agreements reached so far during this negotiation. In effect, it is a combination of good offices and mediation. Even if the United Nations was not involved in this, the parties would need someone to be there in the middle.

Leni Berliner (Council for International Development): First, how do you view the prospects for getting enabling legislation for COPAZ through the General Assembly? Second, what is the reasoning behind having COPAZ make the decisions for which it is responsible?

De Soto: The enabling legislation for bringing COPAZ into existence formally in El Salvador is to be prepared by the members of COPAZ themselves. In fact, that is one of the tasks that they have before them as an informal preparatory body, which is more or less what they are in advance of the cease-fire.

There will be represented in COPAZ not only the government and the FMLN but also all the political parties in the Legislative Assembly. I assume, given the responsibilities that they have, that the parties will be represented by their leaders; this is too important a body for delegation of responsibility. It is an important body for the history of El Salvador, and so I would assume that the passage through the Legislative Assembly of whatever they draft is guaranteed in advance.

With regard to COPAZ's decisionmaking, one would probably have to ask the parties. But I imagine that the reason they chose this method is that they can achieve a more or less adequate balance, which leaves both sides feeling that they are not going to be overwhelmed by the other.

Bonnie Tenneriello (Washington Office on Latin America): To what extent, under the current framework, will COPAZ have a role in drafting proposals such as the reduction of the armed forces?

De Soto: I do not think that COPAZ is likely to get involved in those specific subjects. Those military issues are up to negotiation between the warring parties. It will, of course, play a considerable role in drafting its own enabling legislation. Its main role will be as a kind of clearinghouse for all draft legislation regarding implementation of constitutional reforms and all other agreements reached at the negotiating table.

Third, and this is perhaps a point that I did not highlight enough, it will play an important role in ensuring the agreements that are emerging. I underscore "are emerging" because regarding the transition from the existing security bodies that are controlled by the Ministry of Defense to the new national civilian police, the negotiations are very much in a state of flux. COPAZ's role will be to ensure that this transition is carried out as smoothly as possible on a nondiscriminatory basis in accordance with the agreements reached between the parties. Also, they have supervisory responsibilities. It is specifically described in the heading of the agreement on COPAZ that it will be the control mechanism of Salvadoran society. COPAZ does not have executive responsibilities; it does not do things by itself. It is nominally a recommendatory body, but its recommendations are binding.

Salvadoran Participant: Is it possible that the armed forces will not accept the New York agreement? The activity of the death squads has continued. A day or so before the agreements were signed some people in the repopulated communities were threatened. Although Salvadorans

151

are happy with the agreements, they are also waiting to see what the armed forces and the right wing of ARENA will do. Can the United Nations do something in this regard?

De Soto: Following the summit in Guadalajara, the presidents of Colombia, Spain, Mexico, and Venezuela, who assist the secretary-general most energetically in seeing this through, formulated an appeal to the government of El Salvador to push ahead with the constitutional reforms that had been agreed to in April. The government has since set up and laid out a calendar, and this is proceeding apace. They have, I believe, already ratified the constitutional reforms as far as they affect the judiciary and the electoral system and they have also created a new national prosecutor for human rights.

I understand that they want to hold back ratification of constitutional amendments regarding the armed forces until there is a cease-fire. They are not bound under the Mexico agreements to ratify them immediately and, in fact, there is a specific provision for synchronization with the negotiation process. But I think the dynamic is already quite positive.

With regard to what the attitude will be after the New York agreements, I understand that in general they have been well received by the government party and the parties of the opposition and by the social organizations as well. I do not know whether there have been any pronouncements from the armed forces as such, but the armed forces were well represented in the New York talks. The deputy chief of staff of the armed forces was there and he was in touch with the minister of defense. I have to assume that they are going along with these agreements.

Having said this, we are at a potentially dangerous moment because there are, quite possibly, certain forces in El Salvador that do not share the enthusiasm or the flexibility that was shown by the negotiating parties in New York, perhaps because they were not there. And so we are watching this particular moment with some tension. The secretary-general shared his concerns in a private meeting yesterday with the Security Council. Partly as a result of those concerns, we have the resolution that was adopted yesterday in the Security Council, which I hope will be interpreted in El Salvador as a call for restraint.

Frank Kendrick (Council on Hemispheric Affairs): There is little mention of the two big issues—the end of armed confrontation and reintegration of the rebels into society—in the accord itself. These two issues are left to the agenda for future negotiation. From a somewhat pessimistic point of view, I see these as huge issues, and there is room for a great many stumbling blocks.

De Soto: Certainly. I do not want even for an instant to underestimate the difficulty of the negotiations remaining before us. I would draw your attention to the second and third paragraphs of the preamble of the New York agreements, which say the negotiating parties are "convinced of the need to give a final impetus to the process of the negotiations currently taking place with the active participation of the Secretary General so that the set of political agreements required to bring a definitive end to the armed conflict in our country can be reached as speedily as possible." In the final paragraph of the preamble, the following is written: "Conscious of the fact that in order to achieve the aforementioned objective, it is essential to establish a set of conditions and guarantees which ensure the full implementation of these political agreements by both parties."

The whole purpose of this negotiation is to put together the necessary elements that will allow for reintegration into society of the FMLN. The specific terms under which this would be done and the timing are indeed a matter for negotiation.

Bill Goodfellow (Center for International Policy): What are the obstacles to a cease-fire? How much progress has to be made to achieve one? Could a cease-fire be reached at the Columbus Day session, or are we talking about another month or two or three before enough progress will be made for both sides to declare a cease-fire?

De Soto: If what you are asking is when a cease-fire can be signed and agreed to, perhaps one, two, or three months is close to the mark. This does not mean that the issue will not be addressed at the Mexico talks. It could well be. But I would view that essentially as a first approach to a new design. The problem that we had until now is that we could not agree on the concept of a cease-fire. And the secretary-general is not the one who actually orders the recruitment of troops or finances it. The Security Council does that. And the Security Council needs clarity, above all. They need to know who is gong to be where and when before they send out personnel to monitor the action. So we have to sit down with the parties now and redesign the cease-fire because we were working under a different set of premises than earlier.

Monitoring a cease-fire in a country like El Salvador is a difficult matter in any case, because of its size, geography, and climate and because of the nature of the conflict, in which the warring parties are frequently cheek by jowl. It cannot be easy. It is not like monitoring a cease-fire between Iran and Iraq or on the Golan Heights. The warring parties will have to go to separate places and our United Nations people will have to be in-between. Agreeing on the location and size of those places will not be an easy matter. But it will certainly be far easier than under the scenario of what was sometimes referred to as an armed peace, in which both sides would be maintaining their military capability.

Peruvian Participant: Are you or the United Nations willing to use your good offices to help settle conflicts in other countries, such as Peru?

De Soto: As a basic premise, for the United Nations to get involved in an internal conflict there would have to be agreement on the part of the government of the country concerned to invite the United Nations to become involved in one way or another. And it would have to be on a case-by-case basis. Another basic premise is that the parties involved in the conflict must not only have a desire to bring the conflict to a negotiated settlement but must also want the United Nations to be involved in bringing it to an end. In the specific case of Peru, I do not believe that those premises exist. The government of Peru is not interested, as far as I know, in having an outside party help mediate the conflict. Up until now, the Shining Path has shown no desire to end the war or to have the United Nations involved in bringing it to an end.

Gilbert Richardson (American Association for the Study of the United States in World Affairs): You mentioned that the archbishop of El Salvador is part of the peace process. In light of what happened to Archbishop Oscar Romero and with the assassination of the Jesuits, is the church becoming repoliticized? Could you tell us about the role that the current archbishop of El Salvador is playing in the negotiation of a settlement?

De Soto: The archbishop of El Salvador has been asked to participate in the work of COPAZ as an observer. I understand that he has been designated by the Episcopal Conference of El Salvador as the representative for any tasks that the church may be asked to carry out in the search for peace in the country. The Salvadoran church has been putting forward its views regarding the conflict and what needs to be done to end it. And it has been an active participant in voicing its opinions regarding national affairs. So I do not think that bringing the church into COPAZ as an observer will politicize the archbishop, because to a large extent he is already involved in these matters.

Heather Foote (Unitarian Universalist Service Committee): Would you comment on the tasks of the three separate commissions that are laid out in the accord so far? What are the more salient contributions each is to make toward shifting the relationships between military authorities and constitutional authorities?

De Soto: The Commission on Truth, the establishment of which was agreed to on April 27, 1991, will be a nonjudicial body whose members are to be appointed by the secretary-general of the United Nations. Over a period of six months it is to study and come to conclusions on a selected number (they will determine which cases) of human rights violations in the past decade. They can make recommendations of virtually any nature and both parties are committed to following those recommendations.

The National Commission on the Consolidation of Peace, which was just agreed to in New York, is to follow through on the negotiations. It will be the control mechanism for the process of transition and implementation of agreements, the control mechanism of the body politic—civilian society—as a whole. The members will be representatives of the FMLN, the government, and each of the political parties. The commission will also include observers, the archbishop of El Salvador, and a representative from ONUSAL.

There is also a provision in the armed forces agreements, which are not yet signed but have been widely discussed in public, for an ad hoc commission whose aim will be to purify the armed forces. It will be composed of three civilian Salvadorans appointed by the secretary-general of the United Nations following consultations with both the government and the FMLN. They would have the task, over a period of three months, of reaching conclusions on the future service of all the members of the Salvadoran officer corps, based on three criteria: respect for human rights by both themselves and their subordinates, professional competence as military, and aptitude for service within a newly democratized and peaceful society.

Larry Storrs (Congressional Research Service, Library of Congress): Can you say if there are any understandings between the two sides about the nature of hostilities that would exist during the negotiation process? It was reported that the FMLN proposed a one-year truce to facilitate negotiations and so forth and that it then became part of the agreement.

De Soto: As of now, there are none. These are wartime negotiations. One of the issues on the agenda is working out the terms of a cease-fire. It is true that the FMLN mentioned the possibility of unilateral truces on both sides for up to a year and to last at least for a part of the transition. But this proposal was never pressed at the negotiating table; it was never conveyed to President Cristiani. Both sides agreed to give precedence to the secretary-general's own suggestions regarding the package of guarantees for the reintegration into society of the FMLN.

However, Secretary-General Pérez de Cuéllar and I think that many others are concerned that in view of the approaching peace (if I dare say that we are at that stage), there may be some who are less enthusiastic than others about the prospect of a negotiated political solution and who might view this as a time in which to get in a few last licks. If combat is intensified over the next few weeks or months, negotiating positions could harden. The secretary-general has made known his concern about this and the Security Council has, to some extent, echoed it.

Adelina Reyes-Gavilan (National Endowment for Democracy): The 1987 Esquipulas II Accord called for the establishment in each Central American country of a National Reconciliation Commission. As far as I know, Guatemala has the only working commission so far. The idea of the commission is to broaden political participation and create a national dialogue among competing economic, political, and social sectors. Is there a chance that this idea will be revived during the negotiations in order to broaden popular participation in the process?

De Soto: You have correctly given both the state of national reconciliation commissions in Central America and the philosophy behind them. Obviously you will have noticed that there is a certain similarity between at least the concept of the National Reconciliation Commission and what is in COPAZ, except that COPAZ is considerably more fleshed out.

The membership of COPAZ also is restricted to political bodies, if, broadly speaking, one considers the FMLN to be one. The idea of using the National Reconciliation Commission might have been one way to address precisely the same problem. However, it had the difficulty associated with its birth certificate. As you know, the idea behind Esquipulas II is solidarity among the governments against irregular forces and insurgent movements. For these reasons the FMLN obviously considered it rather inimical. And I do not think that the FMLN would have accepted the National Reconciliation Commission, which in any case was not proposed as a body or as a means of broadening participation.

Todd Howland (El Rescate, Los Angeles, California): Does the United Nations foresee an enforcement mechanism outside of COPAZ for the ad hoc commission on purification of the armed forces? If so, could you elaborate on what mechanism you foresee?

De Soto: COPAZ is going to be enacted into law. The agreements that are being reached between the two sides, except those related to the armed forces, are essentially of a political nature except insofar as they can be implemented into legislation, and in those cases it would be expressly stated as such. In the case of the purification, the president would be committed to implementing within a given period of time what has yet to be negotiated. That is one of the few elements that are still pending negotiation. It is more of a political commitment than anything else. However, all of these agreements will be subject to what I would call a microscope of outside verification. I cannot conceive of a situation in which a decision is taken, negotiated by the two sides, and not implemented; that would be untenable politically.

Joseph Tulchin: There is an actor in the peace process, and one that likely will play a role following any cease-fire, that has not been mentioned. Could you comment for us on the role of the United States in the peace process and what you envision its role to be following the cease-fire?

De Soto: The United States, of course, is an ally of the Salvadoran government in many ways and has been giving it considerable military assistance over the years. It has a large part of the responsibility in seeing the process through and has recognized this responsibility and offered to play a role both bilaterally and as a member of the Security Council in guaranteeing its implementation. So, indeed, the United States has an important role to play, and I am sure that it will play that role.

Gustavo Verganza (La Crónica, Guatemala): The United Nations is involved in Guatemala, but not nearly to the extent that it is in El Salvador. Why has the United Nations not taken a more active role in the Guatemalan peace process?

De Soto: We only enter in where we are invited. However, I should underscore that in the case of Guatemala there is a process of negotiation now under way between the government and the URNG (Guatemalan National Revolutionary Union) armed opposition movement, which is being carried out under the auspices of the National Reconciliation Commission that was mentioned earlier. There is, however, one foreigner present in the room throughout the talks who regularly sees both sides; however, that person, from the United Nations, is there merely as an observer.

I understand that it is the decision of the Guatemalans to do this among themselves and that they may resort to the United Nations for specific verification tasks. Subject to the approval of the appropriate UN bodies, the United Nations would be able and prepared to do that work if it would help produce peace in Guatemala. But we do not go into these tasks uninvited, and we are not seeking a role beyond that which the bodies want to give us.

Phil Kete (FENASTRAS, Washington Office): How can any agreement have authority over the death squads after a cease-fire?

De Soto: The assumption is that it would be difficult for such organizations to operate if they did not have some sort of blessing from those with the power to give such a blessing, even if it is the wink of an eye or looking the other way. Under a reformed, purified armed forces, and under a set of guarantees from abroad, including the participation of the United States, it is hoped that they will cease to have such tacit blessing from the authorities.

Other than that, what is being explored and will in due course be agreed to is a set of fairly elementary, practical measures. They are not in place at this time, but the goal is to ensure that private security bodies are duly registered, that their members are known, and that they are restricted to the use of certain weapons, presumably small weapons. In general, improvement of the judiciary system will perhaps also incrementally contribute to that goal. That is as much as one can want. One cannot wish such organizations away.

Cindy Buhl (Latin American Working Group, Washington, D.C.): One often makes the assumption, when reaching agreements and before they are ultimately implemented, that both parties will operate out of a common definition of what they have just signed and agreed to. We are currently seeing, following your agreement, diverse interpretations of some of the points that have been signed, such as the dissolution of the Treasury Police and the National Guard. One side says that was agreed to; the other side says nothing of the sort was agreed to. How do you help to hold both parties to common understandings of the agreements they have already signed, let alone those that are yet to be negotiated?

De Soto: Constructive ambiguity is useful in certain cases. This is obviously not one of them. The understanding on this point, and this has yet to be written out, is that the existing security bodies, as such, will be disappearing. Certainly the Treasury Police and the National Guard will go. As to the personnel in these entities, that has yet to be decided. But they would cease to function as security bodies as such, as police. A new National Police would be created, possibly utilizing some of the personnel of the existing National Police. There is clear understanding on that, but the fine print has yet to be written.

Luis Parada (Armed Forces of El Salvador, Embassy of El Salvador,

Washington, D.C.): When the conflict ends, there is an understanding that there is going to be a deal as part of which international organizations will help out with the reconstruction of the country and also the reintegration into society of the combatants of the FMLN and the armed forces. Is that a factor that is presently being considered in the negotiations? Is there an effort to establish some coordination that will give these agencies the necessary lead time for budgetary reasons and for planning so that their programs are available when called upon?

De Soto: This is a problem to which some thought is being given. For instance, the government is well advanced in a plan for reconstruction of the nation as a whole, and one of the ideas is to involve at least certain portions of the Salvadoran army in the reconstruction tasks.

Then there is the question of the demobilization of combatants from both sides. Obviously, this will require considerable financing. To this end, the US government is committed to using at least some of the funds that have previously been assigned for military assistance. The US government would assist in the transition to a new civilian life for those combatants on both sides who, in the case of the FMLN, would cease to be combatants and, in the case of the army, might no longer have positions within a reduced army.

It is my understanding that the government has always been prepared to reduce the army once the war is over because the army is its present size only because of the war. Hence, I assume, it would already have advanced-stage plans for such a reduction and for what to do with the personnel. There will be other operations that will be costly, such as creating and training a new national civilian police, the bulk of which would be entirely new personnel.

Unfortunately, lead time is always a problem when one resorts to requests for cooperation from either individual governments or international organizations. Nobody will listen until a peace agreement has actually been signed, and then, of course, we have to ensure that once peace is in place the country or countries concerned are not entirely forgotten.

There are some cynics who say that peace is bad business and war is good business. That is a difficulty that will have to be addressed and is to some extent already being addressed. We at the United Nations are certainly looking into it—though we do not have a treasure trove of resources into which we can dig.

PART 5

CONCLUSION

15

Assessing the Transition to Democracy

Gary Bland

Not very long ago, "Salvadoran democracy" was the catchphrase of US and Salvadoran politicians who dismissed the need for institutional reform and sought the political isolation of the FMLN. For the armed rebels, the term once represented the ideal of popular revolution followed by the establishment of a socialist, one-party regime. To much of the Salvadoran population at home and in exile it had come to symbolize a cruel hoax. What Salvadoran democracy did not stand for was the right of all citizens to be treated as equals in the public decisionmaking process and the obligation of public officials to be held equally accountable to those decisions.[1] But much about El Salvador has changed.

Today, Central America's smallest country is on the road to peace and reconciliation after twelve years of war. The signing of the final peace accord in Mexico City on January 16, 1992, an occasion marked by extraordinary displays of mutual affection and respect among once-bitter enemies, demonstrated a genuine desire on the part of key actors in society to work toward democracy in El Salvador. The series of agreements reached between the Cristiani government and the FMLN touch all areas of society, including human rights protections, reforms in the judicial and the electoral systems, reduction of the armed forces, creation of a new national civilian police, economic and social policy changes, and the disarmament of the FMLN. The full implementation of these measures—though it no doubt will be extremely troublesome—is critical to the country's future. The importance of the political and financial commitment of the United States, the UN, ?nd other international parties to ensuring that they are respected cannot be underestimated.

Now that a cease-fire has been achieved and the process of implementing the peace accords is under way, one can assess El Salvador's

Gary Bland is program associate of the Latin American Program at the Woodrow Wilson International Center for Scholars.

democratic transition, evaluate the prospects for democracy, and consider what shape it will take in the 1990s. I will argue that liberalization and thus the transition to democracy in El Salvador began tentatively in early 1984, in the midst of the campaign for presidency won by José Napoleón Duarte.[2] From 1984 through most of 1991, liberalization continued, but the tenuous political opening coupled with an electoral process were insufficient to constitute democratization. Democratization required, in addition, societal accommodation and the acceptance of political uncertainty in the pursuit of one's interests, two processes that were central to the peace accords and that began in earnest when the two warring parties agreed to settle their differences at the negotiating table in April 1990. The process of democratization itself did not commence for another year and a half, when the government extended basic rights to Salvadoran citizens through the implementation of the first agreements reached between the FMLN and President Cristiani's negotiating team.

Today El Salvador's democratization is proceeding. The implementation of the reforms and the improvement in political conditions demonstrate the movement toward democratic government. Not until 1994, however, after El Salvador successfully completes its "founding" elections, will it be accurate to consider the country a democracy. From that point on, El Salvador should with some good fortune be able to focus on consolidating and improving its newly democratic regime.

Outside of Costa Rica, El Salvador's chances for democracy may be the strongest in Central America (recognizing that such an assessment may be as much a reflection of the poor state of democracy in the region). The Cristiani government and the FMLN not only negotiated an end to the civil war but also laid the foundations of democracy in a society that has never before experienced it. In the words of UN mediator Alvaro de Soto, they virtually produced a "negotiated revolution."[3] Above all, with both sides claiming victory, the peace accords represent a successful accommodation and the strong desire to move the battle for power back to the political arena. These two changes, the implementation of democratic reforms and the good prospects for reconciliation, are providing the momentum for El Salvador's democracy today.

Although current events allow a positive view of the prospects for democracy in El Salvador, many additional considerations cast doubt on the accuracy of that assessment. A much wider range of factors must be addressed in analyzing the prospects for a democratic future of the countries of Latin America.[4] In taking this broader approach, history and political culture, leadership, and institutions must be studied, as must the military, civil society, socioeconomic development, economic policies, and international influences. Addressing these elements in depth is beyond the scope of this chapter, but a brief consideration of each for the case of El Salvador does allow one to be guardedly optimistic about the country's future.

Historical Overview and Political Culture

The case against democracy in El Salvador is not hard to make. Yet despite the legacy produced by a self-serving oligarchy allied with a praetorian military, El Salvador experienced the first stirrings of democratic transition on at least five occasions prior to its civil war. In November 1930, five political parties competed in a reasonably free election and the winner, Arturo Araujo, became president the following spring. The fairly representative junta of 1944 organized free elections and supported the return of political parties, including the Communists, and labor unions. A progressive, Arturo Romero, appeared ready to win the presidency that year. In 1960, a reformist junta rose to power following a coup and announced its intention to hold free and fair elections. José Napoleón Duarte was winning the 1972 presidential vote, in which a broad center-left coalition openly challenged the military's one-party political system, before military leaders intervened. Finally, the reformist coup of October 15, 1979 produced a series of reformist juntas with the participation of the Left that promised broad-based political and economic reform. By spring 1980, however, civilian junta members on the left and center-left felt forced to resign and eventually aligned themselves with the armed opposition.

All of these attempts were quickly thwarted through military countercoups, state-sponsored repression, torture, and murder. Democrats were free to organize and even hold free elections as long as they did not pose a threat to oligarchical interests or the military's hegemony. To the ruling class, thwarting the Salvadorans yearning for democratic reform was imperative. But it grew increasingly difficult and bloody until a large segment of society chose to support radical methods to achieve change and a revolution was born.

As has been well documented, the introduction of coffee as an export crop in the second half of the nineteenth century had an immediate and dramatic impact on Salvadoran life. Much like today, El Salvador sought to insert itself into an increasingly competitive world market. Large private coffee plantations quickly came to dominate the countryside, displacing or virtually enslaving the Indians and farmers who had worked the land communally for centuries. Living in a densely populated country and controlled by vagrancy laws favoring the commercialization of coffee for export, the great majority of Salvadorans had little choice but to work the land under harsh exploitative conditions for bare subsistence wages. Coffee exports skyrocketed in value from 1880 through World War I and by 1929 accounted for nearly 93 percent of all of El Salvador's exports.[5] International prices were high; coffee was king.

Salvadoran society was based on political domination. Early in the twentieth century, El Salvador, not having developed a significant urban middle class, consisted of a tiny, landowning elite and a mass of impoverished campesinos. The ruling class was drawn from this elite, which governed unchallenged in its own interests, such as securing favorable tariff policies and building infrastructure needed to ship their goods to port. Spending on the military was shifted away from defense against an external enemy and toward internal security,[6] in case the landless peasants objected to their treatment. The country was a fiefdom for landowners who reaped tremendous wealth in the course of exploiting the population.

From the rise of large-scale coffee production until the mid-1880s, El Salvador had six constitutions. The constitution of 1886 remained in place until 1944. It was considered liberal, the dominant ideology of this period, which is known for its anticlericism and capitalism. The coup, however, led by a *caudillo* and often supported by a faction of the landed elite, was the primary means of transferring power from the mid-1800s into the early twentieth century.[7] From then on, the presidency was passed from one dominant family clan to another. The first three decades of the century thus witnessed fewer coups and longer presidential terms.[8] Until November 1930, when the oligarchy was divided and Arturo Araujo won the presidency in the first freely competitive vote, the elections that occurred were no more than rubber stamps for the official candidate, who was sure to provide dictatorial rule on behalf of the ruling class. Otherwise, presidents were simply appointed by the leading families.

The depression doomed many a democratically elected regime in Latin America. El Salvador under Arturo Araujo was no exception. The price of coffee dropped by 45 percent in six months (57 percent ultimately), and national income dropped by half from 1928 to 1931.[9] As for peasant tenant farmers, their wages dropped by 50 percent and close to a third were forced off their land for lack of work or inability to pay their debts.[10] Araujo, a landowner with progressive ideals, had the misfortune of taking office in spring 1931, in the midst of massive labor and student strikes. Martial law was declared, and soon the military, upset about not having received its pay and supported by the oligarchy, which distrusted Araujo, easily overthrew his government after nine months. The infamous Gen. Maximiliano Hernández Martínez took over as head of the ruling junta.

The *matanza* of 1932—the massacre of 10,000 to 40,000 peasants in response to an uprising organized by Communist leader Augustín Farabundo Martí, has been amply discussed in the literature on El Salvador. It suffices here to emphasize it was a central turning point in the history of the country, an event that deeply influenced the Right and the Left's view of their enemies in the violent decades to come. The massacre demonstrated the brutal lengths to which the regime that was established over the preceding decades would go to defend the status quo and also instilled a reactionary fear of communism in those who were determined to preserve their societal status. El Salvador then lapsed into the twelve-year personalistic dictatorship of General Martínez, the man who presided over the mass killings.

During the Martínez period, independent organization was effectively prohibited, labor unions were illegal, and repression was widespread. Apart from a few economic reforms, little changed. Traditional patterns of production remained unaltered and, unlike authoritarian regimes in other parts of Latin America during the depression, Martínez did not resort to state-led expansion or other populist experiments to ease popular discontent.[11] In fact, the US ideal of positive government, of the state and economic sector working in tandem to improve the general welfare, was absent; the ruling class remained untouched and committed to its laissez-faire economic philosophy.[12]

Martínez was deposed in a 1944 coup with the support of the United States, which was displeased with his Nazi tendencies. The junta that replaced Martínez "had visions of a democratic El Salvador"[13] and called for elections. In addition, post-World War II prosperity, based primarily on a growing industrial sector and a resurgence of political activity, produced new demands for modernization. This movement was led by Arturo Romero, a popular progressive who formed his own party and began campaigning for the presidency. But the hope for democratic change was soon dashed. A reactionary colonel easily overthrew the junta and unleashed his own terror campaign, persecuting leftists and Communists, exiling the liberal leaders, and prompting an uprising and exile invasion from Guatemala, both of which failed. A series of fraudulent elections in subsequent years produced a president of the coffee oligarchy, a reform-minded military leader, and a dictator whose primary tool of government was repression until another burst of prodemocratic activity emerged on the heels of a coup in October 1960.

A group of maverick junior officers, concerned that the military president's repression would incite a Cuban-style revolution, staged the 1960 coup with the aim of allowing a political opening. With an outpouring of popular support, they established a junta that included three civilians and promised to conduct free and open elections. In a mere three months, however, most of the officer corps, wary of potential division within their institution and encouraged by the oligarchy, launched a successful countercoup and installed a traditional brand of military leader. As for the political future of the country, 1961 marked the installation of a new military party that sought to build a representative coalition that would legitimize the leaders chosen from its ranks and therefore ensure the dominance of the old regime. It would last until the coup of 1979.

The new system involved the creation of the military's National Conciliation party (PCN) and the promulgation of a new constitution by a legislature composed of only PCN representatives. The regime produced token reforms in the countryside and the export sector, and favorable coffee prices provided a temporary respite from popular unrest. But changes in electoral laws allowed the opposition to grow, gaining nearly half of the legislature's seats by 1968 and winning the prospect of a free presidential election by 1972.[14] During the 1960s, the industrial sector blossomed, in part as a result of US assistance under the Alliance for Progress and the economic opportunities provided by the Central American Common Market established in 1961. Although this growth did not threaten the traditional economic dominance of the landed elites, it did produce increasing demands for modernization. Labor unions and popular organizations grew progressively militant.

1972 was a critical year for democracy in El Salvador. The blatant electoral fraud perpetrated again by the military to maintain its control convinced many Salvadoran democrats that peaceful change was impossible and substantially weakened the position of those who continued to believe that reform could occur. Several sectors, from right-of-center to the far left of Salvadoran society, had formed a coalition, the National Opposition Union (UNO), which was aimed at defeating the military candidate for the presidency. In a highly charged and bitter campaign, hard-line conservatives opposed to all reform split from the regime and chose their own party candidates, while Duarte appeared to garner enough support to win. The problem was that the military stopped tallying votes upon realizing that its defeat was imminent and announced the next day that its candidate, Col. Arturo Molina, won the election. A revolt was put down and, though Duarte and his vice-presidential candidate Guillermo Ungo threatened a general strike, they were soon forced into exile. The outcome of the 1977 presidential election, won by the PCN candidate, was no less fraudulent. Revolutionaries further pointed to the futility of attempts to achieve change through elections and drew more adherents to the cause of insurrection.

A fundamental characteristic of Salvadoran political life is a long history of unionization and political organization. By the early 1920s Salvadoran laborers, part of a relatively small, but growing industrial class and deeply influenced by the day's ideologically charged debates over anarchosyndicalism, communism, and Leninism, had organized a major labor federation and were seeking legalization of the Communist party.[15] The party was formed in 1930 and led by Farabundo Martí until he was executed for his role in planning the 1932 uprising. Over the course of the century, oppressive regimes strengthened the tradition of popular protest and further radicalized workers and landless peasants. In the words of Robert Leiken, by the 1960s and 1970s, "Salvadoran political life swarmed with broad-based political parties, grass roots movements, coalitions, demonstrations, [and] popular organizations."[16] Leftists heatedly debated which of the socialist models was the correct path to revolution. The long-outlawed Communist party split in 1970 and, after occasionally violent factionalization, ultimately produced the five groups constituting the FMLN, each with its own ideological strategy and tactics.

Toward the end of the 1970s, the military's one-party system was in severe crisis. As originally conceived, it was to maintain the military-dominated alliance with major economic groups, particularly the landed elite, while eventually incorporating some elements of the middle class. But opposition groups on the right and left developed their own means of representation and their own political platforms, and their limited participation in elections and government for a time kept the radical sectors on the margins. The 1972 and 1977 presidential elections exposed this weakness and produced a highly radicalized society characterized by, first, an absence of political intermediaries between the government and major social sectors and, second, increasing confrontation between those sectors and a military with virtually no ability to manage conflict peacefully.[17] Human rights abuses by the military reached new levels as revolutionary groups and organizations grew in strength.

Amid a volatile insurrectionary atmosphere, the one-party system collapsed on October 15, 1979 when another group of reform-minded junior officers deposed the president, Gen. Carlos Humberto Romero. A new junta that included Guillermo Ungo, two military men, and a progressive businessman and that received support from the Social Democrats (MNR, or National Revolutionary Movement), the PDC, and Communists in the Nationalist Democratic Union (UDN), took charge of the government. They called for the abolition of the Nationalist Democratic Organization (ORDEN, a paramilitary agent of repression in the countryside), worker and peasant rights to organize, land reform,

reform of the financial sector, and a more equitable distribution of national wealth. Nearly all of the revolutionary organizations, however, denounced the junta and Communist collaboration with it as opportunism, compliance with military repression, and incompatible with their model of insurrection.

Accounts of El Salvador during the period from the coup to civil war a year and a half later describe a society in upheaval. Immediately after the coup, military-sponsored violence, including the use of the notorious death squads, escalated. The mass organizations responded with large marches and occupations, only to be met again and again with bullets. Attempts to control the army and to calm the revolutionary fervor of the popular organizations were fruitless. By the end of October 1979 alone the army had killed at least 100 protestors at marches, striking factories, and a funeral.[18]

None of the series of juntas that led the government through the 1982 elections could control the violence perpetrated by the military against tens of thousands of civilians. Rather than continue to serve as a democratic facade for the repressive regime, and finding themselves powerless to implement their reforms, civilian junta members resigned, only to be replaced by others who were further to the political right and were willing to disregard the violence and accept the limitation on their power. This process began when Ungo and the Communists resigned on January 3, 1980, along with thirty-seven high-ranking government officials.[19] The Christian Democrats gradually assumed all the new juntas' civilian positions, believing they could institute reforms and produce democratic change. But this move precipitated a party split that witnessed the departure to the political opposition and eventual exile of many of its activists, including Rubén Zamora.

The late José Napoleón Duarte, a leading Christian Democrat, joined the junta in March 1980. He was appointed president before the end of the year by securing US sponsorship and the military's acquiescence. The junta nationalized the banking system and the coffee trade and began a major land reform; none of these, however, affected the ruthlessness of the army. By April 1980, the rebels had launched their bid to overthrow the regime. The political opposition, soon to be forced underground or into exile, coalesced around the Democratic Revolutionary Front (FDR), and the civil war began. In addition, El Salvador became a central focus of US foreign policy at this point. Although the Carter administration had earlier pressured the Salvadoran army to respect human rights, US relations with the military gradually warmed and extensive abuses continued. And as the conflict intensified after the 1979 coup, Carter's greatest fear became another anti-US revolution in the wake of Nicaragua's Sandinista victory in July 1979; he thus initiated the policy of arming the military. Among the more than 8,000 killings in 1980 attributed to the army and security forces[20] was that of Archbishop Oscar Romero.

The Salvadoran military, delighted that a new, conservative US president had made it clear that he would put anticommunism ahead of human rights considerations in foreign policy, went on a killing spree following President Reagan's electoral victory in November 1980. In the process, the security forces took the lives of five leaders of the FDR in late November and, drawing the US public into the crisis, murdered four US church workers a week later. President Carter cut military aid to the regime following the murder of the North Americans but then quickly restored it as the FMLN (a coalition of the five rebels groups united in October 1980) launched its "final" offensive of January 1981, an unsuccessful attempt to grab power before Ronald Reagan assumed office. It is important to note that throughout the war the FMLN, by, for example, assassinating rightist political figures, executing unarmed combatants, and indiscriminately planting land mines, abused human rights to achieve their ends, albeit not nearly in the wholesale fashion demonstrated early on by the military.

The Reagan administration selected El Salvador as the first test case in its crusade against communism in the hemisphere. Large-scale military and economic assistance to bolster the regime, strengthen and professionalize the military, defeat the rebels, support gradual reform, and manage the transition to democratic government was a central element of the strategy. It also required a deep US political and military commitment and the decision to overlook tens of thousands of human rights abuses by the military. The United States and the Salvadoran army became allies to preserve their perceived security interests: The armed forces (and their right-wing allies) supported elections, civilian governments, and limited reforms that were necessary for congressional support of the administration's policy in exchange for institutional preservation, military assistance, and their own aggrandizement. This relationship ensured that efforts toward a negotiated solution and democratization would be put on hold for a decade, and at a heavy cost.

In summary, El Salvador's political culture is not only absent a democratic tradition, but it is also characterized by a long history of brutal repression of successive attempts by citizens seeking a greater voice in civil affairs to achieve political representation. Time after time Salvadorans sought peaceful reform through elections, only to be thwarted by the entrenched power of a reactionary oligarchical-military alliance that ruled in its own interests. After fifty years of increasing polarization, Salvadoran society erupted and a large segment of the population supported armed confrontation to achieve change. Overcoming this legacy in the postwar era will be one of the greatest hurdles of the transition to democracy in El Salvador.

Theoretical Considerations

Political Leadership

The skills, values, and strategies of political leaders have been defined as essential elements in considering the formation of democracy.[21] In El Salvador since early 1989 leadership has been instrumental in the turn toward peace. Because he was a member of ARENA, for example, Cristiani could pursue dialogue with far greater credibility with the Right than Duarte could ever approach. The accords have conferred legitimacy upon and helped strengthen civilian institutions as well as the democratic leaders of those institutions who played central roles in the peace process. President Cristiani, widely praised for his statesmanlike role in the talks, is a primary example, as is Rubén Zamora, the vice-president of the Legislative Assembly. Today, key leaders are fully supporting the peace accords and rallying their followers around them.

Prior to the civil war, Salvadoran democrats never exercised sufficient power to implement change. Throughout the 1980s, the late president Duarte was the leading political figure in the country, and before his role with the juntas from March 1980 to April 1982 he was considered a force for economic and social reform, negotiation, and an end to military impunity. On the positive side, Duarte's economic reforms of 1980 may have helped weaken the landed elite, and from 1984 to 1989 his presidency allowed limited political liberalization and the continuity of the electoral process. But by the end of his term of office, he was widely associated with corruption, bitter division within his party, and, most important, the failure to achieve peace. Allied with the Reagan administration, Duarte led the government when the military killed tens of thousands of Salvadorans and implemented a failed strategy of marginalizing the FMLN; his tenure served to prolong the war and postpone democratization. If democracy was what Duarte desired, his drift to the right and close ties to the United States probably doomed his effort from the start.

Roberto D'Aubuisson, founder of the ARENA party and whose past involvement in death squad activity has been widely reported,[22] was a source of deep distrust for the Left. (He was revered by the Right.) He alone, particularly through his role in the assassination of leading political figures, greatly contributed to the polarization that the country must overcome. Nevertheless, although terminal cancer limited his political influence, he remained ARENA's *caudillo* and played a critical role in the party's move toward dialogue until his death in February 1992. As Cristiani assumed office it was clear that two major tendencies had emerged within ARENA and that D'Aubuisson was the link between them. Cristiani headed the "liberal," probusiness group that promoted the peace process from a weak position at the start of his administration. The second tendency, on the other hand, was characterized by the traditional politicians on the extreme right who continued to seek the elimination of the FMLN and its sympathizers. Over the course of the peace process, the Salvadoran president, having risen within ARENA's ranks as a D'Aubuisson protegé, received his critical support vis-à-vis party members opposed to compromise. According to Cristiani, D'Aubuisson "had always very openly supported the peace process."[23] A savvy politician who quickly noticed the winds of change (which was recognized early on by the Bush administration), he served as the bridge between ARENA's two wings and helped keep the party united.

At a major ARENA convention the weekend after the signing of the New York accord, to which opposition political parties were invited and some attended, D'Aubuisson made a dramatic appearance before the party faithful. He declared that ARENA stood fundamentally for peace and negotiation, and that the Farabundos (FMLN) were Salvadorans, too. This remarkable gesture received a round of applause.[24] With D'Aubuisson's leadership, ARENA became an increasingly legitimate party; its future stability is now, following his death, open to question.

President Cristiani and some of his leading advisers have been insisting since they took office that their government was serious about peace and would achieve it during Cristiani's term. Now that the cease-fire is in place, one must credit Cristiani for his leadership on the path toward a political settlement. As the FMLN recognizes, he has continually faced extreme pressure from the right, particularly from Vice-President Francisco Merino, but over time and with each new step forward he has been able to gradually either win the support of or marginalize the rightist opposition. After the December peace accord, in a gesture called characteristic of his nonantagonistic approach to the rebels, Cristiani praised the FMLN for their courage in the peace talks.[25]

Certainly one of the most important political leaders is Rubén Zamora, the moderate leftist founder of the Social Christian Popular Movement (MPSC; a party of the Democratic Convergence) and now vice-president of the legislature. Choosing to return to El Salvador in

November 1987 at significant risk to his life, he has helped bring the FMLN to the negotiating table, courageously strengthened the electoral prospects of the Democratic Convergence through two elections, and improved his relations with the Right and military by, for example, acknowledging publicly their efforts in support of peace. A thoughtful democrat who has built ties to the US Congress, Zamora appears prepared to run for president in 1994.

Critical decisions have been made by others in leadership roles; these leaders are likely to influence future events as well. Defense Minister René Emilio Ponce's record includes apparent involvement in death squad activity and serious human rights abuse under his command,[26] and evidence strongly indicates that he participated in the decision to murder the six Jesuits priests.[27] Yet Ponce also traveled to New York twice with Cristiani as the military's leading representative to the peace accords, recognized the need for concessions, helped sell them to skeptical officers (a role for which he received politically astute praise from Zamora), and at the time of the final New York agreement met with FMLN commanders.[28] Ponce strongly expressed his desire to see the war come to an end and acknowledges that the army must respect the elections regardless of who wins.[29]

Joaquín Villalobos, the rebels' leading commander known for his ruthless tactics in the prosecution of the war, wrote in April 1989 that the FMLN sought "an El Salvador that is open, flexible, pluralistic, and democratic in both the economic and political spheres."[30] He signaled a radical shift in the FMLN's approach to the conflict: The rebels now sought victory through negotiations, not on the battlefield. Villalobos, like the rest of the FMLN leadership, has maintained that view; today he continues to speak of pragmatism and social democracy. Finally, there is also the progressive-sounding, neoliberal business sector, as exemplified by Roberto Murray Meza, a wealthy, US-educated businessman in the Cristiani mold who is mentioned as a presidential candidate.

To summarize, the trend in Salvadoran political leadership appears to bode well for the future. Democrats occupy important positions of power and their strategic decisionmaking has allowed them to demonstrate that peaceful and fair political competition (and therefore continued change) is necessary and possible. Others have not had their recently discovered commitment to democracy tested but after twelve years of war apparently believe that democracy can best protect their interests, achieve stability, and bring order to the polity. Finally, and ominously, there is a group of individuals, particularly within the armed forces, that will continue to exist after the FMLN's disarmament. They are not democrats but recognize that their weakened position allows them no alternative at present.

The Military

Ending the impunity of the military is the primary issue in the consideration of democracy in El Salvador today. Historically, this institution has been fundamentally antidemocratic, exercising power with the will to resort to extreme violence in order to protect its interests and those of its allies. During the 1980s, the United States vastly expanded the army and provided it with a measure of professionalism. Massive US aid also produced an increasingly corrupt and powerful institution with no more instrinsic respect for human rights or democracy than it had before the war began. For democracy to succeed, however, the military must end its abuses and respect the rule of law, fully come to understand that its interests are a few among many in Salvadoran society, and be subordinated to elected civilian government. A dramatically reduced societal role for the military is imperative. How successful this process will be remains to be seen.

At least two considerations, therefore, are warranted. First is the package of military reforms that have been agreed to and whether it, in tandem with the strengthening of civilian institutions, is sufficient over time to curb permanently the power of the military. The reforms appear strong on paper: The army will be reduced in size to 31,000 members within two years and stripped of absolute control over admission to the military academy in an effort to improve the quality of recruits. A new, independent national police force will be created with a majority of the recruits sought from among those not involved in the war, and the notorious security forces and counterinsurgency battalions are to be disbanded. Internal security and safeguarding the Constitution will no longer be constitutional responsibilities of the army; except under exceptional circumstances and subject to recall by the legislature, its role will be limited to the protection of the nation's sovereignty and frontiers. Furthermore, civilians will assume most of the intelligence functions, military officers will be evaluated by an ad hoc commission so that those considered corrupt and abusive can be purged, and a civilian Commission on Truth will investigate the most notorious human rights cases and make recommendations regarding the prosecution of them in the courts.

But there is still room for concern. The heart of the officer corps may remain intact and it is unclear to what extent the army will actually be reduced because its true size is open to question. Moreover, powerful hard-line members of the army are known opponents of the peace accords. In the January 1992 round of the military's leadership rotation, while two relatively moderate members were promoted to the rank of general, dangerous hard-liners such as Juan Orlando Zepeda (the deputy minister of defense) were allowed to remain in their high-level positions.

A second consideration is the set of factors that led the military to agree to the substantial reforms reached in the peace negotiations. The army was war weary, especially many lower-level officers and soldiers who bore the brunt of the fighting, and has come to recognize that the FMLN cannot be defeated. The armed forces felt the domestic pressure for peace from all sides, including the Cristiani government. In addition, they have faced substantial international oversight and pressure, especially the possibility of a total aid cut by its benefactor, the US government. Under such scrutiny, they, like the FMLN, did not to want to be accused of undermining the peace accords.

The US Congress should receive as much credit as the Bush administration for ensuring that the military supported Cristiani and accepted concessions during the peace process. Congressional pressure, particularly through legislation introduced by Rep. Joseph Moakley (D-Massachusetts), which had the strong support of the House leadership and would have effectively eliminated military funding entirely, was significant. This bill followed Congress's withholding of 50 percent of the administration's military assistance request in 1990 (only to see it quickly released by President Bush for partial, selective disbursement) and a nearly successful attempt by Sen. Christopher Dodd (D-Connecticut) in July 1991 to pass stronger legislation that would have cut aid by 50 percent (including unexpended aid in the pipeline) and effectively prevented the administration from restoring it.

The Bush administration cajoled the military through its pronegotiation allies—General Ponce and Gen. Nelson Gilberto Rubio, the armed forces chief of staff. Although supportive of the peace process, the administration appeared to balance its every step to help protect Cristiani's right flank, appease US officials who wanted to take a harder line against the FMLN, and avoid a perceived potential loss of influence within the Salvadoran army. Its opposition to military aid cuts is a good example of this approach.

As the momentum for peace grew in El Salvador and internationally with each new accord, the ability of powerful officers who opposed the talks to derail the process diminished; the hard-liners were marginalized. Leading officers have become pragmatic, either recognizing the need for a more professional role in society or preparing for the future because they cannot prevent the changes. A large group may not fully realize what was done in the negotiations. In the end, the military's choice was either to buck the strong tide, which would have exacted a heavy political cost from the institution, or to support the process while defending its interests, particularly by securing a broad amnesty and preservation of the officer corps.

One point is clear: The military leadership is now not full of reconstructed democrats. Rather, most officers have decided to compromise because they believe at this juncture that it is the best way to protect their institutional interests.

In short, the armed forces appear willing to accept their reduced role in civil society as provided by the peace accords, and no time can be wasted in fully implementing them. Long after the cease-fire ends and the FMLN has disarmed, the greatest challenge will be to institutionalize these reforms to ensure that the military respects civilian authority over its interests.

State Structure and Strength

Historically, the Salvadoran state, dominated by economic elites and the military to serve their interests (which they messianically equated with El Salvador's), has been extremely weak. As controlled by the ruling sectors, the state's primary function was not an issue of maintaining the rule of law (unless its interests were involved) or providing for the general welfare but rather a question of how it could be used to enforce the socioeconomic status quo.

Deep polarization accompanied the civil war in 1980 and the state fractured. A large sector, as represented by the FMLN and its political allies, rejected the status quo, refusing to accord legitimacy to the state in its present form and thwarting the establishment of state institutions (and creating some of their own) in conflictive zones. Salvadoran politicians of the Right continued to attempt to reform the existing structures, use them for their own political and economic benefit, and support the US-sponsored strategy aimed at defeating the armed opposition. Meanwhile, the Salvadoran state became increasingly dominated by a larger, far more powerful and wealthier military.

In addition, given the conditions of war, many institutional responsibilities were effectively assumed by the US government and entities such as nongovernmental organizations (NGOs) because the state was incapable of meeting them. US power filled the vacuum by becoming deeply involved in all areas of Salvadoran life. Few major government decisions were made without US consultation; the US ambassador was a major center of power. US army advisers were closely linked to the Salvadoran military leadership and involved in all aspects of the war, including, on occasion, combat. And US officials knew that their involvement in Salvadoran political affairs significantly infringed upon El Salvador's sovereignty.[31] US assistance, for example, was seen in civic action projects, earthquake reconstruction, restoration of rebel-damaged infrastructure, aircraft bombs, and helicopter-gunships. It was this deepening involvement that produced the US public's fear in the early 1980s of El Salvador becoming "another Vietnam." International and domestic NGOs, along with other organizations and private companies, filled the vacuum by providing basic services in many areas where the state has been nonexistent for a decade. Establishing themselves much like a parallel government, these organizations provided and will continue to provide during the reconstruction period communications, health care, education, housing, and other developmental needs for Salvadorans.[32]

As the Duarte era demonstrated, as long as the war continued without hope for resolution, the state would progressively weaken. US involvement precluded Duarte's ability to establish his authority and undermined the legitimacy of his government. Given the stalemate on the battlefield, not until the two warring sides achieved an accommodation and agreements on reform, which would eliminate the justification for military intervention in civilian affairs and for the US role, could the state develop independently and secure the power to serve the national interest.

Today, far-reaching—almost revolutionary—reforms in state structure and operation are being implemented as a result of the peace agreements. Negotiators agreed to reduce the military's power and constitutional duties and shift major new responsibilities to civilian government, especially the legislative branch. These changes, along with judicial, electoral, human rights, and socioeconomic reforms and the return of the FMLN to political life, should help significantly to strengthen the state's ability to act on behalf of the nation as a whole and increase its legitimacy in the eyes of Salvadorans. The authority of President Cristiani, who the FMLN in effect has accepted as the official head of state and who has been widely applauded for his leadership role in the peace accords, also has been reinforced.[33] In addition, increasing the size of the legislature to eighty-four seats, a reform implemented prior to the 1991 elections, has improved the lawmaking body's representative capability, as witnessed by the Left's ability to capture nine seats and play an active role. Prior to this point, the elected sixty-seat legislature served primarily its center-right (PDC) to far right (ARENA and the PCN especially) constituencies, the parties that held seats in the assembly. Only in this limited fashion could it have been considered representative.

The Salvadoran state now must develop the capacity to address the needs of the populace. Where they existed, state services collapsed for the first few years of the war, at which point massive US assistance took hold in an effort to stabilize the system. Public expenditures and spending on social welfare declined dramatically, and military spending escalated.[34] The Duarte government was elected in 1984 on a platform that called for expansion of state services and reform. By the end of his presidency, however, he was badly discredited when those plans produced corruption, inefficiency, and economic failure.

In 1989, the international (as opposed to domestic) consensus in favor of "neoliberal" export-oriented economies and decentralization—a reduced state role—reached El Salvador as well. The technocrats of the Cristiani government have adopted with gusto the policies of streamlined government, export diversification promotion, and macroeconomic reform. The macroeconomic results to date have been excellent, but severe social problems in existence for decades and exacerbated by the war have yet to be touched in a significant way. Popular protest and political opposition to Cristiani's new orientation are already strong, helping further define what is arguably the most serious issue facing democratic government in El Salvador: meeting the rising demands for progress in health, education, and welfare through the use of free market, antistatist economics. The failed coup of February 1992 in Venezuela was a signal to the entire region of the explosive potential of this issue. Moreover, in the postwar period the state apparatus will be required to develop in formerly rebel-dominated zones, to create an administrative capacity, to establish the rule of law, and to provide basic services, a difficult process that will require time, money, and continued reconciliation. Restoring the mayors or other officials in areas where the communities have established their own leaders during the war will prove to be politically contentious. This is another daunting challenge, though an approach that emphasizes decentralization and cooperation would be propitious in this regard.

In summary, Salvadorans have agreed to reform the state so that a great majority of the population ultimately can fully accept its legitimacy. As reconciliation progresses and external actors reduce their involvement, the state's legitimacy should strengthen. It remains to be seen if the Cristiani government's economics of decentralization works in a similar vein.

Political Institutions and the Electoral System

Authoritarian regimes lose legitimacy to the extent that public confidence in democratic ideals increases. But in societies like El Salvador where institutions have been so brutal, distorted, and thoroughly corrupted, the marginalized sectors have dissented and resorted to arms to achieve reform, arguing that conditions cannot be changed through democratization.[35] In El Salvador today, now that a peace accord based on a consensus in favor of democratic government is being implemented, support for democracy can generally be expected to grow at the expense of the legacy of authoritarianism. What remains to be determined is to what extent that growth will occur.

The degree of institutionalization of political parties—their number and configuration within the political system—is far more important to the consolidation of democracy than the size of party memberships.[36] Considering the major parties involved in the most recent election (the PDC, ARENA, and PCN as well as the parties of the Democratic Convergence and the UDN on the left), Salvadorans from across the ideological spectrum are represented. The political equivalent of the reintegrated FMLN, either as one or several parties, will add another significant grouping on the left. Political parties may well proliferate in the coming years as electoral reforms allow for more equitable political competition. A lack of vehicles for representation is therefore likely to be less an issue for democratization than the ability of new political parties, especially those on the left, to (1) develop an organization from the top down to the grass-roots level that will enable it to represent effectively its constituency and (2) secure the freedom to operate freely without fear throughout the country.

The degree of party institutionalization is difficult to measure in any context. Although certainly weak by Chilean standards, El Salvador's older and well-organized parties, such as the PDC, PCN, and ARENA, are well woven into the fabric of political life. Founded in 1960, the PDC, once a mass-based, enormously popular, reformist party, saw its left wing break off in 1980 and some of its right wing form a new party following another bitter split in 1988. The PDC's popularity eroded immensely in the 1980s, but it retains support in rural areas and especially the urban middle class. Once the standard-bearer of the right, the PCN is the former military party whose support, though waning, is derived from the organization it established during nearly two decades of one-party rule. Representing the private sector, the landed elite, and the extreme Right is ARENA, which is positioning itself to win the 1994 elections. Undoubtedly, ARENA will campaign as the party that brought peace and a return to economic growth. The party's wealth and excellent organization throughout the country, as well as the patronage it will be able to provide during reconstruction, make it the potential favorite. Serious concerns, however, surround the stability of the party and its ability to unite around a single candidate given Cristiani's inability to succeed himself and D'Aubuisson's death.

The coherence of the Left and its ability to play a major role in, if not lead, the government is a huge unanswered question. Since the return from exile of Rubén Zamora and Guillermo Ungo in November

1987, the CD has developed a base of support in San Salvador (where it ran nearly even with the PDC in 1991). But it has been far less successful in rural areas because of lack of organization. Campaigning has been dangerous in the countryside, where Salvadorans feared retribution if they voted for the Left, and the party has been unable to field many local candidates. By 1994, the FMLN's network will move above-ground and is likely to secure a base of support in areas the rebels dominated militarily. And because it will be the first vote in the absence of war, interest is likely to be at a high level and turnout should be much larger. Will the Convergence and the FMLN (and perhaps the PDC) form an opposition coalition that can widely mobilize popular organizations, campesinos, and workers on a platform of social justice to win a large share of power? The end of the war and implementation of the peace accords should create complete freedom to organize. But the Left may be handicapped by limited time and by the remnants of state-sponsored intimidation associated with support for their platform. If victorious, will the Left be able to assume power and govern effectively, or will society repolarize to produce political stalemate, government failure to respond to basic needs, and even sporadic violence?

The electoral system established over the past decade is also a significant variable in the transition to democracy. Indeed, the absence of free and open electoral politics was at the core of the civil war. Legislative and municipal elections are conducted every three years (the first was held in 1982) and a presidential election occurs every five years (a process that began in 1984).

The Reagan administration organized the 1982 elections to garner support in the US Congress for its counterinsurgency strategy. Given the reality of El Salvador at the time, it was a classic "demonstration" election staged for foreign consumption at the expense of democratic ideals.[37] About 10,000 Salvadorans were being killed each year, the great majority as a result of state-sponsored violence, and the country was in a state of siege (which was lifted briefly for the vote). Arbitrary arrest, torture, and disappearances were a daily fact of life; free organization and association were severely repressed. And despite the atmosphere of terror, the Reagan administration proclaimed the vote to be a major victory for democracy. In reality, however, the circumstances under which it occurred could only have increased the Salvadoran population's cynicism toward the so-called democratic process.

Although the Left did not participate in them, the elections of 1984 occurred in a relatively open environment and were generally regarded as free of fraud. With strong US financial backing, Duarte was elected president. A year later the center-right Christian Democrats won a working majority in the assembly. In the first year of his term, as the repression waned and political activity reemerged, Duarte suddenly called for negotiations. But his efforts to promote peace during his presidency, like his other campaign promises, proved to Salvadorans to be empty public gestures. Taking advantage of the PDC's subsequent political collapse, ARENA regained momentum by winning a legislative majority in 1988 and then the presidency in 1989 with the victory of its moderate-sounding candidate, Alfredo Cristiani.

By the 1991 legislative elections, the Democratic Convergence, which also had participated in the 1989 vote, and the leftist UDN, a new participant, performed surprisingly well despite serious fraud. Also, the FMLN for the first time did not attempt to disrupt the vote, which was the seventh round of elections since 1982 (including the 1984 presidential run-off vote). Although preelectoral violence increased ominously, abuse against civilians was far below its levels from 1980 to 1983, and the space for political activity was substantially higher than it was in the early 1980s.

None of this is to say that El Salvador was becoming a model of democracy. Elections themselves failed to address the issues that appeared to most concern the large majority of Salvadorans: peace and an improvement in the standard of living. All of the elections were conducted under conditions of war. This failure helped produce deep cynicism surrounding the process and profound disillusionment with government institutions. To the extent that it existed, popular confidence in the democratic process diminished. The elections also produced unexpected results that required additional US engineering of the Salvadoran political system.[38] For example, unable to prevent the far Right from winning control of the Constituent Assembly in the 1982 elections, the Reagan administration dispatched an envoy to prevent Roberto D'Aubuisson from being named interim president. To win the presidency in 1984, Duarte received substantial US support and promised peace and reform, progress on which was essentially impossible given the Reagan administration's policies. His failures produced increased polarization, widespread labor defiance of the government, and further disillusionment.

The electoral process from 1984 onward may have been helpful in providing a framework around which other changes could occur, including human rights improvements, the return of the Left and the Right to political life, and an increase in political space. Elections reflected popular sentiment to a degree, as indicated in the rejection of the PDC in the 1989 presidential election. Nevertheless, intimidation and violence accompanied every election, and in 1991 preelectoral violence was greater than it was in 1989;[39] a UDN mayoral candidate was among those killed in early 1991. Whether or not elections occurred, in the absence of structural change the political space that opened could be easily slammed shut, as evidenced by the rise of targeted killings and reemergence of torture in the late 1980s[40] and the collapse of the opening during the November 1989 FMLN offensive. Moreover, the blatant fraud that characterized the 1991 vote raised serious concerns about the Right's willingness to accept gains by the Left, although acceptance of the final count produced promises of reform rather than a rejection of the process.

The critical juncture for elections will be March 1994. At that time all municipal, legislative, and presidential officeholders will be chosen. It should be the country's first honest vote in which, as a result of the peace accords, all Salvadorans are able to participate openly and see their candidate assume office if victorious. If the election is generally accepted as free and fair, and open to all parties, democracy will make great strides.

Two additional institutions—the legislature's role within the presidential system of government and the judiciary—warrant consideration. A legislature controlled by the extreme Right promulgated El Salvador's 1983 constitution following US-mediated negotiations between the PDC and the parties of the Right. It reflected the balance of power at that time within the government and therefore could hardly have been considered a representative document. In fact, the constitution was written in large part by parties interested in reversing or precluding reforms and democratization. The FMLN's decision to accept reform within the context of the 1983 constitution was a significant concession in the peace talks.

Traditionally, the presidential systems of Latin America have exhibited a powerful executive branch coupled with a weak legislature. In El Salvador, however, the unicameral legislature has proved to be unusually strong. Controlling the Constituent Assembly from 1982 to 1985, ARENA and other right-wing legislators ensured that the legislature received extraordinary powers in the new constitution so that they could block the anticipated reform efforts of the PDC. In 1983, they weakened the 1980 land reform and appointed Supreme Court judges and other court officials, ensuring that efforts to investigate human rights abuse would fail. The right-wing parties also stymied all major PDC reform initiatives.[41] Even from 1985 to 1988, when the PDC controlled the presidency and the assembly, the rightists used parliamentary tactics to curtail reform efforts, cooperating only when necessary to ensure the continuance of US assistance.[42] ARENA again appointed Supreme Court judges and judiciary officials when it retook control of the assembly in 1988. In addition, the Salvadoran legislature was responsible for the passage of a broad amnesty in 1987 and the amnesty granted in late January 1992, which also allowed the FMLN to return to political life. In the postwar era, as civilian institutions of government strengthen, it could serve as an important check on the president and thus ensure a stable balance of power in the decisionmaking process.

This tradition of a relatively strong legislature, which recently has become increasingly representative, can be expected to continue. The peace accords dramatically increase the powers of the Legislative Assembly. For example, all political parties represented in the assembly are represented in COPAZ, the commission responsible for overseeing the implementation of the peace agreements. The assembly is responsible for much of the implementing legislation and will have the power to dismiss the presidentially appointed chief of the new National Civil Police and the head of the new State Intelligence Agency, which it also will supervise.

The absence of the rule of law as a result of an essentially nonexistent judicial system was also a root cause of the civil war. Because the judiciary has changed little, disappearances, government harassment of popular organizations and unions, and other violations of human rights continue today. There may well be a period of violence during the cease-fire period as extreme elements attempt to undermine the accords, as evidenced by a bombing attributed to the Right just hours after the final New York agreement was reached. Nevertheless, for democratization to succeed, abuses must end and all individuals who commit crimes must be subject to punishment. And one can expect that the military and the new civilian police force will have their respect for individual rights and the law tested by the demands of traditionally activist Salvadoran population.

In the past, the governments of El Salvador have had neither the will nor the power to investigate and prosecute individuals who had violated human rights. The judicial system was thoroughly corrupted by a long Salvadoran tradition of judicial decisions made on political rather than legal grounds. Only two years ago, Assistant Secretary Aronson declared that Salvadorans "do not have a justice system worthy of its name."[43] Today, despite some progress toward reform, the system is especially weak in its investigative and fact-finding responsibilities.[44] The fact that only one army officer has ever been convicted of a human rights crime, and that it occurred in the Jesuit case, when the government and military were under extreme domestic and international pressure to bring those responsible to justice, is a testament to this reality. Moreover, the January 1992 amnesty may serve to increase a sense of impunity within the armed forces, especially since the judiciary's ability to take effective action against future human rights violators is so uncertain.

One cannot expect the establishment of a fully effective judicial system for perhaps a generation. Like so many other institutions, however, not only is the the judiciary subject to major reforms, but the political will, perhaps the determining factor for the prosecution of human rights violations, has also shifted. Every Salvadoran interested in a stable future for the country recognizes that such abuses must end and that those who commit them in the future must be prosecuted. US secretary of state Baker's warning to the extreme Right in a speech before the Legislative Assembly the day after the peace accord was signed is an indication of the changed political climate.[45] As a result of the constitutional reforms in the April accord, 6 percent of the national budget now must be set aside for the judicial system and Supreme Court judges are to be appointed by a two-thirds majority of the legislature. The presence of ONUSAL, the UN human rights observer team, has made an impression at all levels and already served to raise the standards for human rights protection. ONUSAL tends to put the armed forces on alert that it will quickly spotlight reports of abuse and, given the political pressure on both sides, the demands for prosecution will be strong.[46]

The peace accords include a host of additional reforms that will aid in the administration of justice, such as modifications in the National Judiciary Council to increase its independence, a legal training school, clear delineation of the responsibilities of the military and civilian courts, and a process for purging the armed forces. While noting its deficiencies, especially with regard to the Jesuit investigation, Rep. Joseph Moakley, chair of the house speaker's task force for the case, reported that the judicial system "is making important progress." He added that "reforms resulting from the peace negotiations should provide the judicial system with important additional resources and should lead to the development, in time, of a professional civilian investigative capability."[47]

Civil and Associational Society

The correlation between the strength of independent associational life and the vitality of democracy is highly positive.[48] The history of El Salvador lends great support to this assertion. Although a thorough assessment of the human rights situation is necessary to consider the state of civil society today, it suffices here to mention that serious concerns remain and the human rights issue will be at the center of the country's future. The work of the Commission on Truth and the evaluations of the military will be delicate, and prosecution is unlikely to occur in all of the human rights cases exempted from the recent amnesty.

However, if one considers the level of terror that reigned in the early 1980s in relation to the rest of the decade and to the atmosphere of reconciliation surrounding the peace process, there have been important gains in the quality of associational life. Because of US pressure and because the repression had sufficiently tamed or eliminated the opposition, killings began to subside dramatically and the space for political activity opened haltingly in 1984. The use of torture declined. As labor restrictions were lifted, trade unions and popular organizations moved above ground, many rural cooperatives emerged, and strike activity increased, all of which stretched the limits of the system.[49] Marches and protests became increasingly accepted; the US Embassy reported over 150 strikes and work stoppages from 1985 to the first half of 1986.[50] By the start of the 1990s, overt violence directed against them largely halted. A peace march in early 1990, for example, attracted tens of thousand of leftist organizations and opposition politicians without incident.[51] Over the course of the 1980s it became possible to criticize openly and discuss the reform of the armed forces. Such activity remained dangerous, for the military and the United States routinely treated many government opposition organizations as fronts for the FMLN, but the overall environment clearly improved.

Although subject to intimidation and owner control, the Salvadoran media have become one of the most freely operating in Central America. As of the mid-1980s, television has adopted aggressive and balanced reporting, even interviewing FMLN commanders.[52] Two newspapers today represent the Right and extreme Right, and two others accept government opposition advertisements, one of which serves as a forum for opposition news and opinion.[53] Radio, in addition, provides a wide variety of coverage. ONUSAL reported in November 1991 that though there are a number of restrictions on freedom of expression, the "media express a multiplicity of viewpoints" and provide Salvadorans with "all kinds of news and information" related to the war.[54]

Important developments are occurring today. First, the civil war is ending, which should eventually lead to a climate of increasing trust and have a positive impact on associational life. For example, the FMLN leadership has returned to San Salvador and, if it remains intact, the rebel movement may either organize its own political party or join a coalition for the 1994 elections. Second, exhausted after twelve years of war, the great majority of Salvadorans appear to be overwhelmingly relieved that the fighting is over and to much prefer peaceful competition in the political arena. The strong statements by the FMLN leadership and President Cristiani in support of a new era of free and open politics demonstrate this sentiment.[55] Perhaps the best example of this attitude at the popular level is the dual rallies held two blocks apart to celebrate the January 16, 1992, signing of the peace accords, one by the progovernment forces and another by the FMLN's supporters and combatants. Such an occurrence was unthinkable only weeks earlier.

The third important development is the increasing democratization of society, and the implementation of the peace accords again are the primary testament to that trend. But leftist unions and popular organizations also are recognizing the need to democratize and, depending on the character of their leaders, some already have done so. For example, the National Trade Union Federation of Salvadoran Workers (FENASTRAS), the country's largest union federation, recently reformed its method of voting for its leadership, a move that can be regarded as an important step toward internal democracy.[56]

To summarize, democratization will not reach its potential until the problems of state harassment of legitimate organizations and murder of its citizens for political reasons are resolved. Salvadorans must be able to freely organize and dissent. In addition, full national reconciliation, a goal promoted by the government and the leftist opposition long before the final peace accord, will require much greater interaction among competing organizations and increased understanding by each of them that their interests are among the many to be represented in a democratic society. Signs indicate that such reconciliation will build slowly, but it will build.

International Factors

It is difficult to underestimate the impact of international factors on the development of democracy in El Salvador. Space limitations prevent more than a mention of the primary historical influence: the United States. Located in "America's backyard," a region perceived as vital strategically during the Cold War, El Salvador became an economic dependency of the United States and was assured of protection against Communist invasion. When it came to the promotion of representative government, however, the United States was either allied with the status quo regime as a defense against communism or uninterested.

President Jimmy Carter initiated the policy of arming the Salvadoran military. But in 1981, Ronald Reagan turned El Salvador into a Cold War battleground, and defeat of the enemy required the conversion of a backward army of some 10,000 members into a fighting force of more than 50,000 soldiers well equipped with modern weaponry. The country became mired in US domestic politics to such an extent that the decisions of the US administration and the reactions of the US Congress dramatically altered the long-running course of events. The United States probably prevented an armed revolutionary victory. In large part because the Reagan administration took the approach that it did and because the Congress ultimately approved of that policy, the attempt during the

1980s to build a viable Salvadoran democracy failed.

To support the fight against perceived Soviet expansionism, the United States provided $4.2 billion in military and economic assistance to El Salvador from 1980 to 1991[57] and inserted itself into virtually every facet of Salvadoran life. During the Reagan years, the objective was to build a democratic center around Duarte, reform gradually the traditional antidemocratic institutions, particularly the military, and wage a counterinsurgency war that would marginalize the FMLN. But building a moderate political center without the capacity to draw power away from the extremes produced an irreconcilable contradiction.[58] The Right could play by the rules of the game—elections and acceptance of civilian government—without losing its power. The military grew stronger and more dominant and corrupt with each infusion of aid. Nor could the Left be defeated without sacrificing the democratic framework and the politically acceptable level of human rights abuse on which the policy was constructed. Furthermore, both the US administration and the Duarte government were sponsoring activities that increasingly polarized civil society, such as attempting to destroy antigovernment unions and denying benefits to organizations that did not support the progovernment line.[59]

To be sure, both regional actors, such as the Contadora group, and extraregional players, especially Western European nations and Canada, played an important role in providing support for social change and a political settlement of the war in El Salvador. In 1981, for example, Mexico and France recognized the FMLN-FDR as a "representative political force" entitled to negotiate with the government. But the ability of these actors to take the lead in halting the war was precluded when confronted with strong US opposition to a negotiated peace. Even so, their influence was significant in other ways. Contadora, for example, provided an alternative policy for congressional opponents of the Reagan policy. Futhermore, Latin American and European nations helped convince the rebels in late 1988, when they were engaged in a radical reassessment of their strategy, to pursue a negotiated settlement.[60]

International nongovernmental organizations (NGOs), a wide array of entities that includes private relief and developmental agencies, solidarity groups, churches, and refugee groups, have had an extraordinary impact over the course of the war. Many of them, such as the Americas Watch Committee, were founded in response to the debate over El Salvador. They have served as an alternative policy voice and source of information, especially for Congress; have effectively kept up the "drumbeat" for human rights protection; and have provided invaluable material and emotional assistance to Salvadorans in need. Serving as a link to the outside world, their presence has helped prevent human rights abuse by effectively serving as witnesses to report such activity. International NGOs prompted the phenomenal rise of Salvadoran NGOs, which have served similar functions; all types of NGOs are continuing their efforts during the reconstruction period.

The Soviet Union and its allies in the Eastern bloc, Cuba, and Nicaragua provided directly and indirectly varying levels of military, economic, and diplomatic support for the FMLN. Communism and socialism certainly provided FMLN leaders and combatants with an ideological basis for the war. El Salvador's history, however, provides ample evidence of the homegrown nature of the conflict; the activity of the socialist bloc may have been helpful at times, but it was neither the root of the conflict nor the determining factor in the FMLN's ability to wage war. The FMLN maintained a solid base of domestic support and could rely on alternative international groups sympathetic to their movement for financial and diplomatic backing. Having developed a highly sophisticated insurgency, even after the FMLN lost its allies at the end of the Cold War it was unlikely to be defeated. But neither was it going to win.

A host of often-discussed international factors pushed the Salvadorans and the United States to seek a peaceful settlement and thus begin the process of democratization:

- The collapse of the Soviet Union and the Eastern bloc, the increased isolation of Cuba, and the election of Nicaragua's Chamorro government helped ensure that the FMLN would seriously pursue compromise. Cuba, given its ties to the FMLN and desire to reduce its isolation, has been credited for aiding progress in the peace talks. By late 1988, it had become clear to the FMLN that the Soviets could not underwrite another revolutionary regime, which encouraged the rebels to seek a negotiated solution and the establishment of a "democratic" government.[61]

- Changes in the United States. The 1988 election produced a more pragmatic US administration seeking bipartisan congressional support for its foreign policy and generally searching to extricate itself from the conflicts in Central America. More important, Congress grew tired of financing the war and a ruthless military, whose core nature resounded with the murders of six Jesuit priests.

- The emergence of the United Nations as a vehicle credible to all sides for mediating the negotiations and providing a peacekeeping force. Alvaro de Soto brokered the talks for two years and former secretary-general Pérez de Cuéllar and his deputy nurtured them to fruition as his term expired on December 31, 1991.

189

- Support for peace from the four "friendly" nations—Mexico, Venezuela, Spain, and Colombia—which as a group played a key role in promoting the talks and ensuring their success.

- The turn toward democratic government and market-oriented economies throughout Latin America and, after the collapse of communism, around the world has influenced El Salvador. The Salvadoran private sector, recognizing that economic growth depended on an end to the war, became a strong supporter of dialogue.

- The Esquipulas II Accord and the succession of summits of Central American presidents since its signing in 1987. The presidents have pushed the process of dialogue by repeatedly calling for the FMLN to rejoin Salvadoran political life. They have helped bolster the prospects for democratic government by supporting the revival of the Central American Common Market and the Central American Parliament.

The Bush administration indicated early on that its approach toward El Salvador would be more pragmatic, but not until after a year in office and after absorbing the FMLN's November 1989 offensive did it declare publicly its support for negotiations as the only means to end the war. Generally, from that point on the administration adopted its policies toward the peace talks with the goals of strengthening Cristiani vis-à-vis the military and the far Right and bolstering the pronegotiation faction within the armed forces. This policy meant advocating the government and the military's position in the talks, even though the reforms being pushed by the FMLN were essential to viable democracy, publicly criticizing the UN mediator, and therefore sending mixed messages to Salvadorans about US goals. It also required, as demonstrated by its reaction to the Jesuit case[62] and the failure to support significant cuts in military aid, sacrificing a stronger position on human rights protection to gain leverage within the Salvadoran army. The administration remains the armed forces' key ally, which may continue to prevent it at times from taking decisive action when necessary if it is contrary to the military leadership's demands. US pressure on the military came largely from the Congress, whose willingness to cut military assistance and independent investigation of the Jesuit case tightened the screws on the members of the armed forces opposed to compromise and disrespectful of human rights.

By September 1991, the US administration appeared anxious for the war to end,[63] and an important change was under way by the time of the New York agreement. The agreement signals the warming of relations between the administration and the FMLN. Prior to this juncture, a series of US messages had been sent to the FMLN indicating that their goals and those of the United States were essentially mutual.[64] At least mid-level

US officials at the United Nations mission met directly with the FMLN during the New York talks, and the leadership became convinced that US leverage was available to them and could be helpful to the negotiations.[65] Moreover, the United States reportedly received FMLN requests and listened to its concerns regarding the talks.[66] In December 1991, the United States publicly expressed strong support for the talks, let the rebels know that it understood their concerns, and established direct contact at a higher level with the FMLN negotiators.[67] A high-level US delegation was sent to the final round of talks in December and the United States "made peace" with the FMLN General Command the day after the New Year's Eve accord.[68] Finally, at the final signing ceremony in Mexico City, Secretary of State Baker met the FMLN leadership. The next day he announced before the Legislative Assembly of El Salvador: "We [fully] support these accords—not as a necessary evil to end a bitter conflict, but because we believe the reforms that have been negotiated in the judicial system, the electoral system, the armed forces, and the police will . . . strengthen El Salvador's democratic institutions, enlarge the scope of human rights, and promote national reconciliation."[69]

A major issue is to what extent the United States and the rest of the international community provide funding for the reconstruction of El Salvador. One would think that the United States, having financed the war, would assume a large part of this responsibility. Yet despite the words of support today, this seems far from certain. Secretary of State Baker has stated that the administration "would like to try and maintain at least, certainly the level of our support, and that we would seek to avoid efforts to reprogram those funds to other purposes."[70] Given Baker's refusal to make a specific pledge of funds, his words are not reassuring. The chair of the House subcommittee on Latin America has noted that the United States is likely to be far less generous in building peace than it was in funding war.[71] Reconstruction of the Soviet Union and Eastern Europe are placing great demands on United States assistance during an election year in which foreign aid, because of the recession, is much more sensitive than it usually is.

The Bush administration has informed the Cristiani government that its aid generally will continue to decline, which is part of the reason why El Salvador turned to the World Bank and other international organizations for support for its original $1.8 billion reconstruction effort. The Agency for International Development's (AID) economic funding levels fell for four years prior to the administration's FY 1993 request.[72] One former senior US economic official believes that after two years US economic support funds for El Salvador will virtually disappear and that development aid will fall significantly as well.[73] The consensus is that the United States wants to "withdraw" from Central America.

There may well be a return to benign neglect.

Internationally, multilateral organizations, countries such as Japan, Canada, Europe, and the four "friends" are being asked to contribute. Some have responded favorably. But, especially in countries like Germany, El Salvador is competing with Eastern Europe and the former Soviet Union's massive demands for development aid. The World Bank presently is helping prioritize elements of the Salvadoran reconstruction plan to see which can be funded and was expected to seek pledges from participating donors by late March 1992.

Socioeconomic Development, Economic Policies, and Performance

The socioeconomic development of El Salvador is a well-documented history of inequality that equals any in the hemisphere. Whether controlled by the infamous "14," 100, or 200 leading families, wealth was extremely concentrated in the hands of a small, landed elite. The great majority of the remaining Salvadorans were landless, illiterate, and living in deep poverty. Estimates vary but suggest that less than 2 percent of the population owned 60 percent of the land.[74] Although in the 1960s and 1970s a small middle class developed in the industrializing urban centers, particularly San Salvador, the country remained predominantly a rural society. Yet another source of discontent emerged during this period, one with which Salvadorans were well-acquainted, as increasing land concentration forced peasants off the farms and into the cities, where many could find only menial jobs. Land tenancy remained an explosive issue at the dawn of civil war and continues to be today.

The economy collapsed during the early years of the civil war conflict and then stagnated in the second half of the 1980s. Although the reforms of 1980 did not break the back of the oligarchy, its power was weakened relative to an enlarged and enormously more powerful military. The nationalizations in the banking and export sectors helped ensure deep and lasting private-sector distrust of the Christian Democrats. Because of the war, resistance on the right and left, and substantial waste and corruption, the Duarte presidency could not restore growth to the economy or deliver his promised social and economic reforms even with the tremendous levels of aid received from the US. By 1989, the real per capita income of Salvadorans was nearly 28 percent below what it was in 1979.[75] Living standards plummeted: The basic family basket of food, clothing, and housing service cost from 100 percent to 528 percent more in 1988 than in 1978,[76] and inflation today continues to erode purchasing power. Salvadorans also suffered severe deterioration in the condition of their health and education.

The rise of the Cristiani government mirrors the post–Cold War international consensus around neoliberal market-oriented economics. A businessman himself, Cristiani has restored private-sector confidence and growth through ambitious economic reform, including privatization efforts, export diversification, free trade policies, macroeconomic stabilization, and tax, price, and exchange rate reform. The World Bank calls El Salvador's 1990 economic performance "impressive"[77] and, according to the Inter-American Development Bank, the country appears to be "heading toward a situation of sustainable growth."[78] Cristiani's stabilization and adjustment policies are credited with producing a growth rate of an estimated 3.4 percent for 1990—the highest since 1978—and reducing inflation by more than four percentage points despite the doubling of oil prices.[79] The International Monetary Fund (IMF), Paris Club, Inter-American Development Bank, and World Bank have responded favorably with loans or credit arrangements.

At the same time, however, the basic needs of a population that was deeply impoverished long before the war and then further distressed during the conflict demand prompt and effective attention. It is no surprise that the government's free market ideology has been heavily criticized as a laissez-faire approach that favors the wealthy and places the costs of adjustment on the shoulders of the neediest sectors of the population.[80] Cristiani has developed a "social safety net" in the areas of health, education, housing, and nutrition, but its level of commitment is questionable and, moreover, it is likely to be inadequate in view of the severe problems facing Salvadoran society. Several of these problems are as follows:

- The number of Salvadorans living in extreme poverty, that is, those who were unable to purchase a basic basket of food, increased from 26 percent of the population in 1985 to 35 percent in 1988. Such poverty is especially severe in rural areas.[81]
- More than 60 percent of infant morbidity and mortality is related to infectious diseases.[82] About 50 percent of children under five years of age are malnourished.[83]
- Because of high population density and poor sanitary conditions, a national health emergency was declared on January 5, 1991, to combat outbreaks of cholera.
- The average Salvadoran attends school for 4.5 years; some 31 percent of the adult population is illiterate.[84]
- Some 42 percent of the population is without access to health services.[85]
- Tens of thousands of returning war refugees are in need of

resettlement assistance. Ultimately, as many as 24,000 could return from Central America and 200,000 from both the United States and Mexico. Many thousands of displaced within the country require aid as well.

In addition, the government faces a stiff challenge to maintain substantial economic growth and provide a far higher level of employment. Although there has been progress in promoting nontraditional exports, El Salvador remains highly dependent on coffee for half of its export earnings. Coffee prices are near historic lows today and Salvadorans cannot count on the good weather that spurred the agriculture sector–led growth of 1990. And although a delay of deportation is likely, the United States is pressing for the return of hundreds of thousands of Salvadoran refugees who have been granted a temporary waiver of departure to their homeland. Their huge remittances do far more to sustain the economy, which is suffering from large fiscal and current account deficits, than the earnings from traditional exports. Meanwhile, a great many Salvadorans at home appear to be finding nothing in the Cristiani government's macroeconomic successes to improve their economic well-being. A recent poll conducted by the Central American University of San Salvador found that 65 percent of the population believed that the economic situation was worse in 1991 than 1990.[86]

As the negotiators affirmed in their agreements to end the war, "One of the prerequisites for the democratic reunification of Salvadoran society is the sustained economic and social development of the country."[87] Their comprehensive accord on economic and social questions address many key issues in this regard, such as providing a method for resolving land tenure disputes through purchase of occupied land with low interest loans at market prices or through government provision of substitute land; consumer protection provisions; the strengthening of social welfare programs; and measures to alleviate the social cost of structural adjustment programs. The end of the war alone will help prevent further decline in living standards and improve the economy, especially if it initiates the transfer of military spending, which comprises an extraordinary 27.9 percent of the national budget,[88] to investments in social welfare.

Nevertheless, serious disputes over the economic and social agreements are bound to arise, especially over land tenure, and the country is in need of substantial long-term international support at a time when great demands are being placed on a limited pool of funds. Cristiani has developed an ambitious $1.8 billion reconstruction plan, but he appears to be settling for an amount of about $1 billion. Although the plan is aimed at developing the conflictive zones and aiding Salvadorans hardest hit by the conflict, it remains to be seen how much funding will be received, how it is allocated, and which sectors of the country benefit most.

The Prospects for Democracy

Today, although it will not be an easy task as international interest wanes over the long term, one can be cautiously optimistic about El Salvador's prospects for democracy. Above all, the peace accords address in a positive way many of the factors that are considered to be essential to the development of democratic government; in this sense, El Salvador *is* starting over. Several institutions either have received major new responsibilities or are being created to fulfill critical duties for the first time. In fact, some provisions of the peace settlement, such as the work of ONUSAL, a public process of purging the military, and the establishment of a new civilian police force, are attracting attention because they break new ground among the democratic transitions of Latin America. The accords, of course, must be fully implemented, and their success today will directly influence the quality of democracy in the years ahead. Fortunately, it appears that most Salvadorans desperately want to live in peace and may go to surprising lengths to work together in a spirit of compromise in an effort to secure it. In addition, international pressure and the presence of more than 1,000 United Nations peacekeepers will help bind the parties to their commitments.

Cause for optimism comes not only from the reforms delineated in the agreements: It also derives from the societal change brought about by the process of coming to agreement, which may leave a permanent imprint on Salvadoran political culture. Although El Salvador's history is a nightmare for the development of democracy, as emphasized by President Cristiani as well as the FMLN at the Mexico City signing ceremony, Salvadorans can learn from the lessons of the past, and indications are that they are willing to do so in their approach to conflicting demands. Reconciliation is occurring, although it may take years to do so fully. For the first time, former enemies are coming together to discuss their differences and are at least willing to acknowledge their opposition's concerns. Meetings between members of the army's High Command and of the FMLN's General Command are the most vivid examples of this process; its significance should not be underestimated.

In addition, a number of today's key leaders are strong democrats (they could be setting standards for other Salvadorans) and the discourse

195

of even those whose democratic credentials are suspect clearly favors democracy. The political party system is fairly well developed, and parties from across the ideological spectrum are poised to play a central role in 1994. Even if serious conflict arises between them, they will likely choose compromise over rejection of the electoral process. Moreover, civil society, notably trade unions and popular organizations, is democratizing.

In short, full implementation of the accord to the satisfaction of both parties is clearly the paramount concern. But, there does appear to be a momentum building slowly from the ashes of war that should for some time bolster the movement toward democracy. Salvadoran society may move only slightly forward by the end of this decade, but it will take a series of major crises to reverse the process under way today, as evidenced by the jubilation that has accompanied it.

Economic progress is a critical variable. Sound policy and the industriousness of the Salvadoran people will be important to the country's return to sustained economic growth. But prosperity will need to be far more evenly distributed to deepen the state's popular legitimacy and thus the stability of the new regime. The success of reconstruction over the next few years will largely determine the extent to which society polarizes over the economic issue. As the elections approach, the Left will continue to demand, with justification, a larger social component in the government's economic plans, but destabilizing rhetoric should be cooled by reactivation of the economy, a desire to remain loyal to the new system, the international consensus supporting a free market orientation, and, most important, a willingness to compromise. Leftist politicians and FMLN leaders today support, if not privatization, at least a mixed economy of both private and collective ownership. Nevertheless, if the Cristiani government is widely perceived as unresponsive to the basic needs of the poor and middle-class sectors, and if the opposition parties take up the banner of populism in strident opposition, the 1994 election may occur in a tense atmosphere of instability—and democratization will face a stiff challenge. Thus, it is all the more incumbent upon the United States and the international community to honor their commitments to the implementation of the peace accords and support successful long-term reconstruction. The United States should remain politically engaged in El Salvador and, as the FMLN argues, keep its military advisers in place. Continued involvement in a carefully balanced fashion is likely to have a positive bearing on the quality of democracy that develops well after the 1994 vote. US domestic problems and the country's commitments elsewhere, Congress's general fatigue with the issue of El Salvador, and Western Europe's concerns to the East are therefore worrisome.

The peace accords should be viewed as the turning point in a process that began eight years ago, one rooted in Salvadoran society and continuing today. In this regard, the Salvadoran experience corresponds to classic theories about democratic transition.

El Salvador's transition should be viewed as passing through three phases. The first phase is the period from 1984 to fall 1991, characterized by sporadic liberalization. A transition begins when the redefinition and extension of rights that define liberalization appear in tandem with the dissolution of an authoritarian regime.[89] Prior to 1984, the regime was neither more open nor less authoritarian than it was prior to the 1979 coup, despite the collapse of the military system, limited reforms, the series of civilian juntas, and the 1982 election of a legislative assembly. From 1980 to 1983, Salvadorans were being killed by the state or with its acquiescence at a rate of at least 800 per month. By 1984, however, human rights violations declined significantly, political activity re-emerged, and sectors of civil society increasingly tested the bounds of acceptable behavior. Despite its conditional nature, this period continued through the start of the negotiations and can be said to have concluded when the first agreements reached between the Cristiani government and the FMLN were implemented in 1991. It must be noted that even if liberalization proves to be uneven, the emergence of increased political freedom is a significant change in the behavior of an authoritarian regime.

This phase confirms a few additional maxims of transition theory. The human rights situation demonstrated that it was predicated on the arbitrary use of government power. It showed that elections alone do not produce democratic government. Also, over time, the freedoms to associate and dissent gradually accumulated and became quasi-institutionalized to the extent that it became costly to eradicate them, the price being in the case of El Salvador a loss of vital US military support and international condemnation.[90]

The second and current phase of the transition is democratization, a period when the rights of citizenship are applied to individuals and institutions or extended to cover issues, such as human rights, or institutions, such as the armed forces, that had not been accorded them or subjected to them previously.[91] In July 1990, the FMLN and the Cristiani government signed an accord on human rights and the following April agreed to a series of constitutional reforms. When the human rights and electoral reforms were ratified by the new assembly (September 11 and 25, 1991, respectively) and when ONUSAL became operative (October 1, 1991), El Salvador began democratizing. With the implementation of the reforms of the final agreement and the return of the FMLN to political life under its terms, this process is deepening. The two

197

most important elements of the accords in this regard are the military reforms and the creation of a new national police force. These two rein in the armed forces so that, as in any political democracy, they can gradually be subordinated fully to civilian rule. The creation of a new civilian police to maintain order and separate the defense and security functions of the state eliminates the military's primary justification for intervention in civilian affairs.

Given the stalemate in the Salvadoran conflict, the rights accompanying democratization—rights that would entail a weakening of the power of the military and oligarchy—could be accorded only through the process of negotiation. The negotiations represented societal accommodation, the "historic compromise" that was necessary to give the process of liberalization credibility in the eyes of the FMLN and ultimately to secure the consent of both sides to play by a new set of democratic rules.[92] They also represent the gradual acceptance of the uncertainty of the democratic process—the growing recognition that no group's interests are fully protected in a viable democracy.[93] A major reason for the Reagan administration's policy defeat is that it promoted societal division. By seeking military victory over the FMLN, deliberately increasing rather than seeking to halt polarization, its attempt to build democracy was doomed to failure.

The third phase of the Salvadoran transition will be democracy itself, and it will begin with the successful conclusion of free and fair "founding" elections, the drama-filled competition for national office that is a major contributing factor in successful democratization.[94] Until the war ended and the FMLN was able and willing to rejoin political life, such an event was impossible. But given the current situation, El Salvador's next set of national elections, scheduled for March 1994, will undoubtedly serve this function. If successful, and the indication as of this writing is that it will be, the 1994 vote will at long last launch El Salvador's democracy.

All eyes in Salvadoran political life are on the 1994 election because it will be a major struggle for power as well as a critical test of postwar stability, a trial that should help consolidate the institutional changes implemented in the preceding two years. In view of the atmosphere surrounding the peace accords, one can reasonably be assured that the large majority of Salvadorans on the right and left will be loyal to the system and that the disloyal extremes face isolation should they pose a challenge. This period will indeed be the heroic moment for Salvadoran political parties, a time when they will occupy the center stage of the political drama. Thus, the fact that all sides of the ideological spectrum—ARENA, the PDC, and the Left (the Democratic Convergence and what becomes of the FMLN's network as it returns to political life)—have known vehicles through which their views can be articulated and represented before the state with some effectiveness is positive.

A radically altered international climate—the end of the East-West competition of the Cold War, the democratic revolution worldwide, and the move away from state-centered government—should work toward stabilizing the transition. The Cristiani government is putting the country back on its feet from a macroeconomic standpoint, which is important to long-term development and to the provision of reconstruction assistance from the United States and international lending organizations. As the combatants disarm, there is likely to be a window of international sympathy for the reconstruction effort that will bolster the momentum of the political arena. Although Salvadorans are not as of this writing speaking with one voice on reconstruction, the peace agreements on social and economic reforms and the government's apparent willingness to consider the views of all sectors in developing its plan should help them take advantage of favorable international sentiment.

A host of factors leave room for serious concern. There is no question that the country faces a difficult two-year transition and problems that stand firmly in the path of democracy. Mutual distrust runs deep. The cease-fire period may be violent as elements that are opposed to the compromises reached, particularly rightist extremists who view the accords as the FMLN's Trojan horse, attempt to disrupt the process of reconciliation.[95] The government and the FMLN will be required to demonstrate the same unity of purpose witnessed when the accords were signed, which is likely to prove increasingly difficult as the "honeymoon" period ends, differences over the interpretation of the accords emerge, elections approach, and politicking begins. Moreover, the strong legacy of authoritarianism—the institutional politicization and corruption—left by decades of military rule, will continue to plague Salvadoran society. Institutions cannot be changed overnight and will remain weak and subject to corruption for some time under the best of circumstances. Human rights abuse remains a principal flashpoint. The armed forces will not recede quietly from civilian affairs. And though US involvement is required, especially in the military sphere, the extent to which it will continue is uncertain.

In addition, the war exacted a tremendous cost from the society. Social problems are immense. Social injustice was a major precipitating factor of the revolution, and conditions for Salvadorans have severely deteriorated over the past twelve years. Salvadorans are likely to expect rapid socioeconomic change over the coming years, but can these expectations be met without renewed polarization, by a government whose policies could produce renewed concentration of wealth and whose active support for progress in standards of health, education, and welfare is uncertain? Last but perhaps most important in this regard is the poor climate for raising funds for reconstruction and development given the demands in Eastern Europe and the Soviet Union; total US assistance continues to decline.

The essence of the peace accords and the future of the country lie in the full acceptance by Salvadorans, especially the military, of both the uncertainty and the certainty that characterizes democracy. In a democracy, no party is able to intervene if the new power struggles are perceived as prejudicial to its interests. Yet, all parties secure a level of certainty in exchange: the knowledge that the game will be played according to democratic rules. To rally the party faithful around the negotiations at that convention in fall 1991, Roberto D'Aubuisson told his followers to accept a return of the FMLN because the Farabundos would be defeated in the political battle. But the fact is that he could not have guaranteed such an outcome. As both of these elements, the uncertainty and the certainty of the process, become institutionalized, democracy will grow.

Socialization, the process by which citizens ultimately achieve equal rights and obligations and derive equal benefits from the product of society, deserves a final consideration.[96] Salvadorans now have chosen democracy, a method that is often slow but has obvious benefits over reactionary despotism and revolutionary socialism, to achieve these ends. Even so, the speed with which they are achieved through institutional reform will explain a great deal about the quality of El Salvador's new system of government.

Notes

Note: In addition to the sources cited below, the observations made in this chapter are derived in part from numerous interviews and conversations conducted from 1991 through January 1992 in connection with the Wilson Center's conferences on El Salvador. I extend my deep appreciation to all of those individuals who gave their time to this research, without which these insights would have been impossible. This chapter was completed in late February 1992.

1. This definition of democracy is found in Guillermo O'Donnell and Philippe C. Schmitter, *Transitions from Authoritarian Rule: Tentative Conclusions About Uncertain Democracies* (Baltimore: The Johns Hopkins University Press, 1986), p. 7.

2. For this discussion of democratic transition, I use the concepts developed by O'Donnell and Schmitter in *Tentative Conclusions,* pp. 6–11.

3. Tim Golden, "Ending a Decade of U.S.-Financed War: The Salvadorans Make Peace in a Negotiated Revolution," *New York Times,* January 5, 1992, p. E3.

4. This framework is based on the concepts developed in Larry Diamond, Juan J. Linz, and Seymour Martin Lipset, eds., *Democracy in Developing Countries: Latin America,* (Boulder: Lynne Rienner Publishers, 1989), pp. 2–52.

5. Victor Bulmer-Thomas, *The Political Economy of Central America Since 1920* (New York: Cambridge University Press, 1987), p. 34.

6. Enrique A. Baloyra, *El Salvador in Transition* (Chapel Hill: University of North Carolina Press, 1982), p. 7.

7. James Dunkerley, *The Long War: Dictatorship and Revolution in El Salvador* (London: Verso, 1985), p. 13.

8. Thomas P. Anderson, *Matanza: El Salvador's Communist Revolt of 1932* (Lincoln: University of Nebraska Press, 1971), pp. 6–7.

9. Dunkerley, *The Long War*, p. 22.

10. Ibid., p. 22.

11. Ibid., pp. 32–33.

12. Baloyra, *El Salvador in Transition*, pp. 11–12.

13. Anderson, *Matanza*, p. 152.

14. Ibid., p. 155.

15. Dunkerley, *The Long War*, p. 21.

16. Robert S. Leiken, ed., *Central America: Anatomy of Conflict* (New York: Pergamon Press, 1984), p. 112.

17. Baloyra, *El Salvador in Transition*, p. 49.

18. Dunkerley, *The Long War*, pp. 139–140.

19. Raymond Bonner, *Weakness and Deceit: U.S. Policy and El Salvador* (New York: New York Times Book Company, 1984), p. 162.

20. Americas Watch Committee and the American Civil Liberties Union, *Report on Human Rights in El Salvador*, January 26, 1982 (New York: Vintage Books, 1982), pp. xxvi–xxvii. Americas Watch took this figure from the legal aid office of the archdiocese of San Salvador.

21. Diamond, Linz, and Lipset, *Democracy in Developing Countries*, pp. 14–15.

22. D'Aubuisson reportedly began organizing death squads in the late 1970s. In the early 1980s, he reportedly conspired to overthrow the government at least once, almost certainly masterminded the assassination of Archbishop Romero, organized death squads from inside the national Constituent Assembly, and was involved in a plot to assassinate the US ambassador to El Salvador at the time, Thomas R. Pickering.

23. As quoted in Richard Severo, "Roberto D'Aubuisson, 48, Far-Rightist in El Salvador," *New York Times*, February 21, 1992, p. A19.

24. This event was described by two sources, one of whom attended.

25. Lee Hockstader, "Cristiani as Peace Catalyst," *Washington Post*, January 2, 1992, p. A20.

26. Rep. Howard L. Berman, Sen. Mark O. Hatfield, and Rep. George Miller, "Barriers to Reform: A Profile of El Salvador's Military Leaders," A Report to the Arms Control and Foreign Policy Caucus, US Congress, May 21, 1990, pp. 13–15.

27. Statement of Rep. Joe Moakley, chair of the Speaker's Task Force on El Salvador, November 18, 1991, pp. 3–6. Citing "experienced, respected, and serious" sources, Moakley stated that "the decision to murder the Jesuits was made at a small meeting of officers held at the Salvadoran Military School on the afternoon prior to the murders (November 15, 1989). Among those present were . . . Gen. Emilio Ponce." Conversations with others who have either been deeply involved in the investigation of the Jesuit case or closely follow the Salvadoran military lend even further weight to this view of Ponce's role.

28. Lee Hockstader, "Seen as Peace Accord's Big Losers, Salvadoran Armed Forces Stoic So Far," *Washington Post*, January 10, 1992, p. A14.

29. Ponce is known as a weak personality who makes decisions based on

consensus and is likely to be passive when confronted with the wishes of his hard-line colleagues. Confidential interview with a US military official, fall 1991. See also Berman, Hatfield, and Miller, "Barriers to Reform," pp. 13–15.

30. Joaquín Villalobos, "A Democratic Revolution for El Salvador," *Foreign Policy*, no. 74 (Spring 1989): 121.

31. Tom Carothers, *In the Name of Democracy: U.S. Policy Toward Latin America in the Reagan Years* (Berkeley: University of California Press, 1991), p. 46.

32. See Gustavo J. Arcia, "The Economic Future of Central America," draft paper presented at Duke Univeristy, Research Triangle Institute, April 11, 1991.

33. According to an FMLN official, "Cristiani deserves a gold medal. I respect him. He has done a great service to the country." As quoted in James LeMoyne, "Out of the Jungle: El Salvador's Guerrillas," *New York Times Magazine*, February 9, 1992, pp. 29, 56.

34. From 1979 to 1987, government expenditures on defense and interest spending increased from 13 percent to 41 percent. Social and economic expenditures declined from 33 percent of GDP from 1980 to 1983 to 19 percent in 1988; over the same period, real spending per capita on social welfare fell 40 percent. See "El Salvador: The Rehabilitation of the Social Sectors," report prepared by the World Bank for the first meeting of the Consultative Group for El Salvador (subject to final approval), World Bank, May 15–16, 1991, p. 1.

35. Diamond, Linz, and Lipset, *Democracy in Developing Countries*, p. 20.

36. Ibid., p. 21.

37. Edward S. Herman and Frank Brodhead, *Demonstration Elections: U.S.-staged Elections in the Dominican Republic, Vietnam, and El Salvador* (Boston: South End Press, 1984), p. 5.

38. Terry Karl, "Exporting Democracy: The Unanticipated Effects of U.S. Electoral Policy in El Salvador," in *Crisis in Central America: Regional Dynamics and U.S. Policy in the 1980s*, Nora Hamilton et al., eds. (Boulder: Westview Press, 1988), pp. 187–188.

39. Presentation by Cynthia Arnson, associate director, Americas Watch Committee, at the Woodrow Wilson Center, Washington, D.C., April 25, 1991, the text of which is published in this volume.

40. Americas Watch Committee, *El Salvador's Decade of Terror: Human Rights Since the Assassination of Archbishop Romero* (New Haven: Yale University Press, 1991), p. 18.

41. Benjamin C. Schwarz, *American Counterinsurgency Doctrine and El Salvador: The Frustrations of Reform and the Illusions of Nation Building* (Santa Monica: RAND, 1991), p. 59.

42. Ibid., p. 59.

43. Assistant Secretary of State Bernard A. Aronson, transcript of hearing before House Foreign Affairs Subcommittee on Western Hemisphere Affairs, January 24, 1990, p. 37.

44. Report of the Economic and Social Council, "Situation of Human Rights in El Salvador," United Nations General Assembly, forty-sixth session, October 11, 1991, p. 23.

45. Referring to a bombing attributed to the extreme Right hours after the final agreement was announced on December 31, 1991, Baker called those who threaten the peace process "traitors to the Salvadoran nation." He added: "The United States (and, I believe, others in the democratic community) will provide whatever assistance is possible to the Government of El Salvador to ensure that anyone who threatens the peace process through violence is prosecuted to the

full extent of the law." Although the extent to which it is honored remains to be seen, this declaration certainly represents an important change in attitude. Secretary of State James A. Baker, III, "The Hemisphere's Hopes for Peace," *U.S. Department of State Dispatch*, Bureau of Public Affairs, Washington, D.C., vol. 3, no. 3, January 20, 1992, p. 34.

46. These observations about ONUSAL are drawn from a presentation by David Holiday, Americas Watch office, San Salvador, at the Washington Office on Latin America, Washington, D.C., October 11, 1991.

47. Statement of Rep. Joe Moakley, chair of the Speaker's Task Force on El Salvador, November 18, 1991, p. 2.

48. Diamond, Linz, and Lipset, *Democracy in Developing Countries*, p. 35.

49. Americas Watch Committee, *El Salvador's Decade of Terror*, p. 27.

50. Confidential interview, July 29, 1989.

51. "Conmemoración del primero de mayo: signos de concertación," *Estudios Centroamericanos* (ECA), April/May 1990, nos. 498-499: 320-321.

52. Tom Barry, *Central America Inside Out: The Essential Guide to Its Societies, Politics, and Economies* (New York: Grove Weidenfeld, 1991), p. 186. See also, "The Situation in Central America: Threats to International Peace and Security and Peace Initiatives," Second Report of the United Nations Observer Mission in El Salvador (ONUSAL), New York, November 15, 1991, p. 36.

53. Barry, *Central America Inside Out*, pp. 186-187.

54. "The Situation in Central America: Threats to International Peace and Security and Peace Initiatives," November 15, 1991, p. 36.

55. At the January 16, 1991, ceremony in Mexico City, Shafik Handal declared that the FMLN signed the accord "to create a politically, ideologically, economically and socially pluralist country as the basis for participative and representative democracy and stable peace." Cristiani recognized that the conflict was deeply rooted in Salvadoran society and declared that "we want a democracy with no limits other than the law. We want it to be extremely democratic. We are committed to promoting human rights, not only political but social and economic rights." "FMLN's Handal Speaks" and "President Cristiani Speaks" *Foreign Broadcast Information Service Daily Report*, January 17, 1992, pp. 21, 27.

56. Telephone interview with Tom Gibb, freelance journalist for the *Washington Post*, October 29, 1991.

57. Figures drawn from table prepared by K. Larry Storrs and Marian J. Cotter, "Table 1. U.S. Aid and Credits to El Salvador, FY 1980-1992," Congressional Research Service, September 20, 1991.

58. Carothers, *In the Name of Democracy*, p. 45.

59. A confidential 1986 CIA memorandum (apparently to the US secretary of state) notes that a leftist union, the National Union of Salvadoran Workers (UNTS), has "charged AIFLD [The American Institute for Free Labor Development], the [US] embassy, and the PDC with attempting to destroy UNTS (A charge we accept)." AIFLD, the document adds, should continue "to pick off UNTS member unions one-by-one." AIFLD activities were almost entirely funded by the US government. Document reprinted in Frank Smyth, "Union-busting in El Salvador: AIFLD and Duarte's Christian Democratic Party," draft paper prepared for the Johns Hopkins University School of Advanced International Studies, September 1987, p. 25. See also Americas Watch, *Labor Rights in El Salvador* (New York: Americas Watch Committee, 1988), pp. 14-15, 102-103.

60. See Gary Bland, "The Prospects for Peace in El Salvador," *SAIS Review*

(Summer–Fall 1990): 193–196.

61. Bland, "The Prospects for Peace in El Salvador," pp. 194–195. According to an FMLN official, "There are people in the FMLN who would never have signed this accord if it had not been for the collapse of the socialist camp."Quoted in LeMoyne, p. 56.

62. For example, US Ambassador to El Salvador William Walker insinuated that the FMLN was responsible for the murders as late as January 1990. Also, the administration referred to Rep. Moakley's statement in November 1991, which implicates high-level Salvadoran army officers in a cover-up of the Jesuit killings, as simply accusations.

63. For example, on August 1, 1991, the United States and Soviet Union sent letters to the UN secretary-general asking him to become more directly involved in the peace talks and citing the UN as a venue. (One can be certain that the New York talks were coordinated in advance with US officials.) Also, the Bush administration had criticized mediator Alvaro de Soto for not moving more aggressively to resolve differences between the two sides. See Shirley Christian, "U.S. and Soviet Help Sought in Salvadoran Talks," the *New York Times*, August 21, 1991, p. A7.

64. The most public of these was the US ambassador to El Salvador's meetings with FMLN commanders in a proguerrilla zone. According to an individual who helped arrange the meetings, the ambassador traveled to Santa Marta on two occasions despite strong opposition from within the embassy, and both were planned in advance. See also Lee Hockstader, "U.S. Envoy, Colonel Meet Salvadoran Rebels," *Washington Post*, September 13, 1991, p. A33. Hockstader quotes the ambassador as saying that the Labor Day 1991 trip was an initial attempt to open lines of communication and create trust.

65. The US alternate representative to the UN, in making a strong call for free and safe political expression (and commending the FMLN for its "flexibility and seriousness" in the talks and noting that the United States "takes seriously the security and economic concerns of former combatants after a peace settlement"), called the talks in New York in September 1991 a "break-through." See Statement by Alexander F. Watson, "The Situation in Central America: Threats to International Peace and Security and Peace Initiatives," United States Mission to the United Nations Press Release, December 5, 1991. At the January 16, 1992, signing ceremony, the FMLN representative declared, "The FMLN wishes to recognize the U.S. Government for its cooperation so the negotiations would bear fruit, particularly the round of negotiations last September in New York." See "FMLN's Handel Speaks," *Foreign Broadcast Information Service Daily Report*, January 17, 1992, p. 22.

66. Confidential interview with a US official, February 5, 1992. According to this source, all meetings were conducted with the Cristiani government's knowledge.

67. See Watson statement. Joseph G. Sullivan, deputy assistant secretary for Central America, and Peter F. Romero, director of the Office of Central American Affairs, met with the FMLN in early December 1991, according to a confidential interview with an FMLN official, February 12, 1991, and Tim Golden, "Salvador War Ends for U.S. and Rebels," *New York Times*, January 5, 1992, p. 9.

68. See Golden, "Salvadoran War Ends." There are excellent reasons to doubt that the breakfast meeting between the FMLN commander and Assistant Secretary of State Aronson, which led immediately to Aronson's meeting with

the entire FMLN leadership, was, as portrayed by the reporter, accidental.

69. Baker, "The Hemisphere's Hopes for Peace," p. 33.

70. Transcript of briefing by Secretary of State James A. Baker, III, en route from Mexico City to San Salvador, prepared by the Office of the Assistant Secretary/Spokesman, San Salvador, January 16, 1992, pp. 1-2.

71. Rep. Robert G. Torricelli (D-New Jersey), chair of the House of Representatives' Subcommittee on Western Hemisphere Affairs, has remarked, "It has unfortunately become something of a national tradition that we are willing spend billions to win a military conflict but withhold millions that would insure that peace is sustained." Quoted in Tim Golden, "From Politics to Violence: Salvador Warily Prepares for War's Aftermath," *New York Times*, January 19, 1992, p. 3.

72. Storrs and Cotter, Table 1. Also, K. Larry Storrs, "El Salvador Under Cristiani: U.S. Foreign Assistance Decisions," Congressional Research Service, updated February 5, 1992, p. 1. The FY 1993 request shifts $40 million in military aid to economic assistance; the total level of aid would decline slightly for the fifth consecutive year.

73. Confidential interview, December 23, 1991. The administration's FY 1992 and FY 1993 requests for development assistance are $55 million. This official predicted that development assistance would fall to $30-40 million in two years.

74. Walter LeFeber, *Inevitable Revolutions: The United States in Central America*, (New York: W. W. Norton Company, 1984), p. 10.

75. U.S. Agency for International Development, El Salvador Selected Economic Data, 1978-1991, table published on July 22, 1991.

76. *Health Conditions in the Americas* (Washington, D.C.: Pan American Health Organization, 1990), vol. 2, p. 139.

77. "El Salvador: Recent Economic Developments and Macroeconomic Projections," report prepared by the World Bank for the first Consultative Group Meeting for El Salvador held in Paris, May 15-16, 1991, p. 1.

78. *Economic and Social Progress in Latin America–1991 Report* (Washington, D.C.: Inter-American Development Bank, October 1991), p. 89.

79. *Trends in Developing Economies: 1991*, (Washington, D.C.: The World Bank, 1991), p. 186.

80. See, for example, "Carta abierta al Señor Presidente Alfredo Cristiani y a su partido ARENA," ECA, April/May 1990, nos. 498-499, pp. 380-382.

81. "El Salvador: The Rehabilitation of the Social Sectors," p. 2.

82. *Health Conditions in the Americas* (Washington, D.C.: Pan American Health Organization, 1990), vol. 2, p. 140.

83. "El Salvador: The Rehabilitation of the Social Sectors," p. 2.

84. Ibid., p. 2. The literary figure can be found in *Human Development Report 1991* (New York: United Nations Development Programme, 1991), p. 128.

85. *Human Development Report*, p. 122.

86. "Poll Indicates Worsening Economic Situation," *Foreign Broadcast Information Service Daily Report*, December 10, 1991, pp. 11-12.

87. Draft, "Economic and Social Questions Working Paper" of the parties to the negotiations, United Nations, December 31, 1991, p. 1.

88. *World Development Report 1991: The Challenge of Development* (Washington, D.C.: World Bank, 1991), p. 224.

89. O'Donnell and Schmitter, *Tentative Conclusions*, pp. 6-7. I use their definitional framework for this section.

90. Ibid., p. 7.

91. Ibid., p. 8.

92. Ibid., pp. 43, 49–60.

93. Adam Przeworski, "Some Problems in the Study of the Transition to Democracy," in *Transitions from Authoritarian Rule: Comparative Perspectives,* Guillermo O'Donnell, Philippe C. Schmitter, and Laurence Whitehead, eds., (Baltimore: Johns Hopkins University Press, 1986), p. 58.

94. O'Donnell and Schmitter, *Tentative Conclusions,* pp. 57, 61–62.

95. As of this writing, however, ONUSAL is reportedly experiencing extraordinary cooperation on the part of the FMLN and military in the process of disarming the rebel movement.

96. O'Donnell and Schmitter, *Tentative Conclusions,* p. 12.

Index

207

About the Book

The brutal civil war in El Salvador appears to be nearing an end, an outcome that many observers of the country doubted was ever possible. For both sides, though, the central issue of the war remains: to what degree has democracy taken root in El Salvador, and to what extent can the country strengthen democratic, civilian-controlled government institutions?

This timely book, based on meetings held at the Woodrow Wilson Center in April and October 1991, highlights the key questions regarding El Salvador's transition to democracy. Does the electoral process allow for a fair and impartial reflection of the popular will? Is US policy aiding the cause of democracy—or strengthening an all-powerful military? Can peace last without progress on human rights and economic growth that ameliorates the country's widespread poverty? Contributors from the public, private, and academic realms address these issues, providing up-to-date information. The book includes chapters and discussion by veteran journalist Tom Gibb, Assistant US Secretary of State Bernard Aronson, and Alvaro de Soto, the mediator in the talks between the FMLN guerrillas and the Cristiani government. To conclude, Gary Bland summarizes the evidence presented and adds his own observations regarding the prospects for democracy in El Salvador.